THE RAINBOW AIN'T NEVER BEEN ENUF

THE RAINBOW AIN'T NEVER BEEN ENUF

ON THE MYTH OF LGBTQ+ SOLIDARITY

KAILA ADIA STORY

BEACON PRESS, BOSTON

BEACON PRESS
Boston, Massachusetts
www.beacon.org

Beacon Press books
are published under the auspices of
the Unitarian Universalist Association of Congregations.

29 28 27 26 8 7 6 5 4 3 2 1

This book is printed on acid-free paper that meets the uncoated paper ANSI/NISO specifications for permanence as revised in 1992.

Text design and composition by Kim Arney

Library of Congress Cataloguing-in-Publication Data is available for this title.
Paperback ISBN: 978-0-8070-2279-5
E-book ISBN: 978-0-8070-0480-7
Audiobook: 978-0-8070-1856-9

This book is dedicated to my rose of a wife, Missy. Your encouragement, support, and unyielding love brought me the reassurance I didn't know I needed. There is no way to quantify how much I love you.

To my brilliant parents, Sylvia Rogers and Dr. Ralph DeWitt Story, whose support, courage, love, and guidance aided me in completing this book. All that I am and have hoped to be has been shaped by you both. You both remain my first and greatest teachers.

To Denver Lamont Story-Jackson, my cuddly fur baby and exquisite writing partner, your naps and inquisitive looks always brought me light on my darkest days.

To all of my Black queer and trans ancestors, thank you for your guidance and protection during my life and during this process.

This is for you.

CONTENTS

PREFACE

ON REMEMBERING AND HONORING THE RAINBOW

I have always been both unequivocally and unapologetically Black, with a capital B.[1] My grandparents came from Mississippi, Georgia, and Alabama, and my parents, who were brought up in Cleveland and Middletown, Ohio, raised me to be proud of my history and culture and taught me to celebrate my Black heritage daily. Due to my public school education being bereft of anything substantial about Black people, during my adolescent and teenage years, my parents supplemented my education in order to fill in the social, cultural, and political gaps in my curriculum. They taught me that despite our society's anti-Black and misogynist leanings, Black girls and women continued to persevere, overcome, and accomplish. They taught me to see my Black girl self as an identity that was powerful, beautiful, and something that should be affirmed. They taught me that if I was presented with antagonism, indifference, or alienation due to either my race or my gender when I entered public spaces, I should demand to be seen in the way they saw me. My parents had the fundamental belief that the way they saw me was the truth, and that society would try its hardest at every turn to convince me otherwise.

As I grew up, I discovered that my parents were right. In public, I was constantly put in the position to dispel the racist and sexist perceptions of either my race or my gender. I was policed by strangers as well as by my white peers at school through looks, questions, and what we now call microaggressions. From asking questions about how I washed my hair to being shocked that I did in fact know and have a relationship with my father, my white peers continuously treated me as either a curiosity or a problem. I recognized that I was treated differently from others, and it initially stung emotionally, the intellectual aftermath of those moments only reinforcing what my parents had told me all along. If my peers, like society at large, didn't see me outside of the tropes of racism and sexism, then they were lying to me about myself. When I came into my queerness in my teens, and my feminism as an adult, my parents, without question, embraced and celebrated all parts of my identity, giving me the permission to be my full self. This gave me the emotional fortitude to fully accept myself, saving me from the anguish of familial rejection, an experience that far too often negatively shapes queer and trans folks' lives. The rest of the world, however, wasn't as hip as my parents. Society was exhausting and dehumanizing, demanding that I present all of my selves for their consumption.

As a Black feminist queer femme, every aspect of me makes sense. But traditionally, I confuse a world that still sees feminism as a thing that white girls knit pink hats for, and Blackness as the hypermasculine antithesis to queer and trans identities. I spent much of my early adulthood burdened by limiting aspects of myself in order to make others feel more comfortable. In college, I remember being expected to separate my feminist self from my Black self within the "safe space" of my women's and gender studies classrooms.[2] While some of my white peers were passionate about gender equality, they had only been introduced to feminist principles through a white supremacist lens. Because of this, they were often hostile when I wanted to discuss how race impacted gendered oppression or liberation. They viewed racial inquiries about gendered experiences with suspicion and began to see me as confrontational, divisive, and angry because I sought to interrogate how their ideas of feminism applied to Black women and girls. They would say things like, "We're talking about all women!" or, "We're looking at gender inequality as a whole, not just how it impacts specific groups!" This happened repeatedly throughout my undergraduate career, so I couldn't wait for graduate school to study Black studies, where I assumed that all of my identities would be embraced and celebrated. But I was wrong.

While my Blackness was certainly celebrated, taught, and honored, my lesbian and feminist identities were viewed in this overwhelmingly Black space the same way as my Black identity was viewed in my undergraduate feminist spaces. My queerness and feminist politics in Black studies spaces was framed as a "white thing," and my feminist and lesbian identities were treated as problems that needed to be corrected through Afrocentric graduate education.[3]

Luckily for me, among my undergrad and grad student cohorts, I was given the gift of having a few peers who weren't antagonistic to my Blackness, and who didn't view my queer or feminist identities as a symptom of white supremacist indoctrination. In both spaces, I was able to meet a couple of folks who chose to embrace me and all of my identities with compassion and celebration. Some even challenged those who demanded that Blackness had to be anti-feminist and homophobic to be authentic, while others challenged those who did not want to talk about race but wanted to call themselves feminists.[4]

By the time I landed my academic position in Louisville, Kentucky, in 2007, I continued to mistakenly believe that my experiences with identity erasure would stop, but they didn't. For example, around that time I began to indulge in the daily (and expensive) habit of requiring an iced coffee from Starbucks. The coffee shop was close to my apartment, and after going there every morning before teaching classes, I began to develop a friendly rapport with the baristas. One morning, I decided to bring my best friend Jaison along so he could get a coffee too. The barista greeted me as they usually did, but as soon as they saw Jaison, they shouted: "OMG this must be your husband! I'm so glad to finally be meeting him!" Jaison and I immediately busted out laughing and said, "Umm no, we're actually both really gay! We're just good friends!" The barista, now turning red and embarrassed, replied, "Oh my goodness, I'm just so sorry," to which I responded, "Don't be, hunny! We're excited that we're gay! We actually love it!"

A couple of years later, I got engaged to the love of my life, Missy, and eagerly began planning our wedding. Of course, Jaison went with me to every appointment and was just as excited as I was. A local organization called the Fair Event Vendors Wedding Association hosted a "Love Won Wedding Show" in 2015 after the Supreme Court legalized same-sex marriage throughout the nation. Jaison and I arrived at the event eager to meet all of the wedding vendors that were LGBTQ+ inclusive and to have our pick of which would be best suited for my nuptials. Our enthusiasm, however, began to fade shortly after we arrived. At each station, every vendor kept assuming that Jaison and I were the ones getting married, not that I was a lesbian marrying a woman and that Jaison was my gay good friend who was there to help me plan my wedding. One vendor even told Jaison that he was a bad groom because he didn't know the exact wedding date when she asked him. After the event, Jaison and I laughed all the way home because we had once again been mistaken for a couple, and not seen for who we truly were. Both of us used our laughter in these moments to mask the actual emotional trauma that was taking place internally.

For both Jaison and me, these dehumanizing experiences, where our queerness was muted or rendered invisible, happened often. It was transparent that people were reluctant to truly see us as Black queer people because of the longstanding assumption that queerness and Blackness could not be housed within the same body. This widespread and false assumption is one that exists throughout our culture. Across geographic and, to some extent, generational lines, many people connect queerness directly to whiteness. These strangers unknowingly erased Jaison's and my queer identities because our Black identities made our queerness invisible to them. Despite decades of Black LGBTQ+ artists, activists, and thought leaders articulating their intersectional struggles to the nation, and despite them making social and political inroads that benefitted LGBTQ+ communities, the country at large remained completely oblivious of that history, and of Black LGBTQ+ folks' places within it.

Jaison and I, both being aware of that history, also recognized that any social and political advancement that LGBTQ+ people benefitted from in any contemporary context was only due to the valiant efforts and courageous strides of Black and Latinx LGBTQ+ folks. Our personal experiences with queer erasure were not new to us. Both of us were used to the deflation and exhaustion that come from society not viewing our full dimensionality. These experiences were not particular to us. They were, and are, shared experiences that Black and Latinx LGBTQ+ people face daily.

Black lesbian poet Pat Parker articulated the same fatigue about not being fully seen for who she was back in 1978. Parker's poetic wish, the ability to bring her whole self into any public space without having to say to one of her identities, "No, you have to stay home tonight," was a dream both Jaison and I shared.[5] Parker felt that if the day ever came when she could bring all of her intersectional identities into any public space—her Black self, her gay self, her woman self—and not have any of those identities be dismissed, antagonized, or rendered invisible, it would be on this day that we would have a revolution. Parker's activist work and poetry continually calls out the harmful social and cultural practices of gay racism, anti-Blackness, and Black homophobia to create a better world for Black LGBTQ+ people, and she isn't alone in her sentiments either. Other Black queer and trans activists, like Marlon Riggs, Essex Hemphill, Audre Lorde, Barbara Smith, Joseph Beam, and Marsha P. Johnson, had also done the work of calling out these injustices, either through their art, protests, or prose.[6] They too were tired of navigating between and being impacted by America's homophobia and transphobia as well as white and cis LGBTQ+ communities' racism and cisnormativity. While Parker and other Black LGBTQ+ community changemakers of the '60s, '70s, and '80s were hopeful for the day when their embodied identities would be treated with love and dignity, that day still hasn't come.

Until recently, our collective Black, queer, and trans struggles with being unseen happened in person, giving us the freedom to leave public spaces when we felt unwelcome. The face-to-face dismissal, albeit dehumanizing, still offered the possibility of escape. We could all retreat to safe spaces that we fostered with our families, both blood and chosen, where we could access social and emotional respite from the hostility of the outside world. However, with the advent and widespread adoption of social media in the mid-2000s, public and highly visible antagonism against Blackness, LGBTQ+ folks, and Black feminists by social media users began to follow us throughout our lives and within our homes. Now, Black LGBTQ+ people, as well as Black queer and trans feminists, deal with anti-Blackness, homophobia, and transphobia face to face *and* online, compounding the impact of dismissal, queer erasure, and transphobia.

While some users turn off their notifications to certain posts, block offensive users, or delete various apps altogether, we still confront what happens on social media in our workplaces and classrooms, when we talk with family over dinner or watch the news. While we struggle with the visible harms that social media inflicts, we recognize that it also has a another, more positive function. Social media is an accessible and highly visible public space for minoritized people to assert their identities and promote their advocacy for Black and Latinx LGBTQ+ communities. It allows Black feminists and theorists a nonacademic public platform to spread the gospel on the harms that come from people not thinking inclusively and intersectionally. At the same time, social media continues to function as a space where racists, sexists, and anti-queer and anti-trans people have established a public soapbox to continue their war on anyone who represents difference. Essentially, social media is a platform for everyone. It provides hope and possibilities of freedom and liberation for some, while creating additional nightmares for many.

Forty-two years after Parker's book *Movement in Black* was published, many cis folks, both white and Black, gay and straight, still find it difficult to respect or understand people with intersectional identities.[7] During LGBTQ+ pride month in June of 2020, many white cis gay men grew even more antagonistic to the idea of honoring intersectional identities post-Stonewall. Before Juneteenth became a federally recognized holiday, avid Trump supporter and journalist Chadwick Moore tweeted, "I'm sorry blacks, but you already have a month. Juneteenth isn't a thing. Don't colonize our month as well. Thanks! Signed, the gays."[8] Moore's tweet elicited righteous indignation and outrage from users who shouted through their keyboards that his racist tweet erased Black LGBTQ+ people completely. Many pointed out that his tweet did not consider that Black LGBTQ+ people could and would celebrate Juneteenth and Pride month simultaneously, as both holidays were reflective of their intersectional identities and their communities' demands for freedom and equality. What Moore's tweet also did was to whiten the historical account of Stonewall and erase the activism of Black and Latinx LGBTQ+ people. His tweet made plain for many within mainstream communities that cis white gay men have always, and still do, struggle with racism. Moore's tweet erased trans folks completely; by ending his tweet with "signed, the gays," Moore revealed that many white cis gay men do not acknowledge, see, or embrace trans folks as part of LGBTQ+ communities.[9]

Within February of that same year, Black straight and cis rapper Lil' Boosie Badazz expressed his outrage at NBA player Dwyane Wade's daughter, Zaya, coming out as trans.[10] Bossie was angry that Wade and his wife, the actress Gabrielle Union, accepted their daughter's identity. He was also angry that other folks had joined in to support Zaya and her family. On February 18, 2020, Boosie went on his Instagram Live to tell Wade that "he had gone too far" in supporting his daughter's Black trans identity, ranting that Wade's child was too young to make this decision and pleading with the basketball star not to start his child on hormones or allow her to get gender-confirmation surgery.[11]

Paradoxically, Lil' Boosie Badazz's anti-trans rhetoric in regard to Zaya Wade, which he tried to dress up as an attempt to promote good parenting and protect children, came only a couple of months before the rapper took to Instagram Live in May of 2020 to brag that he was "training these boys right," in reference to him hiring a sex worker to perform oral sex on his twelve-year-old son and nephews.[12] In the video, the rapper loudly boasted that hiring a sex worker for his underage son and nephews should be thought of as a normal parenting pastime because "that's how it supposed to be." He then went on to say that his son and nephews get to "watch as much porn as they want," because that's better than "them watching cartoons with two men kissing."[13] While many social media users called for the rapper's arrest for facilitating the rape of his underage son and nephews, others applauded his actions, including famous YouTuber King Kashez, who stated that the practice of hiring sex workers for adolescent boys "is normal in the hood," and the only reason "the rest of the world ain't used to that" is because it's something that primarily takes place "in Black families."[14]

Lil' Boosie Badazz's insinuation that the Wade family's support of their daughter was an example of bad parenting but hiring a sex worker for his twelve-year-old son and nephews was good for the kids is as absurd as it is dangerous. The rapper's line of thinking shows the severe ideological disconnect that comes from being socialized to only think heteronormatively and misogynistically. This blinkered thinking in fact caused real harm, leading to his nephews' rape and subjecting them to watching pornography. The Wade family's support of Zaya's bodily autonomy and agency is not where the danger lies. The real danger is Lil' Boosie Badazz's denial of the bodily autonomy and agency of his son and nephews, and it is only the rapper's heteronormative, transphobic, and misogynist thinking that leads him to conclude otherwise.

Similarly, it was only Chadwick Moore's white supremacist and transphobic thinking that allowed him to conclude that Juneteenth, if made into a federal holiday, would "colonize" pride month for LGBTQ+ people. Moore's white supremacist thought process prevented him from seeing that Black LGBTQ+ people also exist, and that they would most certainly welcome a national holiday that celebrated their history and culture. The problem is that Moore and Lil' Boosie Badazz's lines of thinking on human identity and sexuality are not limited to themselves. Rather, their perspectives are representative of so many others who can only think in limiting and narrow ways about historically excluded groups due to their racist, sexist, homophobic, and transphobic beliefs.

What made 2020 even more startling was that Chadwick Moore and Lil' Boosie Badazz weren't the only celebrities who made it their missions to use their social media platforms to attack people based on their differences.[15] Everyday folks also joined in, taking the opportunity in person to confront and attack people, and using social networks to spout their reductive views to the masses.[16] Despite all of the work done by Black feminists, Black queer and trans theorists, and Black and Latinx LGBTQ+ activists, white cishets and white cis gays and lesbians still struggled with difference when it wasn't white. Despite Black and Latinx LGBTQ+ creatives making groundbreaking shows like *Pose*, *P-Valley*, *Twenties*, and *Legendary* to teach mainstream communities that Black and Latinx LGBTQ+ people established the ball scene, started the Stonewall uprisings, and are the real reason behind Pride, many white cis gays and lesbians in 2020 still refused to acknowledge this history due to their reluctance to let go of their white supremacist, sexist, and transphobic beliefs.

I wrote this book to dispel the myth that the rainbow should be viewed as a symbol of internal communal solidarity—because such solidarity is sadly lacking. In the chapters that follow, I argue that LGBTQ+ communities still struggle with the same repugnant beliefs that lead mainstream society to harm LGBTQ+ people of color.

Criticism alone isn't enough to help our communities heal from these harms, and to that end I also highlight the work of Black and Latinx LGBTQ+ theorists, activists, and educators who are staging their own social and political interventions in the face of unaccountable white cis gay and lesbian communities. So much good work is being done to help uplift our communities, and I want to give voice to those whose work I find particularly admirable and effective.

Fifty-three years post-Stonewall, white cis gays and lesbians have used the symbol of the rainbow to project to the outside world that LGBTQ+ communities exist as unified fronts in the face of gender and sexual tyranny. In my life and scholarship, I have seen that such a united front seldom exists, and that using the rainbow in this way only absolves white LGBTQ+ folks of their racist and anti-trans views. This book, which is rooted in the spirit of Parker's and other Black LGBTQ+ mavericks' unactualized dreams of truly being seen for who they really are, is an attempt to let readers know that the rainbow ain't never been enuf.

INTRODUCTION

ON WHY THE RAINBOW AIN'T NEVER BEEN ENUF

Coming out wasn't hard for me. Both of my parents immediately expressed their unyielding and overwhelming love and support for my newfound lesbian identity. Friends and comrades did the same. Their support gave me the social, cultural, and ideological freedom to navigate my new queer and Black life with confidence and excitement. Filled with queer enthusiasm, I ventured to Ann Arbor's Kerrytown neighborhood to the one queer bar we had, \aut\ Bar.[1] I didn't have a fake ID and neither did my first out gay friend, Tim, but we decided to take our chances in getting into the bar and it worked. In thinking back on how it was possible for our teenage selves to get into a grown nightclub, I now realize that the white ownership might have viewed Tim and me as being much older than we were. Statistically speaking, Black children and teens are not granted the same veil of innocence as white children and are often perceived and treated as adults.[2] Take the 2015 case of Timothy Loehmann, for example, the white police officer who shot and killed twelve-year-old Tamir Rice just for playing cops and robbers by himself in a park. Loehmann's defense attorneys argued that when he pulled up to the park, he didn't see a twelve-year-old playing with a toy gun; rather, he saw an eighteen-year-old man brandishing a lethal weapon.[3] Or maybe the club owners just saw me as one of the Black girls that Monique Harris talks about in her book *Pushout: The*

Criminalization of Black Girls in School. Harris argues that Black girls are often viewed as older by white adults and administrators due to historical and contemporaneous racist and sexist cultural beliefs about their embodiments. Maybe in this instance, like Harris contends, my Black girl body was viewed as less innocent, as hypersexual, or as just old enough to not be carded.[4]

While Tim and I were eager to flirt and converse with other queer folks, we were disappointed to find that most of the conversations we engaged in centered on our race, racial stereotypes, or assumed racial personae. Before I was even able to say "Hello," white gay men would smile at me and yell, "Hey, diva," or "What are you doing here, girlfriend?" They would snap their fingers at me like Blaine Edwards and Antoine Merriweather on the show *In Living Color*, and they would reduce Tim to stereotypes about Black men's primal sexual prowess, hinting at how he must be well endowed.[5] These were my first experiences not only with LGBTQ+ nightlife but also with gay racism. In my young mind, I thought that queer or trans folks could not be racist. Whiteness at this point in my life wasn't a signifier for racist thoughts or derogatory racialized and sexualized stereotypes. I was naive in my misconception that a marginalized group of people would not hold these kinds of sentiments.

I left Ann Arbor for Chicago to attend DePaul University, before moving to Philadelphia for graduate school at Temple University. In both Chicago and Philly, my experiences in queer spaces mirrored the same queer racism I found in Ann Arbor. I experienced racist statements and ridicule in almost every club and venue that I visited, especially when it was a place that was frequented and dominated by white queer and trans folks. My friends and I would be made to endure an onslaught of racial and gendered hostility, confusion, and questioning of our group's true intentions about being in the space. These occurrences weren't peripheral ones, either. When I would make new Black queer and trans connections and friendships, we would bond over our similar encounters with gay racism. My friends would spill tea about being confronted with reductive notions of Blackness or the Latinx identity when trying to engage in regular conversations.[6] They would speak about overhearing white gay men refer to their sexual tastes with racialized phrasing like, "Hunny, he's a bean queen," and "Everybody knows he's a rice queen."[7] My trans and gender nonconforming friends would share how they pretended not to hear cis gays say things like "tranny," or "he/she," and instead they would move to the opposite side of the bar in an attempt to enjoy their cocktails without being forced to grapple with the reality that our communities still have serious problems when it comes to embracing racial and gendered diversity.[8] Our reality solidified Baldwin's conclusion, "the gay world . . . is no more prepared to accept Black people than anywhere else in society."[9] It made us understand that a radical politic was not an automatic outgrowth of a person's queerness or trans identity.

However, LGBTQ+ communities' problems with racial tension and transphobia did not start with my or my comrades' experiences. In fact, "Since the early 1970s, male sexism had led many lesbians to organize separate groups for women [and] by the end of the 1970s, a similar process was underway among gay people of color antagonized by the persistence of white racism in the institutions of the gay community."[10] Before and after Stonewall, white gay and lesbian activism had always suffered from a lack of insight when it came to understanding systems of domination in intersectional ways, ultimately severing queer liberation from other forms of gendered, racial, and economic empowerment and misrepresenting how power operates within LGBTQ+ communities.[11] When gay racism and queer transphobia are also coupled with generational neoliberal thought and indoctrination, a narrow-minded and homogenized apolitical queer person is produced.[12] A homonormative person. A queer-identified individual who is politically neutered and socially compliant, whose politic does "not contest dominant heteronormative assumptions and institutions, but upholds and sustains them, while promising the possibility of a demobilized gay constituency and a privatized, depoliticized gay culture anchored in domesticity and consumption."[13] Neoliberalism, which gave birth to the homonormative constituency, was and is an outgrowth of the economic libertarian philosophy, which began to pick up social currency within the world's top leaders in the '80s and continued to gain more favor in the '90s.[14] All the while it slowly transformed us into consumers rather than citizens, asserting that our only democratic power was in our ability to buy and sell. Neoliberalism sold the world's constituency the myth that the "free market," and its ability to facilitate competition among corporations, would eventually benefit the most vulnerable by first benefitting the wealthiest.[15] By privatizing public services (healthcare, education, welfare), deregulating tax and wealth, emphasizing rugged individualism, undermining the collective bargaining power of trade unions, and deeming identity politics irrelevant to access and prosperity, neoliberal politics asserts that our power and freedom lie not within our collective endeavors for structural change but with our material independence from one another. "Queers who operate out of a political culture of individualism assume a material independence that allows them to disregard historically or culturally recognized categories and communities."[16] Identities and communities that have been vital to the advancement of racial, gendered, and class equity. Consequently, narrow and homogenized queer political identities are birthed and reproduced that not only reflect the anti-Black, anti-trans, and classist beliefs of society but also reflect the tenets of neoliberal thought.

The Rainbow Ain't Never Been Enuf: On the Myth of LGBTQ+ *Solidarity* is a critical analysis of the white supremacist, anti-Black and anti-trans ideologies and praxes that exist within and outside of mainstream queer communities and popular media. I discuss how neoliberalism intensifies these internal racial, class, and gendered tensions through the proliferation of homonormative political praxes, which seek to deny and attempt to hide the common struggles of racism, sexism, classism, and transphobia that many Black and Latinx LGBTQ+ folks repeatedly experience, and which emphasize rugged individualism, not collective liberation.[17] Further, this book discusses how many white gays and lesbians still struggle to find solidarity among other queer people when those queer folks do not reflect their race or their same economic standing. It delineates how many of them still use their racial privilege and material independence to assimilate into mainstream culture, and how this access to the mainstream allows them to overlook how the dynamics of racism and anti-Blackness remain ever-present in the lives of Black LGBTQ+ folks.

The Rainbow Ain't Never Been Enuf also examines how popular media has a predilection for only showing narrow representations of LGBTQ+ identities—despite myriad watershed moments within popular culture and the many critical interventions created by Black queer theorists, activists, and artists across generations—in order to argue that queer and trans identities are still whitewashed and classed within media. Black and Latinx queer and trans people still face invisibility not only within mainstream popular media but also within queer directed and produced media, and this limited scope with which the media presents queer lived experiences subjects many Black LGBTQ+ and queer people of color to hypervisibility within normative "gay" public spaces, leading them to face further scrutiny, policing, and antagonism within these spaces and within their day-to-day lives. This book demarcates the assumptions and amplification of hegemonic queerness as "unraced," which has allowed white queer people to disavow their racial privilege while simultaneously reifying queer people of color as racialized others, and it will also outline the silencing practices of homonormativity, cis privilege and normativity, and gay racism.[18]

This work asserts that these routine action(s) ultimately cast queerness and Blackness as mutually exclusive categories, eroding and obscuring the genealogical reality of Black queer and trans legacies and futures. I highlight images and/or cultural productions that provide an alternative way of presenting and thinking about LGBTQ+ life narratives (visuals art, performance, literature, music, etc.). Using the analytic frames of Black feminism, Black queer theory, and Black queer history and politics to support my assertions about the consequences of the invisibility, I share some of the narratives I sought out and used along my own journey that aided me in my pursuits of justice, hope, and joy within my own Black and queer life.

I incorporate my personal experiences with gay racism, transphobia, and homonormativity to explore this space as well as urge my readers to create their own counternarratives of self, based upon their various intersecting identities in the face of these repugnant realities. The power within one's story is evident in numerous other Black feminist, queer, and trans works. The experiential knowledge one gains from living in a world that is antithetical to their existence creates a particular kind of insight into how to dismantle the various power structures that are often at play when it comes to both experiencing oppression or benefitting from privilege. In academia this reflexive exercise has been defined as autoethnography, utilizing one's personal narrative and journey to analyze culture and phenomena critically.

Autoethnography connects self-reflection to wider cultural, political, and social prisms. This ideological and theoretical tradition provides the necessary clarity and perspective for understanding our journeys and actualizing our empowered senses of self. From popular media to everyday life, Black queer and trans folks are still continually plagued by the same circumstances and ideologies of those who came before them. Regardless of white cis gay and lesbian efforts to portray LGBTQ+ unity, this book aims to open the closet door and present the realities of various divisions in an effort to improve our community connections and relationships.

CHAPTER ONE

ON THE MYTH AND REALITY OF THE RAINBOW

When I was a girl, my mama and I would frequently travel to Ohio from our home in Ann Arbor, Michigan, to visit her family. While I loved spending time with my grandparents in their tiny town of Middleton, I would often beg to visit my aunt and uncle in Cincinnati under the pretense of playing in their large and lavish house. Truthfully, I just wanted to see their art. All of the Black art. They had busts, sculptures, and paintings on almost every wall, and I would gaze for hours at every item. There was a particular piece that captivated me each time I laid my eyes on it. The painting, which I found out later was a poster, had a melancholy-faced Black woman sitting in what looked to be a bathroom or subway terminal because of the white-tiled walls behind her. There was a phrase written next to the woman's despondent face, etched in exquisite rainbow lettering. It read: "for colored girls who considered suicide when the rainbow is enuf." It wrecked me every time I read it. I would wonder, *Why was this beautiful Black woman contemplating suicide? And why was she referring to herself as colored when it was 1988 and most Black people I knew called themselves Black American or African American?* In fact, the only time I ever heard the term *colored* used was when my paternal grandmother explained to me to never let anyone, especially white people, call me "colored" or "Negro." She said racial terminology for Black people had changed over time and those terms weren't acceptable anymore. Prior to seeing the poster, I had never heard of suicide in reference to Black women. The only knowledge I had of suicide was when it was uttered during a Lifetime movie my mama made me watch during one of our weekend movie marathons. Even then, there weren't any Black women in that film, or in any Lifetime movie in the 1980s that we watched. Even though I had all of these silent contemplations about my aunt and uncle's magnificent poster, I never posed these questions to them or my mama. Instead, I would just stare at it in awe anytime I visited.

I wasn't introduced to Ntozake Shange's work and didn't learn about the political and cultural significance of *for colored girls who have considered suicide/when the rainbow is enuf* until I was a graduate student and had the opportunity to read her 1975 choreopoem. *for colored girls* is a Black girl's song, an ancient yet contemporary tune that allows a Black girl like me to begin to know herself, see herself. It allows Black girls to become familiar with their own voices, souls, and genders. Shange's work enlightened me to the complexities of living within the intersection of gender and race, and how those complexities related to the life chances and choices for me as a Black lesbian woman. Although I had been living within this identity all of my life, I had not yet thought about my existence theoretically: how my reality was interconnected with those who came before me and with those that would come after me. Shange's work showed me how my sociopolitical embodiment directly affected my ability to even dream about something as universal as love. Like Shange's characters, I would have to navigate a racist, homophobic, and sexist world that chose not to recognize my humanity, nor my fragility as a sentient being in ways it did for others. Through its words I realized that I wasn't the only Black girl, now woman, grappling with these realities.

The next time I visited, I asked my aunt Gail if I could have her poster. She promptly said no. For my aunt, the poster represented more than art, as it did for me. It represented her own song and the discovery of her voice. The reasons I wanted it for myself were the same reasons she didn't want to give it to me. Luckily for me, though, after some negotiation my aunt gave it to me, and it has remained with me ever since. This is part of the reason why I chose *The Rainbow Ain't Never Been Enuf* as the title for this book.[1] Shange's work, love, and now ancestral light for Black girls has remained a great influence on my work. Her metaphorical use of the rainbow as a symbol of the multifaceted and complex lived experiences of Black women struggling with and surviving racial and gendered oppression, within and outside of Black communities, is a brilliant illustration of the difficulty of unearthing and unraveling the complex and intricate nature of a people who represent multiple axes of difference. As a Black lesbian feminist and femme-identified academic specializing in Black queer and Black feminist studies, I thought that it was only fitting to borrow and honor this metaphor of the rainbow to explore the white supremacist and dominant representations of LGBTQ+ people's lived experiences and identities, which have become ubiquitous throughout popular media.[2]

The rainbow is a longstanding image for queer and trans communities. In fact, it was a tiny rainbow in the corner of a shop located in Ann Arbor, Michigan's gayborhood that drew me in.[3] I was still a gayby at the time and the rainbow represented a pathway into a new queer world.[4] The shop turned out to be an LGBTQ+ bookstore that housed documentaries, films, and books about LGBTQ+ history, politics, and life. I would spend hours after school devouring the anthologies dedicated to coming-out stories, watching what happened at Stonewall, and flipping through the photography books that showed our community members in beautiful and resilient ways. It was also in this bookstore that I learned that in 1978, artist and peace and AIDS activist Gilbert Baker was commissioned by the openly gay politician Harvey Milk to create the rainbow flag to represent the multidimensional nature and pride of LGBTQ+ people.[5] Each color of the rainbow was intended to represent the diversity and solidarity of our communities, visually capturing our nuances, our differences and sameness, and our complex identities. The flag was created as a symbol to not only spread love and inclusivity but also to counter sexual and gendered regulation within mainstream society. Leaders, community change makers, and inclusive businesses display the flag in stores, offices, and schools as a symbol of solidarity with LGBTQ+ folks and to express their support and welcome of people belonging to such communities. However, throughout time, some of the most vulnerable yet resilient people within our communities have not found the rainbow marker to symbolize diversity, inclusion, or solidarity. For many, it has symbolized terror—racialized and gendered terror to be specific—causing many to disidentify from the flag's symbolism, use, and consumption.[6]

For example, in 1973 when Sylvia Rivera took the stage at one of the first gay Pride parades and celebrations in New York, she was booed, told to "shut up," misgendered, and subjected to objects being thrown at her by the mostly white, mostly cis, and strikingly racist audience. She repeatedly stated "Y'all better quiet down."[7] As an activist, Rivera, along with Marsha P. Johnson, founded the Street Transvestite Action Revolutionaries (STAR) shortly after the Stonewall rebellion in 1969, and both she and Johnson worked tirelessly to protect transgender and street youth whose needs and identities weren't being recognized by early gay groups.[8] Desiring to untether the Mafia's control over LGBTQ+ bars and night life, Johnson and Rivera created the first LGBTQ+ shelter in the US, the first sex worker labor organization, and the first trans women of color organization. They expanded their mission and goals to other cities until the organization's collapse in the mid-1970s.[9] Marsha "Pay It No Mind" Johnson stood at the helm of LGBTQ+ rights for nearly twenty-five years, serving as a central figure and activist, not only for queer and trans rights but also an advocate on behalf of sex workers, prisoners, and victims of police brutality. She became a resounding voice for those living with HIV/AIDS, and for those Black and Latinx LGBTQ+ folks who had to navigate and suffer through gay racism. As a political agitator who lived at the intersections of racism, homophobia, and transphobia, Johnson, along with Rivera, helped to transform public consciousness when it came to queer liberation. Yet, in 1992, Johnson's body was found floating in the Hudson River, and the circumstances surrounding her death remain a mystery to this day.[10] Rivera died of liver cancer in a homeless shelter in 2002.[11] Thus, even before Baker's creation of the Pride flag, many Black and Latinx queer and trans folks dealt with antagonism, violence, ridicule, disregard, and neglect by members of their own communities, despite the mainstream perception of unity.

So, I wasn't surprised to learn that in 2017 the office of LGBT Affairs in Philadelphia, Pennsylvania, was met with backlash when they unveiled a remix to Gilbert Baker's 1978 version of the Pride Flag with the addition of the colors black and brown to the bottom of the rainbow.[12] Many people that I was in community with saw the gesture as moving in the right direction, finally illuminating the need to confront issues of racism, sexism, and transphobia. The office's More Colors, More Pride campaign seemed to feel similarly and expressed in their press release that, "in 1978, artist Gilbert Baker designed the original rainbow flag. So much has happened since then. . . . Especially when it comes to recognizing people of color in the LGBTQ+ community. . . .To fuel this important conversation, we've expanded the colors of the flag to include black and brown."[13] While marginalized folks saw this move as one that spoke to their everyday experiences, many white cis gays and lesbians felt that the revised version of the flag was racist and unfair, and some even felt that the color white should also be added in the interest of keeping things equal. Some took to Twitter to express their anger and frustration with the new flag, while others wrote op-eds to express their discontent.[14] Michael J. Murphy, a white, gay associate professor of gender and sexuality at the University of Illinois–Springfield, asserted his frustration with the Philadelphia office's decision in his piece "We Don't Need a New Pride Flag: Gilbert Baker's Still Works Just Fine," where he contended, "None of the original stripes represented a specific racial, ethnic, gender, or sexual identity";

therefore, there was no need to alter the original version.[15] Professor Murphy validated the impetus for incorporating the additional stripes in the flag in the beginning of his essay, acknowledging that queer communities in fact have a problem with racism, stating, "New pride flags come from a sincere place: a desire to create an inclusive visual symbol for the diverse LGBTQ+ community . . . and respond to real and serious problems and deserve to be taken seriously and considered on their merits." But he still waxed poetic over how the new stripes were reductive and reminiscent of the "scientific racist thinking that distinguished "the races" according to the color of their skin."[16]

In the years that followed, other cities, countries, and Pride festivals began to adopt the new version of the Pride flag to show solidarity with those of the LGBTQ+ community who don't feel represented by the original flag. A London volunteer who leads the LGBTQ+ social and support group Rainbow Noir wrote an op-ed for the UK news outlet *Gay Star News* in response to the anger about the modified flag, following Manchester Pride's announcement to adopt it for their festival.[17] "We are worn out; physically sick and tired from having to defend our right to be seen, both individually and as queer, trans, and intersex people of color (QTIPOC) collectively."[18] They argued throughout their essay that the rainbow flag for many Black and Brown queer and trans folks has never felt like it was created for them, and that the "racism and silencing that has ensued since Pride's announcement is a painfully clear example of why the stripes were included in the first place."[19]

On June 27, 2018, Stonewall, the United Kingdom's leading charity for the equality of LGBTQ+ people, released a report about the extensive and longstanding discrimination and racism within the LGBTQ+ community. They reported, "Half of Black, Asian and minority ethnic (BAME) LGBT people (51 per cent) faced discrimination or poor treatment from the wider LGBT community."[20] They further stated that the "situation is particularly acute for Black LGBT people: three in five (61 per cent) have experienced discrimination from other LGBT people."[21] The study, which was based upon five thousand participants, revealed the longstanding problem that queer and trans communities are also plagued by racism, sexism, cisnormativity, and even homonormativity.[22] Before I came out, I wasn't aware of this fact, either. I neither recognized nor thought about the fact that LGBTQ+ communities, like Black communities, weren't monoliths or communities made up of unmitigated unity. I never thought about how intricate, nuanced, complex, and diverse they were. After I came out, my experiences began to reflect the respondents' voices, not only those in the Stonewall study but also sentiments voiced by the activist collective Rainbow Noir. When I came into my own grown Black queerness, I finally understood that some white queer and trans folks would never cede their own racial privilege over creating the necessary solidarity with queer and trans people of color. It was and is this reality that has led me to interrogate my own relationship to the rainbow flag, trouble the contention that LGBTQ+ communities have always been and are harmonious, borrow from the genius and nuance of Shange's use of the rainbow, and assert that whiteness, cis-ness, wealth, and the like aren't the only signifiers or representations of queer and trans identities.

CHAPTER TWO

YOUR BLACK AIN'T LIKE MINE

There's this new app that I have been having fun with since COVID-19 upturned all of our lives. It is called reface, and it allows you to place your face in music videos, gifs, even movies, on the body of whichever celebrity you choose. From Lizzo to Beyoncé to Kim Kardashian, from Nicki Minaj to Rachel McAdams, the app allows its users to reimagine themselves and visualize a new them. Different hairstyles, bodies, even skin tones can all change with one swipe.[1] During shelter-in-place, I began creating movie after gif after music video, swapping my face and placing it on a variety of celebrity bodies. I was surprisingly disappointed in the outcomes. Seeing my skin tone, body size, and hair altered did not excite me in the least. I downloaded the app because I thought it would be fun to see myself in various movies or videos, being glamorous and indulging in a celebrity culture that usually left folks who looked like me out of it. But the app didn't do that. I had to be altered to fit within the frame of the app in order to participate in this way. Seeing the way the app transformed me made for a startling and disturbing reality. It turned out that I didn't like me with a different body or hairstyle or skin tone. Although I didn't download the app to create a "better," or more "enticing," version of myself, I did recognize that the way the app modified my being to reflect what Western culture has deemed conventional notions of attractiveness. It made me lighter and thinner. It changed my curl pattern so it was looser and my hair was no longer loc'ed. After hours of playing with the app, I hoped that for other users disoriented by the change in their appearance, the app offered the realization that despite our internal or external struggles with our bodies, hair, skin tones, etc., we actually like ourselves better as we are.

Yet, learning to like myself as I am has not been easy. It has taken years of struggle and decades of unlearning the values that our culture dictates to all of us when it comes to the ways we value or devalue ourselves. Being socialized within a culture that engenders the subjective rejection of ourselves, uses media as a neoliberal tool to show us our deficits, and pushes products that serve as correctives to these projected shortages leaves many to relearn their self-identity outside of these constraints. Many, myself included, must understand that who we are in our origination is okay, worthy even. Our bodies are, in fact, matter, made up of parts and flesh that sense, feel, and require touch. Our bodies are also more than that, as Carla Peterson asserts. Our bodies are "never divorced from perception and interpretation."[2] Even if some people are able to see their bodies' characteristics, features, and tones as temples that are sacred, this doesn't stop others from seeing something else. People outside of ourselves often project the white supremacist, fatphobic, and misogynist Western body politics onto our bodies, despite our own subjective resistance to it. Therefore, even though some of us might view our Black bodies as beautiful, regal, and sensual, others might see our bodies as dangerous, libidinous, and even criminal due to the projected normative constraints that exist within our body politics. These diametrically opposed viewpoints of the same body are reflective of how the body has always been viewed and analyzed as not only matter and flesh but also as a social body that physically and ideologically locates itself within society.

Within Western borders, the value of the individual human body has been so important to Western social, cultural, and political agendas that its perceived corporal value (based on race, national origins, and gender) inevitably translated into its perceived ideological, political and social value.[3] Therefore, in this sense our perception of our own bodies and others' bodies is often measured by this antiquated prescription. Western societies have inscribed individual human bodies to such an extent that a body's corporal worth directly translated to its psychic worth, turning the body itself into a readable text.[4] Thus, the body is "always in view and on view. As such, it invites a gaze, a gaze of difference, a gaze of differentiation—the most historically constant being the gendered gaze."[5] Typically, gender and race discourses surrounding the body have historically been treated as separate and distinct dialectics.[6] However, in this work, they will be treated as one and the same, due to their historical and contemporaneous influence over one another. This influence created a complex interplay that in turn shaped and invented the ways in which we come to know and view minoritized bodies. Although the body has been seen as a text that is gazed upon by its viewers, early Western philosophical discourses contended that some human bodies were read, and other human bodies were attached to minds, which allowed them to be the readers.[7]

The philosophical assertion of Cartesian dualism left certain bodies attached to minds and certain bodies attached to matter or flesh: "women, primitives, Jews, Africans, the poor, and all those who qualified for the label of different in varying historical epochs have been considered to be the embodied, dominated therefore by instinct and affect, reason being beyond them."[8] Therefore, if we think of the body as a physical text that can be read by "dominant" and "subordinate" bodies, through a sociopolitical and differential gaze, then we can begin to understand how for centuries Western society has valued certain bodies and suppressed others.[9] Reading bodies were deemed normative bodies, and non-reading bodies were viewed as abnormal or atypical. These presumed corporal differences that were established in the eighteenth and nineteenth centuries created a very important discursive staple. Black bodies were subjected to the ultimate scrutiny based on racial prescriptions of humanity. Female bodies were regarded with a similar if not the same type of scrutiny.

European women's bodies were viewed as dangerous and suspicious due to the fact that they had anatomy unlike that of males; African bodies were deemed hypersexual and ultimately nonhuman because of their polarization to whiteness.[10] Colonial expansion, enslavement, and "science" all contributed to the ways in which minoritized bodies came to be regarded within visual and actual European culture.[11] While the scientific community concluded Africans were biologically inferior, the institutions of enslavement and colonization advanced the conclusion that Africans were also inferior ideologically and socially. The Black body through the institutions of enslavement and colonial expansion therefore was turned into a corporal possession that only mattered as it was physically productive for plantation work. Enslavement as an institution visually and aesthetically altered the African body to such an extent that it left its corporal value open to interpretation and perception. Since African bodies were being viewed through a white supremacist and misogynistic "scientific" lens, their worth hinged on the ideological and imaginative convictions of Europeans.

In *Bodies That Matter: On the Discursive Limitations of Sex*, Judith Butler retraces the origins of materiality and asserts that when matter (flesh or corporeality) is not associated with reproduction, it is generally linked to origination and causality.[12] In their discussion of matter, Butler locates the substances of which any physical object consists or is composed, and these substances themselves assume histories and forms that are rooted in a matrix of origination and composure inevitability colored and framed by European rationality and power, and leading one to intelligibility—a subjective reading of matter.[13] Consequently, if the body is matter, how that body comes to materialize, mean, or matter is contingent on its origination; it is not a given but is produced. Bodies are produced through acts of performativity, which are tethered to a "historicity" of discourse and a "historicity" of norms that constitute our collective discourse about bodies. Therefore, the normalization of the body depends largely on reiteration and exclusion.

Performativity is not "willful" or "arbitrary" but has been confined to the domains of intelligibility, which are bound with the effects of a "historicity of discourse" and "historicity" of norms, which have constituted the power of discourse.

The institutions of enslavement and colonial expansion gave white enslavers the power to define and determine the worth of Black bodies by physically and ideologically removing them from their respective social contexts. As a result, enslavers reinvented the materiality of African bodies, turning them into Black commodities (which inevitably excluded them from conceptions of normalcy). Placing themselves in a position of authority over African bodies, they simultaneously placed themselves in a position to reproduce the intelligibility of African bodies. Accordingly, Europeans began to recreate and rewrite the origins, transformation, and potentiality of African bodies through the institutions of enslavement, colonization, and eventually science.[14] Hence, African bodies existed during enslavement and colonization as commodified possessions and were regarded within the realm of science as either apes or subhuman creations that happened to be bodies. The materiality of their bodies became less significant and in fact disposable, therefore scripting African bodies as having no origins, no transformative abilities, and no potential, inevitably making them not matter. As a consequence of this process, African bodies became the mere corporal manifestations of the European imagination. The social and ideological assignment of Black bodies as deviant, impulsive, hypersexual, imitative, and criminal by European science, culture, and society obscured the social and political relations of their African ancestry and customs, and the value attributed to their bodies as possessions was therefore solely based upon their presented appearance. Europeans then measured that appearance against bodies they deemed normal or typical (which were inevitably their own).

This antiquated, white supremacist, fatphobic, and misogynistic European—now American—body politics continues to inform our collective consciousnesses through the dissemination of popular media. Invading our lives, it exalts mostly white, cis, straight, light-skinned, and thin bodies, while simultaneously utilizing the praxis of invisibility and neoliberal product-pushing to show all of us who do not embody the aforementioned characteristics that our bodies and beings have little worth and value. If this is our inheritance, then how does one begin to value, love, or truly see their own body if love and value are not reflected back to them? How does one begin to see themselves as desirable if their beings and bodies are not shown to them in any favorable or worthy light? The politics of representation and the politics of desirability have always shared an integral relationship to one another, informing each other and converging within the realm of popular media. Popular media is usually the first source of our negative views about ourselves, stressing our imagined deficits, and exaggerating our lack of worth. The politics of representation and desirability are not only vital to shaping the ways that we see and value ourselves, but they are also imperative when it comes to viewing and evaluating other bodies that are not our own, and therefore determining other beings' worth based on our subjective evaluations of their bodies.

In *The Body Is Not an Apology*, Sonya Renee Taylor discusses how all forms of media serve as an intersection where the politics of representation and the politics of desirability meet. If minoritized people do not see themselves represented within mainstream or queer art forms, this absence facilitates a negative self-perception. Taylor's assertion hints at how media is the mechanism by which this negative relationship is created, eroding our own subjective ideals about our desirability.[15] The invisibility politics at work within media presents us with a "constant barrage of shame discrimination and body-based oppression" that leaves us all in need of "something radical to challenge these messages."[16] Mainstream media embedded within our current neoliberal political landscape aid in shape-shifting us from citizens into consumers, from human subjects to commodified objects. By not adequately or accurately representing minoritized bodies, while exalting bodies that are already socially located in spaces of privilege, the media inevitably produces the psychological and bodily deficits within its consumerist populace as well as the urge to seek ready-made solutions for their projected inadequacies. We see bodies as normative in our youth that we come to see as nonnormative or atypical in adulthood. And while neoliberalism continues to reshape our everyday lives, reiterating that our worth begins and ends with our buying power and our ability to consume, if one does not see their embodied reflections within media, they in turn begin to devalue that embodiment and diminish their perception of their own social worth.[17]

My first thoughts about desirability started at the movies. It was in that dark theater where I was, like Toni Morrison's character Pauline in *The Bluest Eye*, introduced to the destructive concepts of romantic love and physical beauty.[18] As a child of the '80s, some of my favorite films to watch were *Annie*, *Heathers*, and *The Breakfast Club*.[19] I had to creatively watch most of them, as they did not reflect my embodiment back to me. None of the main characters, even the ones in the background, were Black, so I had to relate to the films through their overarching themes and messages. There were two other films I loved that did include Black characters. In fact, most if not all of the characters in *The Color Purple* and *The Women of Brewster Place* were Black, and some of them were even Black and queer. After coming into the realization that I was also both Black and queer, I began to seek out more films that reflected my identity and embodiment.

It was the '90s and I was a teenager. I had a car, and in between my deli job at the mall, track practice, and band rehearsal, I would take my mom's Blockbuster card and rent everything they had in the gay and lesbian section of the store. The first films that I rented were *The Incredibly True Adventures of Two Girls in Love* and *The Watermelon Woman*.[20] While I enjoyed both films because it was the second time in my life that I was introduced to characters that were both Black and queer, both films left me with the uncomfortable feeling that if I was going to live my life as a lesbian, then my world would have to become white. In *The Incredibly True Adventures of Two Girls in Love* the protagonist was white and in *The Watermelon Woman* the protagonist was Black, yet in both films each character pursued interracial relationships, and because of those relationships, both characters' worlds became all-white worlds. While *The Watermelon Woman* delineated the complicated feelings that existed for both characters when it came to dating interracially in a racially segregated and polarized world, *The Incredibly True Adventures of Two Girls in Love* pretended that race didn't exist at all, never once having the main characters, nor any of the characters, address or discuss issues of race. Instead, the film's content concentrated heavily on what it was like to have two people date across class lines. In addition, in both films each of the Black characters seemed reluctant about pursuing a lesbian relationship, while the white characters were portrayed as pressuring them, relentlessly, to engage in interracial and queer intimacy. In both films the Black characters had limited contact with Black family members. In *The Watermelon Woman*, the Black main character had two Black lesbian friends who were a couple, and every time they appeared all they did was interrogate their friend about pursuing an interracial relationship.

Alongside my viewing of these films, I had begun to formulate my own attraction to white girls. These girls often displayed an irreverence to societal expectations of femininity and gendered expectation. They were usually athletic, physically strong, and did not seem to care what boys in our school thought about them. They mirrored the soft studs/butches in these films, but often my crushes on them were unrequited because either they were not out to themselves or to others.[21] Or, even worse, they would try to solidify a connection with me through a racist microaggression[22]—"jokingly" calling their backsides "ghetto" if they were large in any aspect, or asking me some question about a popular rap song to make sense of it for them. This space was where I was introduced to, and became familiar with, my own intersection that Taylor spoke of—where the politics of representation had informed my own politics of desirability. Hari Ziyad asserts that "desire is political," and that it is "both affected by and simultaneously shaping systems of power and oppression."[23] Further, Ziyad contends that "desirability politics deal with the questions of how social ideas for attractiveness can have a pull, and how one can also pull back."[24] I did not understand desirability politics then as I do now, so I thought my initial crushes on white girls had to do with my own personal preferences, seeing my specific taste as innate or natural, not taking into account that what I had been watching had influenced my views on what I saw as attractive, desirable, or sexy.

The Black lesbians in the films I had watched seemed to come to know their own desirability only through the lens of whiteness, and I began mimicking this praxis back to myself. The characters only came to understand that they were attractive as queer people because someone who embodied white queerness told them so, pursued them, dated them. I soon began to recognize that my teenage crushes were nothing more than manifestations of Black queer invisibility. In watching these films, I did not see myself, nor did I once see a character that would desire someone like me. My desperate need for queer affirmation had facilitated these crushes. I began to pull back, recognizing that I didn't actually want them so much as I desired to live out my queerness, and their white bodies had come to represent that queerness to me. White queer bodies were overly represented in the films I was watching, and even after I checked out more lesbian directed and produced films like *Go Fish* and *Bar Girls*, those films continued to follow the same pattern. Black lesbian women could actualize their queer identities only through white queer intimacy and relationships.[25]

While I found no issue, and still don't, with queer interracial relationships, I didn't feel as if they reflected what the queer world was actually like. When I entered queer spaces, blatant looks and expressions of racism, hostility, and racialized exoticism framed my reality. Questions about my hair, what my parents did for a living, and so on were asked in an attempt to place me and decipher my worth. The films I had watched, which I used as teaching tools to help me navigate queer life, made it seem like these types of interactions among queer folks who were racially and culturally different didn't exist. I didn't understand how insidious transgressions happened continuously in queer venues between white queer folks, Black queer folks, and other queer folks of color, and in the films everybody would end up in bed together or continue to pursue relationships with one another. Gay racism and homonormative politics manifested in almost every corner of my young Black lesbian life, but the cinema that was specifically geared toward me and my community never showed me two Black lesbian women loving or pursuing relationships with each other. I did, however, find some respite in the films and television show created and directed by Patrik-Ian Polk. *Punks*, *Noah's Arc*, and *The Skinny* all showed me Black queer men loving one another, desiring each other, and sharing communal space in stories framed by laughter, joy, and struggle.[26] While Polk's creations mirrored my own experiences as a Black queer person more closely than the prior films did, they still did not show me Black lesbian women desiring one another, pursuing each other, or living their lives together.

By the time I entered graduate school, I had ended my pursuit. I still used television and films for entertainment purposes, but I had given up on the expectation that I would see me, or my loved ones, reflected in these media. That was until my mama called and told me that there was a new Showtime series called *The L Word* and instructed me and my friends to start watching.[27] I was intrigued and a little bit excited about the potential of this new show. I remained hopeful that me and my Black queer comrades would not only be able to enjoy the show but also be able to see Black lesbian representation. Yet, after six seasons of the show, I had no such luck seeing any reflection of Black queer life, intimacy, or relationships.

From Bette and Tina to Alice and Tasha, every time the show presented a Black lesbian woman, she was deeply tied to a white lesbian woman. Occasionally the *L World* showed Bette's Black father, but there were few other Black characters. Tasha, the Black butch lesbian character on the series, didn't have any people. No Black queer friends, comrades, past lovers, or even a mama or daddy. No aunts, no childhood friends who functioned more as cousins. Tasha, like Bette, existed in a world shrouded in whiteness. Even when the show added Latinx characters, Papi and Carmen, both of their worlds were also cloaked in whiteness, and when the audience finally got to meet their families, the portrayals were mired in racist stereotypes. The Black and Latinx lesbian characters in the show continued to be isolated, forgotten, or cast out from their home communities, friends, and family. These characters were in such desperate need of queer-affirming contact, and seemed to find it only through forming community with and dating queer white folks. They all needed to be convinced that it was okay to exist in a queer world and unabashedly lead queer lives, and the white queer characters gave them the courage to do so.

Although I should have known better (after all I was in my midthirties), I once again became hopeful about the potential expansion of Black queer visibility and intimacy in popular media. After all, the Supreme Court had finally made same sex marriage legal in the US, popular media had more mainstream reach due the success of shows like *Will and Grace.*[28] Ellen DeGeneres was now a cover girl with her own daytime talk show.[29] Streaming capabilities had been created, and everyone had begun binge-watching shows routinely.[30] I thought, surely now was the time where that expansion would be realized. I was wrong. While hit television shows like *The Fosters* and *Empire* and hit streaming shows like *Orange Is the New Black* all made bold moves to depict intimacy, sexual scenarios, and romance as it happens and unfolds within queer relationships, and popular new online outlets like *Huffington Post* and *NewNowNext* showcased same-sex weddings and proposals, there was still an absence of Black lesbian representation.[31] Any time Black lesbian intimacy, love, and/or desire was depicted within these new outlets or television shows, it continued to perpetuate the idea of Black lesbians existing solely in tandem with their pursual of, and romantic relationships with, white women. Whether it was a story about weddings or a television show that sought to tell the love story of two lesbian characters, the union was always interracial. Popular and queer media seem still beholden to the idea that Blackness and queerness are mutually exclusive categories, and that the story of Black lesbian identities can only be told through a white lens. This promotes narrow-minded and homogenized representation of apolitical queer folks who are almost always cis and mostly white. It furthers misconceptions about queerness for mainstream viewing audiences by presenting queerness in line with domesticity and consumption. These limited media portrayals aim to showcase queer stories without disrupting heteronormative notions of identity, and instead, frame queer lives to run congruent with these normative notions.

Consequently, if our own recognitions of desirability begin with antiquated body politics and are then further exacerbated through neoliberal media's insistence on only presenting certain bodies and identities as beautiful and sexy, this ultimately creates the false notion that our bodies and identities are not worthy of space, recognition, or celebration. This insidious dynamic not only shapes the ways in which individuals value or don't value their own subjective existences but also permeates our institutions. In the Unite for Reproductive and Gender Equity op-ed "What Are the Politics of Desirability?" author Tristan asserts that it is vital to our survival for everyone to pay attention to how the politics of desirability and the politics of representation pervade our lives daily. Tristan contends, "It is important to recognize when you are participating in these harmful stereotypes about who deserves to be loved," arguing that various identities get their understandings of their value from seeing and not seeing their embodiment and identities portrayed within media. So, "while many may think of who we are attracted to as personal preference, . . . [i]t's impossible to separate one's desires from the culture and society in which they were formed."[32] Therefore, if certain bodies are exalted while other bodies are absent or condemned, institutions, like schools, law enforcement, and other state-sanctioned structures, begin and continue to mirror these identical sentiments within their organizational configurations. Thus, Black queer bodies, trans bodies, fat bodies, and disabled bodies are continuously met with indifference, disregard, and invisibility within and outside of the realms of media.

In concert with our culture's obsession over adult bodies, our culture fixates on the bodies of children, not only categorizing, valuing, and defining them as precious or pedestrian but also agonizing over where to place them within the parameters of our Western body politics. For a body in our culture to signify meaning and value, its physiological assessment of worth at birth usually relies upon its various traits. Due to the white supremacist, misogynistic, and ableist nature of our culture, these valuative markers are often based on the sex, race, and abilities of a baby's body. As a consequence, sex designation has been and remains vital to our culture's designation of ideological and social worth. We see this especially in the omnipresence of gender reveal parties. Created in 2008 by Jenna Myers Karvunidis, because she saw herself as a person who likes "to have fun," gender reveals are an immensely popular phenomenon today.[33] According to historians, however, the more universal practice of American families hosting baby showers did not begin until the 1930s with the publication of Emily Post's book *Etiquette: The Blue Book of Social Usage*, in which Post calls them "stork showers."[34] Whereas baby showers are parties thrown by expectant parent(s) who have already been made aware of the projected sex assignment of their child, gender reveal parties are when the expectant parent(s) find out in front of all of their guests, customarily in an over-the-top way.[35] While Karvunidis's party ended with tears of joy, cheers, and cake eating, others have not. At least five reported fires have ensued because of gender reveal parties, with the most recent being the devastating 2020 El Dorado, California, fire.[36]

This obsession with the projected sex designation isn't just facilitated by parents' curiosity. We live in a culture that makes expectant guardians and parents feel immense pressure, not only from their loved ones and families but also from the neoliberal and heteronormative undercurrent that pervades our society and demands our consumerist population to wield our buying in response to an upcoming birth, adoption, or even fostering of a child. Our culture isn't fixated on the gender binary just due to our society's need for antiquated gendered organization; rather, this obsession is also due to neoliberal gendered and heterosexist product pushing. Baby dolls, kitchen sets, vacuum cleaners, and the color pink for girls; action figures, toy guns, wrestling mats, and the color blue for boys. Toys for children therefore do not just function as playthings that bring joy and delight but act as socializing tools for those children to then grow up and fit within our narrow conceptions of human identity. Cishet folks are beholden to these restrictive sex/gender designations and performative expectations not only because they may hold misogynist, homophobic, or transphobic views but also because they are deeply invested in a way of life that reflects and affirms their lived experience. However, most human identities cannot fit neatly and/or easily within these tapered gendered or sexual roles. Most Black queer and trans folks, who often diverge from these problematic and exclusive customs, await hatred, violence, and even death as a consequence of such resistance.

A recent Pew poll discussed by GLAAD (Gay and Lesbian Alliance Against Defamation) indicated that while "nearly 90% of Americans say they personally know someone who is lesbian, gay or bisexual," only "20% of Americans say they personally know someone who is transgender."[37] Media representation of minoritized identities has become especially vital for people who otherwise do not lead diverse and inclusive lives. In addition, it is also extremely important for minoritized people to be able to see their reflections within popular and alternative forms of media for their own development. As Laverne Cox asserts in the Netflix documentary *Disclosure: Trans Lives on*

Screen, popular media representations of trans folks are critical to their own ontological existences as individuals who transgress the rigid gender binary.[38] Popular and alternative forms of media serve as a window into the lives of folks that some of us would not get to know otherwise. Through television and film, we are introduced to story arcs that do not mirror our own and characters who participate and indulge in things that we otherwise wouldn't. Through them, we are able to build an understanding about the lives and experiences of those who differ from us. Similarly, minoritized individuals are also able to utilize media as a teaching tool for their own embodied affirmation, psychological confidence, and confirmation that who they might eventually become will be embraced within our society, regardless of initial rejections by family or peers. Popular and alternative forms of media create diverse worlds and inclusive experiences for us every time we pick up a remote. However, if those glimpses are limited, or if that diverse representation is narrow, stereotypical, or even violent in certain aspects, what does that do to individuals who are already made vulnerable by their respective social locations within our culture?

As an extremely curious person, I have always sought out various forms of media to learn about others. Learning about trans identities was difficult for me, a queer cis person, because just as my examples of Black lesbian identities were limited, my exposure to trans people and their lives was also slight. One of the first lesbians I met was at the nightclub I used to frequent during my teens.[39] Her name was Erin, and she gave me all types of Morticia Addams played by Angelica Houston vibes.[40] She was statuesque, gorgeous, and the kind of bartender who always gave you a heavy pour. I lived for her. After a couple months of brief small talk, she began to talk about the difficulties of being a trans lesbian, and how a lot of lesbian women she encountered were transphobic, volatile, and/or made uncomfortable by her trans identity. I recognized in that moment that out of all the films I had watched that had a queer focus, none of them had been about trans identity. I also recognized that Erin was the only trans person I had ever met in the small township I was growing up in.

The next day I went to Blockbuster and asked an employee there if they had any films that focused on trans identity. He said, "Oh yeah we have that film *The Crying Game*."[41] I rented it and went home to watch it right away. I was overwhelmed with sadness and shocked at how the beautiful trans protagonist, Dil, was treated. Not only was her straight-identified cis male companion, Fergus, mortified that she was a trans woman, but he subsequently punched her in the face and began to vomit in her bathroom. Although the two eventually fell madly in love after their initial encounter, Dil was still made to dress as a conventional man in order to evade capture from the IRA and was subsequently put in a position to have to kill her former lover's rival, Jude, who discovered that Dil had been having a liaison with his former comrade Fergus. The film ends by Fergus taking the fall for Dil, protecting her identity and allowing her to evade capture from the IRA. Although my initial takeaway from the film was that the director, Neil Jordan, was trying to present a sympathetic portrayal of a trans woman, showing that trans women were beautiful and loveable, I also found the initial violence and repulsion of her lover after he learned she was trans to be a deplorable and disgusting representation of trans identity—not only for trans folks to witness, who might view the film to see a glimpse of themselves but also for cis viewers watching the film to understand trans identity and what the lives of trans folks are like.

Unfortunately, *The Crying Game* was not the only film or television show that portrayed trans people's lives in relation to violence and rejection. In the Netflix documentary *Disclosure: Trans Lives on Screen*, Nick Adams of GLAAD argues that *The Crying Game* ultimately created a trend in popular media of portraying romantic encounters between cishet male suitors and trans women that start with an initial reaction of disgust. This narrative became the overwhelming crux in these representations.[42] He contends, "In the same way that *Psycho* created this ripple effect of cross-dressing psychopathic serial killers, *The Crying Game* created a ripple effect of men reacting with vomiting when they see a transgender woman."[43] Similarly, Michael D. Cohen asserts that in his initial viewing of the film in his youth as a trans person, he feels, "Emotional even when I talk about it. The repulsion . . . because that's how I felt about myself for so long. Like will people be repelled. Will people be . . . you know, the word disgust."[44] He goes on to further articulate, "You know there's so much shame that people have to fight through and come out the other side of, and then it emerges again in weird and insidious ways somewhere down the road."[45]

This is not the only way trans characters are subjected to violent depictions. In his chapter "Unlosing Brandon: Brandon Teena, Billy Tipton, and Transgender Biography," J. Jack Halberstam argues that there have typically been three ways that the trans biography has been presented within the realms of popular media and news.[46] Halberstam defines them as the *projects of stabilization*, *rationalization* and *trivialization*, and argues that transgender identity as it is expounded upon in these realms is "used as a marker for all kinds of people who challenge, deliberately or accidently, gender normativity."[47] The *project of stabilization* is described as anytime a trans person's body, story arc, or life narrative is presented as a way to counteract "the destabilizing effects of the transgender narrative," which then "are defused by establishing the transgender narrative as strange, uncharacteristic, and even pathological."[48] This project can be seen in films like *Judith of Bethulia*, *Terror Train*, *Psycho*, *Dressed to Kill*, and *Silence of the Lambs*, which all show trans lives as strange, atypical, and pathological.[49] This project emphasizes not only that trans individuals should be seen as strange and atypical but that their uncharacteristic identities inevitably turn them into psychopathic deviants bent on killing others to satisfy their acute tastes.[50] All of these use trans characters' identities to reify gender normativity and to solidify the necessitation for all to operate within the gender binary, establishing it as the only normal way to express and live one's gender.

We can see the *project of rationalization*, manifest in the television show *Bosom Buddies* and in the films *Tootsie*, *Just One of the Guys*, *Mrs. Doubtfire*, and *Big Mama's House*, where the characters transgress the gender binary only momentarily, either out of economic need or in order to occupy a space that they would have traditionally not been allowed in due to the constraints of gender normativity.[51] In *Disclosure*, Laverne Cox asserts that these comedic portrayals of gender transgressive expression and identity are dehumanizing to trans people, like the portrayals of trans people as dangerous psychopathic killers. "These images are so disparaging towards all women, and we see comedians dressing up as women in order to get a job in *Tootsie* or affordable housing in the case of *Bosom Buddies*. These are all real obstacles for actual trans people."[52] Not only is the *project of rationalization* utilized by mainstream media in order to proclaim that individuals who disrupt, diverge, or contravene societal gender expectations only do so to advance their goals of financial stability, but this cinematic rendering of trans identity as temporary, or a phase in one's life, also serves to placate "mainstream viewers by returning the temporarily transgender subject to the comforting and seemingly inevitable matrix of hetero-domesticity."[53] In all of the aforementioned examples, the characters return to gender normativity because they ultimately fall in love with another character that believes them to be another gender, and in order to actualize the romantic connection to the other character they must confess that they are in fact not the gender that they have been pretending to be, and ultimately state their rationalization for doing so.

Finally, the *project of trivialization*, or any form of storytelling that functions as a cautionary tale against trans identities and the transgender subject, can be seen in the films *A Florida Enchantment* and *Beyond the Valley of the Dolls*, as well as in a television episode of *The Jeffersons* where George's old friend Eddie, from the army, returns as Edy. It is also depicted in the films *Fast Break*, *Soldier's Girl*, *TransAmerica*, and *Dallas Buyer's Club* where we see each trans character treated as an anomaly.[54] Each trans character exists only to expand the worldviews of the other characters. They teach the other characters, enduring the rage and violence when their trans identities are revealed, and are only able to find peace with themselves as trans subjects when the cishet characters in the film or television show accept them for who they are. In each instance the trans subject's own interior struggle with their identities is superseded by the cishet characters' struggle to make sense of their identities, as they grapple with how to untether the trans subject's identity from their own evaluations of their cishet identities. Consequently, these films and guest appearances on television by a trans character ultimately belittle trans identities and instruct audiences to see trans subjects as non-archetypal individuals whose lives are so out of the ordinary that if they do encounter hostility, violence or rejection from others, it is due to their own gender transgression, and not to transphobia or the narrow constraints of the gender binary.

In addition to these harmful depictions of trans women and trans femininities, in more depictions of trans masculinities we see these same limiting story arcs for trans characters—even in more contemporary depictions. Not only are trans masculinities or trans male characters not seen in popular media as much, but when characterized in queer media, their depictions have been not just problematic but also deleterious. Max, a trans man character on the Showtime series *The L Word*, started as a loving, thoughtful, and shy character when they were introduced in the show as Moira, a butch lesbian from the Midwest whom one of the main characters meets in a bar during a visit to her hometown. Jenny and Moira begin a romantic relationship and Moira then returns with Jenny to Los Angeles to meet Jenny's friends and community, and to begin a new life on the West Coast.[55] While in LA, Moira discovers through the friendships she creates that she in fact is not a butch lesbian but rather a trans man who shortly thereafter begins his journey into self-actualization by beginning to transition. After Max begins his transition, he reemerges as an angry, violent, and abusive boyfriend.

In *Disclosure*, Zeke Smith asserts that "Max is the first recurring trans masculine character on a television series. Then Max starts testosterone, and Max goes from being nice and likeable to raging A-hole."[56] Max's journey of self-discovery unveils a startling and transphobic perspective of trans masculinities through a lesbian lens. In addition, Brian Michael Smith in the same documentary states, "As someone who was transitioning at the time of this show that was problematic for me because *The L Word* is a lesbian show, and so they were looking at trans people through a lesbian lens."[57]

Not only were audiences expected to view Max's character as unreasonable, unstable, and ultimately a threat to their happy lesbian community, but audiences were also expected to view Max as a traitor: a traitor to women, to their community, and ultimately to their own feminist ideals. In *Disclosure*, Zeke Smith states, "The writers and producers of *The L Word* approach to Max is that they are seeing trans men increasingly enter the lesbian community and viewing them as traitors to feminism."[58] Not only is this characterization of Max on a popular lesbian show harmful to cis lesbian viewers because of it engendering a transphobic and suspicious perspective about trans men and trans masculinities, but in rendering Max's character as anti-feminist, it also hurt many trans men who loved and watched the show as well. These men were simultaneously re-entering their home lesbian communities with their new identities only to encounter transphobia and hostility from lesbians. Zeke Smith concludes, "As an audience we are not supposed to root for Max, we're supposed to root against Max."[59]

The ways in which queer and trans political allegiances functioned on *The L Word*, through the characterization of Max and the other cis lesbian characters on the show, is a consummate example of just how dangerous homonormativity and neoliberal politics can be for real queer and trans communities. Instead of showing any of the characters engrossed in collective endeavors for structural and institutional change with regard to anti-Blackness, anti-queerness, or anti-transness, the show portrays its characters' attempts at freedom and power through their reliance on consumption, domesticity, and homonormative and anti-Black conceptions of their identities. The characters' queer and/or trans identities were narrow and homogenized queer political identities that not only reflect the anti-Black, anti-trans, and classist beliefs of society but also reflect the tenets of current neoliberal thought. When the show did try and insert any kind of political aggression within the characters' story arcs, those politics did not contest or diverge from dominant heteronormative or homonormative assumptions. In fact, they often upheld them, sustained those assumptions, presenting the audience with a demobilized gay and trans constituency that was deeply invested in domesticity and consumption, instead of freedom or liberation.

The intersection where the politics of representation and the politics of desirability converge for transgender folks operates within three working frames. The first are the films and television shows that characterize trans identities and lives as undesirable ones—lives that are framed by rejection from loved ones, family, comrades, and the like. In addition, these characterizations also demonstrate to their audiences that if a trans person or body is desired by another character in a film or television show, it is only because there is something fundamentally wrong with the pursuant. The suitor is either a misfit, an outcast, or otherwise so desperate for romantic and intimate connection that they end up pursuing someone who, unbeknownst to them, transgresses gender normativity. This is why we see countless examples in popular media of characters who are mortified, repulsed, become violent, or have another kind of visceral reaction when they are made to recognize that who they were about to become intimate with isn't who they thought they were. Not only do these frames posit the trans body and individual as strange or non-representative of others, but they also assert that trans people are liars who deceive their love interests about who they really are in order to be loved or desired.

These distorted depictions of trans people and trans lives in popular and alternative forms of media facilitate real-world outcomes for trans folks, especially for Black trans women and Black nonbinary folks. The gay/trans panic defense "legitimizes and excuses violent and lethal behavior against members of the LGBTQ+ community."[60] This defense strategy "asks a jury to find that a victim's sexual orientation or gender identity is to blame for the defendant's violent reaction, including murder."[61] In 2019, the Human Rights Campaign reported that "22 transgender people and gender nonconforming people were killed," and almost all of them were Black transgender women.[62] In 2020, "at least 28 transgender people have been murdered, or their death [has been deemed as] suspicious," with most of them being either Black trans women or Black nonbinary people.[63] The politics of invisibility and hypervisibility are tethered when it comes to the representation of Black trans women and Black nonbinary people in media. These politics operate on the same axis, making Black trans women and Black nonbinary individuals virtually absent while at the same making certain depictions of them hypervisible. Black trans women are often given roles as sex workers or drug-addicted outcasts in guest appearances on television, and in films when they do appear. Or, even worse, their presence is completely absent, exacerbating the alarming idea that in order to have and live a trans experience one must be white.

Western body politics, which asserts that certain bodies are normal and others deviant by white supremacist, fatphobic, misogynist, homophobic, and transphobic paradigms, bleeds into our culture, infecting our society that has already been altered by neoliberal ideals. Due to their assimilative praxes, Western body politics both emphasize and erode the specificity of divergent identities as insignificant. Assimilationist politics is one of the main organizing principles of neoliberalism in that it needs to erase the specificity of all subversive identities in order to subsume them under the auspices of buying power and accumulating assets, which separates us from one another—not only financially but also ontologically. The power of marginalized individuals and communities has always been through collective organizing and resistance to the oppressive regimes that have attempted to snuff them out through institutional means. Lack of access to housing, food, and other resources creates immense vulnerability and isolation. If our window into other worlds and lives, namely media, engenders a harmful and ideologically violent body politics in tandem with a neoliberal politics, it ultimately reveals the blatant disregard with which Black trans bodies are viewed and valued. If we do not see them, or if we only see them through distorted and violent lenses that depict them as atypical, then it is no wonder that trans and nonbinary bodies, specifically Black trans and nonbinary bodies, are often met with harm, violence, and even death. Not only does the media excuse the violence that Black trans women face through its distorted characterizations, but the neoliberal state then sanctions their deaths through its homophobic and transphobic laws.

This is the historical paradox that has resulted from trans representation in popular film and television. In *Disclosure*, Nick Adams asserts, "For decades Hollywood has taught audiences how to react to trans people, and sometimes they're being taught that the way to react to us is fear. That we're dangerous. That we're psychopaths or serial killers. That we must be deviants or perverts."[64] So, creating trans characters and trans stories that show audiences the interiority of trans lives is a vital endeavor, not only for people who do not have the fortune of knowing anyone who is trans but also for the affirmative potential of that reflection to audiences who are trans. On the flip side, having a character vomit or become violent upon recognizing a trans character, or dismissing trans identities as example of strangeness, can result in actual abuse or even murder. The hypervisibility of problematic trans portrayals in popular media, as well the invisibility of Black lesbian intimacy and desirability, must evolve past these distorted representations and begin to present racialized queer folks and trans folks with dignity, dimensionality, and humanity. If our entertainment cannot move forward, how can our society?

>>>>>>>>>>>>>>

Black trans actress Angelica Ross made history as the first trans actress to ever star in two recurring television shows, playing the tough sleepaway camp nurse, Rita, in Ryan Murphy's *American Horror Story: 1984* and as Candy, an overlooked but fierce and beautiful ball walker in the widely watched FX series *Pose*.[65] Activist Raquel Willis was appointed executive director of *Out* magazine in 2018, making her the first Black trans woman to stand at the helm of leadership in one of country's longest-running LGBTQ+ publications.[66] Lena Waithe's television series *Boomerang* ran for two seasons, and her show *The Chi* introduced audiences to Black trans actress Jasmine Davis, who played the illustrious Imani, a Black trans woman engaged in a mutually respectful and loving relationship with the tender-hearted gangster Trig, played by R&B singer Luke James.[67,68] Both best-selling trans author Janet Mock and actress and trans advocate Laverne Cox have become household names.[69] South Sudanese model Aweng Ade-Chuol married her fiancée, Alexis Ade-Chuol, and in an Instagram post that went viral, she announced to the world that she had just married her best friend.[70] *Pose* is simultaneously teaching audiences about the 1980s AIDS epidemic and how transphobia was rampant within queer nightlife.[71] It's showing us how the Black and Latinx queer house ball scene was the birthplace of voguing and how the function of Black queer and trans rhetorical practices are often employed as a form of resistance.[72] Black actress Gabrielle Union and her husband, three-time championship NBA player Dwyane Wade, made their love and advocacy for their child, Zaya, who is trans, known through their social media platforms. On a recent episode of the podcast, *All the Smoke with Matt Barnes*, Wade expressed his admiration for his child's strength and courage when it came to how Zaya emotionally handled the ridicule of online trolls.[73] Concurrently, the mission statement of the most ever-present movement and network for collective change of our time, Black Lives Matter, reads that it seeks to "affirm the lives of Black queer and trans folks, disabled folks, undocumented folks, folks with records, women and all Black lives along the gender spectrum."[74]

All of these wildly popular and symbolic representations of Black queer and trans lives are exactly what I needed growing up. I craved seeing Black queer and trans bodies playing robust three-dimensional characters that embodied complex and intricate political identities—manifested within newsfeeds, illuminating my movie and television screens. It is so important that current Black creatives like Lena Waithe, Issa Rae, Michaela Coel, and Ava DuVernay are producing, writing, and showing us our reflections. Films like *Gun Hill Road* and *Ma Vie en Rose* are just what general audiences have needed for so long, films that tell our stories in robust and multidimensional ways.[75] They introduce characters not only to represent Black, queer, and trans storytelling but also to reflect a cinematic counternarrative that redirects their art away from longstanding white supremacist, homophobic, and transphobic tropes.

We are currently in a moment of ideological ruptures within the American television and film canons. Black queer and trans creatives are severing their art from the master narrative that kept telling them and us that Black trans and queer bodies could not serve as objects of desire, nor could they be exalted, worshipped, or obsessed over in the same ways that many people exalted white cishet actors.[76] Yance Ford in the documentary *Disclosure* asserts that "children cannot be what they cannot see, and it's not just about children. It's about all of us. We cannot be a better society, until we see that better society. I cannot be in the world, until I see that I am in the world."[77] While I am immensely grateful for Black queer and trans media makers showcasing our stories and lives for general audiences, we still need to see more white cishet media makers evolve past these antiquated, harmful, and often violent depictions. This is just the beginning of manifesting a Black queer and trans utopia. We are just getting started.

CHAPTER THREE

WE AIN'T HAVING A BALL

I created my Introduction to LGBTQ+ Studies course shortly after being hired by my university in 2008. As an educator, I've found that the beginning stages of systemic change are formulated when a student recognizes that marginalized folks are not just a part of history but also its architects. Because of this, I believe it is important that my Black LGBTQ+ students understand that knowledge has been socially and culturally constructed. Therefore, one of my pedagogical aims continues to be providing my students with the opportunity to both challenge and transcend that which has previously sought to define them. It is this type of learning that both empowers and transforms students, not only in the classroom but in their everyday lives. Since homophobia, transphobia, and white supremacy continuously frame their lives within and outside of queer communities by configuring borders around their day-to-day and ensuring that they doubt their intellectual, personal, or spiritual viability, forcing them to grapple with their own self-worth, I have always approached teaching as a way to counter this onslaught within their minds and lives. In many ways this reflexive praxis has been my most steady form of activism.

"YAAAASSS Dr. Story! You look fierce!" A consistent greeting from the nightclub to the classroom. It's usually a relatively young white cis gay man who gives me what he thinks is a culturally relevant salute. Or even worse, he makes the statement as if he owns the phrasing, and when asked where he learned that specific term or expression, he proudly explains how Mama Ru taught him all about it on *Drag Race*.[1] This cyclical encounter was another reason I felt the desperate need to create my Introduction to LGBTQ+ Studies course. I needed these young, white cis gays and lesbians to know that all of their new rhetorical phrases and terms that they thought they learned from popular programs such as *RuPaul's Drag Race*, *Married to Medicine*, and *Real Housewives*, terms such as *yas*, *werq*, *shade*, and *gag* were actually rooted in the Black and Latinx ballroom community, whose members created these resistive linguistic practices in direct response to state violence, sanctioned oppression, and homonormativity.[2] I also needed them to know that if they used these terms, phrases, or gestures in their everyday speech and interaction with others, they also needed to learn and practice the specific politic that comes with them—especially seeing as how much of the language and culture have been co-opted for mainstream consumption to the point that many are unaware of their roots. I definitely wanted all of my students to know that Stonewall was a series of uprisings in response to police brutality and inequity and not a party as it is often mistaken for today. I also needed these young people to understand that most of the queer liberatory privileges that they currently enjoy are due to the valiant efforts of Black queer and trans folks, specifically Black trans women.

While working on this book I've fallen in love with the television series *Lovecraft Country*.[3] Not just because Black creative Misha Green is ensuring that American audiences know that Black people have existed free, joyous, and radical at every point in history but also because in the fifth episode of the first season, the character Montrose Freeman attends a Black drag ball in the 1950s to support his longtime lover, Sammy.[4] Sammy places second at the glamorous affair where all of the attendees are decked out in feathers, glitter, male and female artifice, and even satin gloves.[5] Montrose watches his drag beauty with trepidation at first, glancing from behind a pole in the room in order to ensure all the guests don't see how entranced he is by Sammy. As Sammy sashays around the room, however, the pair lock eyes and move to the dance floor. As they dance slowly, the music picks up its tempo, and Sammy whisks Montrose away to join the rest of the drag queens on the floor, who lift Montrose in the air, spinning him around as glitter cascades down from the sky. Montrose closes his eyes, frees up his stiff body, and embraces the glitter that is raining down on him, giving the audience the feeling that the spin, the ball, and his lover placing second is a sort of rebirth for him. Montrose, a character who has thus far in the series attempted to keep his queerness hidden, finds comfort in this very Black queer space. He is free from the anti-Black and anti-queer sentiment of the outside world.

Watching this scene reminded me of my own experience at one of the first balls I ever attended. Although I was less apprehensive than Montrose, as it was 2009 and I was friends with many of the ball kids, I was still unsure. For instance, the start and end times threw me off, but the timing of balls is intentional. Since their inception, balls are purposely set to begin late in the evening and end early the next morning so as to not subject their participants to street harassment or other forms of physical or rhetorical violence.[6] In college and then graduate school, I could never attend the balls because the hours they ran were not conducive to my schedule, even though I loved to hear about them. The first ball I did attend was in Louisville, Kentucky, and it was thrown by my best friend Jaison Gardner, one of the founders of the Louisville ball scene. The venue was small but inviting, and all of the performers were extraordinary. For me, my first ball and every other one thereafter was a manifestation of what Black queer freedom dreams look like when materialized. Balls are spaces to trouble monolithic conceptions of Blackness. Balls are events where performers and spectators disrupt the heavily regulated mainstream notions of racialized sexuality and gendered performance, as well as unsettle and redefine notions of masculinity, nonbinary identity, and femininity. Balls are celebrations and rearticulations of family, and a way for the most marginalized within Black and queer communities to disidentify from dominant and normative tropes to remix them and make them their own.[7]

Before ever attending an actual ball, though, I was introduced to the ball scene through the cult classic *Paris Is Burning*.[8] The 1991 documentary brought the underground world of Black and Latinx queer and trans houses, balls, and new conceptions of families to the attention of the mainstream public. Through a series of interviews with the filmmaker, Jennifer Livingston, the house mothers, ball walkers, and various house members share their insights and perspectives on the ball scene in Harlem, New York, and how it came to be. In one of the interviews with house mother Pepper LaBeija, Pepper discusses the former and original mother of the House of LaBeija, Crystal LaBeija. In responding to Livingston's question about who they are, Pepper vibrantly says, "I'm not the founder. Crystal's the founder. I just rule it now, with a soft glove."[9] It was not until 2019, after Kino Lorber restored Frank Simon's 1968 documentary, *The Queen*, that I was visually introduced to Crystal. The film chronicles the 1967 Miss All-American Camp Beauty Pageant in which Crystal LaBeija competes as Miss Manhattan.[10] The competition concludes with Rachel Harlow winning, and while the documentary does feature a contestant pool, band, and audience that is racially diverse, once the crowning commences, Crystal goes into an immediate rage. After realizing that her wing-tipped eyeliner, beautiful lashes, cascading gown, and bold bright pink lip were not enough for the judges to designate her as the winner, and instead earned her only a fourth runner-up, she subsequently walks offstage before the judges crown the quintessential blonde, slim, and blue-eyed Harlow as the winner.

When Harlow begins to head backstage, Crystal is already in the midst of her rant. She begins to read Harlow, the judges, and the pageant organizer, Flawless Sabrina.[11] Another Black contestant who is also backstage and who shares Crystal's rage asks her, along with other contestants: "Do you think she deserved it? Answer me; you're not speaking for the damn camera. You have a mind." Crystal responds by saying, "She is not beautiful. She has no qualifications and she's bodiless." The other Black queen continues to reiterate her initial question to the other contestants, who are now completely silent and allow Crystal to continue with her perspective regarding the winner and the pageant. "No Darling! She didn't deserve it! You know she didn't deserve it. All of 'em, the judges knew it too. And her explanation for why she wanted the money. To put it in the bank, ha-ha-ha! She's not getting any money. Because Sabrina's not going to pay her. They're good friends."[12] At this point, Harlow and all of the other contestants are frozen, not just by Crystal's assertions about Harlow but by Crystal's accusation that Flawless Sabrina had rigged the pageant in her friend Harlow's favor. While Crystal continues to hurl her accusations and insults around the room, a white contestant whose face is semi-obscured from the audience's view interrupts her to say, "It's in bad taste and you're showing your colors. . . . You should have—"[13] Crystal quickly responds to the heckler by raising her voice, saying: "I am doing it bad, but I've got a . . . I have a right to show my color, darling. I am beautiful and I know I'm beautiful."[14] Another Black contestant who supports Crystal's viewpoint speaks up and says, "Don't talk about she's showing no color."[15]

Crystal's electric anger and poignant analysis about the fixed competition has now become a viral sensation on YouTube.[16] Her sentiments have also made their way into *RuPaul's Drag Race's* infamous "snatch game," where season nine contestant Aja embodied Crystal and even parroted her by saying, "I'm beautiful and I know I'm beautiful, damn it."[17] While Aja's stellar performance as Crystal is overwhelmingly humorous to watch, Crystal's rage and heartbreak during that 1967 competition was not. And it was not that particular pageant that ignited Crystal's wrath or even fueled her rage. Rather, what drove her ferocity was all of the pageants before that one, pageants where she had given her all without winning or placing highly even though she had deserved to. In addition, Crystal's experience at the Miss All-American Camp Beauty pageant was not an isolated or individual experience. The other Black contestants who cosigned her tirade had similar experiences. Black drag queens were regularly slighted when it came to winning prizes and placing highly in categories, and most, if not all, knew it had to do with their race.

Drag pageants date back to the 1860s with the annual "Odd Fellows Ball" being one of the first to capitalize on the inclusive energy of the times.[18] Taking place at the Hamilton Lodge in Harlem, the Odd Fellows balls were racially integrated affairs where the contestants and audience mingled with one another. They grew in popularity during the roaring twenties, attracting thousands of participants due to what was known as the "pansy craze," when it was deemed socially and culturally acceptable to embrace queer entertainment and such identities became trendy. As the balls reached their height in the 1930s, societal panic over their popularity ensued, and it became apparent to Mayor Fiorello LaGuardia that something needed to be done. Consequently, Mayor LaGuardia began to utilize the NYPD to openly harass, antagonize, and arrest any ball attendees who were caught between Fourteenth and Seventy-Second Streets, citing drag as an arrestable offense. This left only two neighborhoods where gender lines could be disrupted, blurred, or contested within New York City: Harlem and Greenwich Village. However, despite the balls' outward appearance of being inclusive and allowing Black contestants to compete, Black participants still felt immense pressure to either lighten their skin and/or acculturate their appearances to appease the anti-Black judges who never awarded a Black contestant a first-place prize in the first sixty-nine years of the Odd Fellows ball.[19]

After the 1930s, the Odd Fellows balls ended, and public drag pageants and balls went underground, not to reemerge until the 1960s, benefitting from the revolutionary thoughts that sought to undo strict and heteronormative conceptions about gender categories, sexual expression, and sexual identity.[20] By the 1970s, ten years after Crystal LaBeija's rant, Crystal formed the House of LaBeija and inevitably shaped the Black and Latinx ball scene and culture that we have come to know today.[21] No longer trusting the racially integrated ball and pageant scenes with Black and white contestants but mostly white judges who never recognized the talent and beauty of Black performers, Crystal, along with other Black and Latinx drag queens, femme queens, and ball kids became the creative architects of a scene that embraced and awarded the most vulnerable populations of New York City.[22] Yet, winning prizes and garnering fame from peers was not the only reason the scene was created. These Black and Latinx queer infrastructures known as houses and families were also a direct response to the inequity, homophobia, and generational poverty that plagued their participants.

Frank Leon Roberts, ball walker and ball aficionado, argued in his essay "There's No Place Like Home: A History of House Ball Culture" that the creation of queer families, houses, and balls as they manifested in New York during the late 1970s and early 1980s also had to do with the "spiraling decline of the city's welfare and social services . . . early gentrification of urban neighborhoods through private redevelopment . . . [and] decreases in funding for group-homes and other social services targeting homeless youth."[23] In addition, there was "a sharp rise in unemployment rates among Black and Latino men," which Roberts argued was further exacerbated by the HIV/AIDS crisis and the benign neglect with which the Reagan administration treated the issue.[24] This oppressive, violent, and dehumanizing reality for Black and Latinx LGBTQ+ folks, particularly youth, contributed to the birth of the Black and Latinx ball scene.[25]

Within a ten-year span, eight major houses were formed. These families and houses not only served as spaces of refuge for the Black and Latinx queer youth involved but also allowed them to escape, at least momentarily, from the heartbreaking rejection by their birth families and the outside world. In the scene these young people learned fundamental life skills through the creative kinships formed between house mothers, fathers, and siblings. Young people were taught how to better navigate generational poverty by pooling their money and resources together within their respective houses and chosen families. In addition, the scene also engendered ball kids to recognize and see the beauty in themselves and their collectives by awarding them trophies for their skills in walking and competing, and for their subjective nerve to embody identities that white supremacy, homophobia, and transphobia reject. The late Dorian Corey, mother of the house of Corey, articulated the type of self-actualization that balls gave to their participants when she said, "In real life you can't get a job as an executive unless you have the educational background and the opportunity. Now the fact that you are not an executive is merely because of the social standing of life. . . . Black people have a hard time getting anywhere and those that do are usually straight." She continued by saying, "In a ballroom you can be anything you want. You're not really an executive, but you're looking like an executive and therefore you're showing the straight world that I too can be an executive. If I had the opportunity, I could be one . . . and that is like a fulfillment."[26]

The New York ball scene in the 1980s had a profound influence and expansive impact on ball communities across the country. From the Midwest to the South to the West Coast, participants mirrored and differed from one another depending on region and cultures, but all of them enacted the same kind of affirmation and fulfillment. Each scene added their own spin on voguing, queer families, and houses. While the commercial success of the film *Paris Is Burning* certainly allowed more people outside of queer communities to become familiar with the ball scene, it was the queer art form of vogue, both the dance and the creative, resistive language, that inevitably catapulted the Black and Latinx ball scene into the mainstream. Starting with the infamous Malcolm McLaren song "Deep in Vogue," released in 1989, to Madonna's "Vogue," released in 1990, ballroom became a part of popular consumption. This gave many ball kids the hopeful assurance that greater success, acknowledgement, and even income were to come. But sadly, as with many marginalized groups, this was not the case. A new trend began of pop stars, such as Madonna and Janet Jackson, hiring ball kids to dance in their music videos. Willi Ninja, mother of the house of Ninja, was highlighted in

McLaren's "Deep in Vogue" music video before becoming a featured dancer in two of Janet Jackson's videos for her *Rhythm Nation* album. José Gutiérrez and Luis Camacho of the house of Xtravaganza were dancers in Madonna's *Vogue* video. However, during the culminating part of Madonna's song, where she vocalizes icons who embody the attitude and personae of voguing, she only mentions white cis and straight icons, not the architects of the ball scene. While Jackson initially selected Ninja to be highlighted in a central role in two of her videos, both Jackson and Madonna inevitably made Ninja, Gutiérrez, and Camacho serve as backdrops or props in their videos.[27] And though many of the queens featured in *Paris Is Burning* went on various talk shows to discuss the ball scene, drag, and voguing, this visibility fizzled out quickly along with popular conversations about the topic. Meanwhile, ball life continued despite the rise and fall of public interest, but many of the original founders endured various health complications due to HIV+ statuses, diabetes diagnoses, or ill health due to the lack of access to equitable health services throughout their adult lives.[28] Ultimately, the formative legends of ballroom passed away in isolation, broke and unclaimed.[29] The roots of the scene became obscured and its architects forgotten.

In Wolfgang Busch's documentary *How Do I Look*, which chronicled the Philadelphia and Harlem ball scenes over a decade, many of the entertainers who had been featured in *Paris Is Burning* were able to express their dismay, anger, and sadness over what had happened to the scene as a result of the success of the film and the mainstreaming of the culture. Carmen Xtravaganza, speaking to Busch about Livingston and her film, said, "I felt that she took advantage of all of us. All of us. You know. But I didn't benefit nothing out of it."[30] Marcel Christian LaBeija, ball historian and helper to Livingston and her crew while filming the documentary, told Busch, "She was an all-white crew and she was coming to Harlem on an adventure like that and she was well received, people respected her and liked her and treated her well . . . but in the brochure, *Paris Is Burning* was advertised as a film about prostitutes, welfare recipients, and messengers. That's what was actually wrote up in the brochure . . . that's when I really had a thing against her."[31] When Busch asks Octavia St. Laurent, "So, how do you feel about *Paris Is Burning*?" Octavia, whose back is to the camera, turns around to say, "It's a terrible movie."[32]

Many within various ball communities felt that Livingston's documentary focused too heavily on what they as a community deemed the negative aspects of ball life. Namely, the practices of shoplifting and sex work. They noted that Livingston presented these endeavors as a natural or innate part of Black and Latinx queer life, rather than a direct response to the sociopolitical inequities that the community had to navigate, endure, and survive through.[33] Due to Livingston giving absolutely no context for the sociopolitical conditions that framed ball life, many within ball communities felt that these aspects of her documentary gave mainstream audiences who did not live Black and Latinx queer or trans lives a negative representation of the ball scene, its architects, and its participants.

Despite the culture and its participants being taken advantage of by Livingston and others who sought to capitalize on the scene's innovativeness, many ball kids, mothers, fathers, and siblings are now able to make a substantial living due to the mainstream visibility of Black and Latinx ball culture. Members of the house of Ninja showcased their runway walking skills and makeup artistry on popular television shows like *America's Next Top Model*.[34] Further, with the birth of the new Black and Latinx queer youth scene in New York, as chronicled in the documentary *Kiki*, past aspects of families from the golden age of balls in the 1980s are simultaneously intertwined with new ways to enact change within impoverished Black and Latinx communities, allowing many ball kids to flourish in and relish ever greater visibility.[35] The success of the television show *Pose* has rectified and rearticulated the origins of the Black and Latinx ball scene, and in many ways undoes the obscene exploitation by mainstream culture.[36] Because the ball scene and its communities exist in the margins of society as a subculture, they are difficult to access. When their work, art, and experiences are shared with the mainstream public it is often through exploitation, appropriation, or co-optation. As general appreciation for ballroom culture grows, it is important to center the creators of this influential culture that continues to shape popular discourse. Our society's neoliberal subjugation commodifies actual lived identities into banal consumerist ones, putting emphasis on what individuals should be able to acquire through financial means, since racial and cultural identities are continually obscured through neoliberal praxes.[37] Neoliberalism posits that our society's problems with racism, sexism, homophobia, and transphobia are solely individual-level problems, considering them reflective of personal struggles as opposed to institutional or systemic issues. Neoliberal politics not only turns struggles for freedom into capitalist trends, but they also seek to commodify and repackage these things for flat and narrow public consumption, so that the realities of the struggles can be easily dismissed and co-opted.

An example of neoliberalism's anti-Black and anti-queer politics at work is the distribution of the 2015 film *Stonewall*, which whitewashed the impetus for the 1969 Stonewall uprisings.[38] In the film, the protagonist Danny Winters, played by actor Jeremy Irvine, leaves his small Indiana town for New York City after being kicked out of his house by his homophobic parents. Once in New York, Winters is exposed to the recurring anti-LGBTQ+ discrimination facilitated by NYPD and decides that it is time to do something about it. Ignoring the warnings from his gay, queer, and trans mentors in his newfound community in the city, who caution him against acts of radicalism, Danny ends up throwing the first brick that begins the three-day rebellion known as the Stonewall riots.[39] Not only does the film convert the Stonewall Inn into a mostly white gay and cis bar, but it also centers a white cis gay man as its protagonist, and as one of the first agitators of the rebellions, erasing the real clientele of the bar, and rewriting the Black and Latinx queer and trans roots of the three-day mutiny. Mainstream visibility of marginalized identities and communities should not signify racial and cultural erasure. This ahistorical and cinematically violent depiction of the origins of queer liberation is an unequivocal example of how severe gay racism, homonormativity, anti-Blackness, and trans erasure can manifest within and outside of queer communities—harmful not only to the respective members of Black and Latinx queer and trans communities but also to the general public who could have immensely benefitted from a more accurate and nuanced depiction of this important historical reckoning.[40]

Reality television stars and shows have now begun their own versions of co-optation that replicate the sanitizing and civilizing of Black and Latinx queer and trans identities. Many reality stars have incorporated ball gestures and rhetoric into their speech as a way to be seen as more unique and creative. In *The Real Housewives of Atlanta*, Marlo Hampton's fame and visibility has always been deeply tethered to her creative use of speech, which has always been a literal parroting of the resistive language practices of the Black and Latinx ball scene. Her use of sayings like "Yaaass hunty," and "Werq b**tch," have earned Marlo a continual role on the show, which has generated more financial stability for herself and loved ones as well as helped her to gain recognition and notoriety as being someone to watch. In season five, Marlo's candor got her into trouble, not only with the show's producers but also with the show's franchise creator, Andy Cohen.[41] Angry that she was not invited to Sheree Whitfield's party, Marlo told Sheree, "And anyway, that's why you don't have a man, go and hang with them f*gg*ts."[42] While Marlo later apologized, and continued to appear on the show, her use of a pejorative and dehumanizing gay slur illuminates how a person can "Columbus" gestures, speech, and performativity from a marginalized community and at the same time not hold a Black queer politic.[43] To "Columbus," or the act of "Columbusing," occurs "when you 'discover' something that's existed forever, but outside your own culture, nationality, race or even, say, your neighborhood."[44] So while

Marlo has been made famous by mimicking the words and phrasing of the Black queer ball scene, she certainly in that moment was not adhering to a Black queer politic. Further, the incident also showed how a person can share space and community with Black queer and trans people and still not see, nor give them, the humanity they seek.

Marlo, however, is not alone in being someone who consistently "Columbuses" Black and Latinx ball vernacular while simultaneously spewing Black queer antagonism when it suits her purposes. Tamar Braxton, celebrated reality star for her time spent on several popular reality shows, including *Braxton Family Values*, where she became a standout cast member for her use of ball terms and phrases in interviews with the show's producers, in an attempt to make herself a more provocative cast member than her costar sisters. In season after season of the *Braxton Family Values*, Tamar would call herself "Muvva," refer to herself in third person, and say phrases like "She tried it," "YASSS," and "Werq hunty."[45] On the daytime talk show *The Real*, which she cohosted until 2016, Tamar continuously used ball phrases incorrectly.[46] The most consistent one was the phrase "Get yo' life, get yo' life," when she was trying to read someone or signify her dismay about a certain issue.[47] The phrase is actually supposed to be said "Get life," and is used as a salute or cosign to a friend, loved one, or comrade who achieves something.[48] Tamar's inaccurate execution of the saying did not stop her from continuing to say it incorrectly, and like Marlo, when Tamar was upset about something she chose to express her disdain through weaponizing homophobia, just as Marlo did on the *Real Housewives of Atlanta*.[49]

In 2019, Tamar Braxton took to Instagram after having a conversation with a friend about how a potential lover refused her friend's sexual advances by continuing to sleep in the same bed with her without pursuing sexual intimacy. After the two spoke, Tamar began to rant on the social media site about the conversation, instantaneously weaponizing Black queer antagonism and making the racialized and heteronormative assumption that if this prospective Black male suitor did not attempt to turn things sexual, he must be gay.[50] In the post, Tamar wrote, "The truth is ladies that these dudes out here really do be gay. . . . They want DICK!! Periodt!! . . . If he lays with you for 3, 4, 10 days and he don't touch you . . . HE WANT A MAN!!!"[51] Not only did Tamar's post assert that there was something fundamentally wrong if a Black man was, in fact, gay, but her comments also conveyed that if a Black man did not exhibit a ferocious sexual appetite towards a cis straight Black woman, then he somehow must be gay. The post has since been deleted after she issued a swift public apology.

Both Tamar and Marlo's articulations about Black queerness were disparaging and dehumanizing. They enjoy the spoils of borrowing a marginalized community's speech, and yet do not celebrate and/or fight back against the systemic and institutional structures that seek to harm Black queer folks or Black trans folks. Embodying a Black queer and Black trans politic means not only to stand in solidarity with these folks and communities but also to stand with them in sociopolitical ways. Further, having a Black queer and Black trans politic demands that one actively pursues the eradication of institutional and systemic structural harm that seeks to dehumanize Black queer and Black trans folks. The hypocrisy of saying phrases like, "She tried it," "Yassss!" "Slay," "Beat," and the like, and then harming the community your entire personality is crafted from, is a form of violence. Not speaking up about the gendered violence that is continuously wielded against Black trans women and other Black queer folks is a form of not just Columbusing but also of tokenism and cultural appropriation, even if the violator is Black themselves.

Given the fact that cis and straight Black women often share intimate spaces with Black queer folks and Black trans women, whether it be by raising them, supporting them, or loving them, in many aspects this act of Columbusing can be precarious. The realm of reality television often encourages this behavior to ensure ratings. So, while many might argue that what Tamar and Marlo do regularly is a form of appreciation or parody, ultimately it falls into a space of exploiting Black queer and trans culture. Both Tamar's and Marlo's relationships to Black queerness have been through service-orientated relationships; Black gay men have been employed by them as their stylists, makeup artists, or hairdressers. While these can be seen as intimate relationships, knowing a person only through a domestic capacity does not necessarily constitute real and actual intimate exchanges.[52] Therefore, Tamar and Marlo's theft of ball culture gestures, speech, and expressions should be seen in the same way that we view the behavior of the Kardashians: a family that has risen to fame by parroting Black women's everyday styles and expressions, by erasing the Black precedents in which these styles and expressions are rooted.[53] The Black queer and trans roots of ball culture expressions continue to be erased not only by white pop stars like Madonna but also by these cis, straight, Black women who are immensely invested in maintaining their marketability and appeal.

This perpetual theft and heteronormative erasure of the queer and trans roots of the Black and Latinx ball scene has now become so ubiquitous that in 2014, CNN anchor Don Lemon conducted a cross interview with op-ed writer Sierra Mannie, who penned a piece for *Time* magazine while she was a senior at the University of Mississippi entitled "Dear White Gays: Stop Stealing Black Female Culture." She echoed my consistent encounters with white cis gay men in particular using histrionic gestures and phrases that mimic speech patterns rooted within the Black and Latinx ball scene.[54] Unlike my assertion that this mimicking was specific to the resistive and joyous language practices of Black queer culture, Mannie argues that these practices originated from Black cis women and are then co-opted by white cis gay men who want to indulge in what they view as the fun aspects of Blackness without fully having to engage with the consequences.[55] Lemon also invites op-ed writer H. Allen Scott, who was enraged by Mannie's arguments, to speak on the issue. Scott is a white gay man who vehemently disagrees not only with Mannie's op-ed but especially with her assertions that queer folks are able to hide their queerness while Black women cannot benefit from the privilege of hiding their Blackness.[56]

During the interview, Lemon allows for both Mannie and Allen Scott to give their perspectives about Mannie's op-ed. When neither concedes to the other's point of view, Mannie continues to proclaim that these gestures and language are rooted within Black cis and straight woman's culture, which counters H. Allen Scott's argument that they are embedded within gay culture. Although H. Allen Scott uses the documentary *Paris Is Burning* as an example of this, he also uses the 1970 film *The Boys in the Band* in an attempt to convince Mannie that her assertions are wrong.[57] Even though Mannie never backs down from her point of view and anchor Don Lemon continues to support Mannie's contentions throughout the interview, both Mannie and H. Allen Scott completely erase the actual Black queer and trans intersections that created the gestures and language in the first place. H. Allen Scott conflates the virtually all Black and Latinx queer and trans cast of *Paris Is Burning* with the virtually all white and cis gay cast of *The Boys in the Band* to serve as the stronghold of his argument, not recognizing that one was fictious and the other real, as well as not seeing how this conflation aides in the erasure of the creators of this language. Mannie, on the other hand, who recognizes the value in proclaiming that cis and straight Black women are in fact cultural innovators and creators themselves, and who as a Black woman knows that there is creative dialogue between Black queer and trans folks and Black cis and straight Black women, still does not mention both groups in her argument or the interview, inevitably aiding in erasure in the same vein as H. Allen Scott.[58]

The interview reflects not only how harmful but also how insidiously perpetual Columbusing can be to marginalized communities when the act manifests within the realm of popular culture. When one person and/or a community are not held accountable for either their co-optation, their misuse, and/or their erasure of a particular idea, trend, or performativity, it becomes difficult to identify the actual originators of the pastime. And while stealing a particular hairstyle, way of dress, or turn of phrase may not seem that detrimental on the surface, when it occurs continuously to one of the most politically and socially vulnerable populations, it is not a benign act but rather an act of violence—especially when the poachers do not embody or articulate a Black queer and Black trans politic.

The Black queer and Black trans innovators and creatives of the ball scene who instituted queer and trans families and houses, invented voguing, and wove improvisation throughout their balls resisted the racist, homophobic, and transphobic paradigms that neoliberalism engenders. They did so in order to cultivate their own survival, joy, and opportunity for themselves and others within their communities. The erasure, misuse, and co-optation of these structures and their roots by folks who have yet to grasp the ways in which these communities are routinely harmed is a maddening reality that must end. This pilfering cannot continue if we as a nation and as communities articulate our deep investment in inclusive and consistent coalition building across lines of difference. Instead of pocketing the creative and festive gestures and resistive linguistic practices of the Black and Latinx ball scene for our own subjective amusement or entertainment—or even worse, doing it to make ourselves seem more interesting—Columbusers of the culture need to instead learn about the struggles that compelled people to create the scene in the first place, and attempt to ensure that those inhumane circumstances no longer exist. Educators, activists, and content creators owe it to everyone involved in the ball scene and everyone within vulnerable Black and Latinx queer and trans communities to do better.

CHAPTER FOUR

THE STAKES IS HIGH

I began writing this book during the COVID-19 pandemic. As of this writing, there have been more than 1.1 million COVID-related deaths in the US.[1] Yet, there has been another epidemic within this pandemic that is also at work, and that is the anti-trans violence directed at Black trans women. Black trans women continue to be harmed in the worst ways and are violently accosted or killed throughout the US. In 2023, at least thirty-three transgender or gender nonconforming people were killed by violent means, the majority of whom were Black trans women.[2] The intersection where Blackness and transness converge is the center of epidemic levels of dehumanizing violence.

Nothing seems to keep Black trans women safe, not even if they are celebrities with a global reach. In November of 2020, trans actress and activist Laverne Cox was hounded by a stranger in a park while walking with a friend. Cox "and a male friend had been walking earlier that day in Los Angeles' Griffith Park when a man 'very aggressively' asked for the time. Cox's friend told him what time it was, after which the man asked, 'Guy or girl?'" After Cox's friend deduced that the man was attempting to undermine Cox's womanhood, he told the man to "[expletive] off," to which the man responded by hitting Cox's friend. The fight prompted Cox to call the police, but as soon as she began to dial the phone number the man disappeared. Cox believed that the man wanted her to answer his questions so he could gauge whether or not she was trans. Even though Cox has received overwhelming support from her fans, loved ones, and comrades for being vocal and visible about who she is, she has also received insulting questions about her body, antagonism about her trans identity, and threats of violence regarding her womanhood. Cox, an international celebrity, still wasn't able to remain safe from being ridiculed and harassed about who she is.[3]

Cox's experience in the park illuminates how transphobia and the accompanying verbal violence doesn't cease, even amid a global pandemic. This is the harmful, scary, and inhumane reality that Black trans people, specifically Black trans women, encounter and endure simply because of who they are and what they signify to narrow-minded, transphobic, and violent people. Our culture, an innately individualized one due to its capitalist origins and social emphasis on rugged individualism, has been inherently hostile to initiating any system-level intervention in response to community crises. The neoliberal politics that pervades our lives and our communities not only exacerbates this systemic neglect but often facilitates the various forms of harm that many of us must confront. We continue to ignore forms of violence like homelessness and systemic poverty that have existed for generations, and if we specifically look at the experiences of Black trans women, our country fails to address how they are disproportionately affected by incidents of rhetorical violence that often escalate to physical violence.

As Black queer and Black trans folks attempt to pursue joy, safety, and freedom, societal constraints remain ever-present for both of these groups, within and outside of their own LGBTQ+ communities.[4] Despite the mainstream perception that LGBTQ+ folks are a monolith of shared experiences, the rainbow isn't enough to unify us against the cisnormative and/or racist queer ideological fissures that remain within and outside of LGBTQ+ communities.

Black trans folks constantly deal with misgendering, deadnaming, and other cis microaggressions both within queer venues and online spaces, and among mainstream communities.[5] These practices can often negatively affect one's mental health and well-being.[6]

In addition, some cis white gay men, like conservative Milo Yiannopoulos, use their celebrity platforms to troll and disparage trans people online. In 2016, while speaking at the University of Delaware, Yiannopoulos referred to trans people as "mentally ill," urging his audience to begin strategizing about how to eradicate the liberal lobbying groups that support them.[7] These forms of harm that are propagated by queer folks are not only detrimental to trans and nonbinary people individually, but they also hurt queer and trans communities as a whole. Additionally, many white gay cis folks are able to distance themselves from other queer people because of their racial privilege, and they can assume a sense of authority over trans and nonbinary folks through their gender identity, oftentimes in tandem with their racial privilege. Some even go as far as to advocate against trans people and weaponize their privilege, both intentionally and unintentionally, to harm Black trans people. The racist, sexist, and cisnormative politics of desirability and embodiment then further exaggerates the harm that ensues.[8] This inevitably leads many queer folks to reproduce multiple dehumanizing paradigms like femmephobia, ableism, and fatphobia, and even to propagate transphobia and misogynoir.

For Black and Latinx LGBTQ+ people, siblings (also known as sibs), is a term that originated from the ballroom house system and has since evolved to mean queer and trans kinships. The conception of a "chosen family" has served as a socialized form of protection throughout queer communities. Having been historically excluded from white queer gatherings, Black and Latinx queer and trans folks formed their own communities and found family among each other.[9] Since many Black LGBTQ+ folks confront adverse reactions when coming out to their biological families as either gay, trans, or nonbinary, many have found emotional solace and various forms of care within their chosen family units. These kinships are typically made up of people that support each other in financial and/or emotional ways. In many instances these creative family units can lift Black LGBTQ+ people up in ways that biological familial connections do not, either because of capacity or because of transphobia and homophobia. These formal and sometimes informal connections to others outside of one's biological family often create a communal form of love and regard that Black LGBTQ+ people are often unable to find within the larger world. The mother of the house of Corey in the 1980s, Dorian Corey, put it best when she articulated what purpose queer families and/or gay houses actually serve in the Jennie Livingston documentary *Paris Is Burning*.[10] She states, "The hippies had families. A family is a group of human beings in a mutual bond."[11] Another example of how Black queer and trans families operate can be seen within the popular HBO Max show *Legendary*, where Black and Latinx queer and trans families compete against one another for bragging rights within the ball scene.[12] Chosen family is one of the many ways Black LGBTQ+ people have been able to maintain an emotional equilibrium amid a world that is anti-Black, transphobic, homophobic, and the like.[13] However, even within the safety of families, trans people are not immune to transphobia. Trans people often confront various forms of violence within queer spaces. Nowhere is this more obvious than on queer and trans dating sites. On dating apps such as Scruff, Jacked, and Grindr, these problematic notions of desire and identity continue to result in the physical and psychological vulnerability of Black trans women, nonbinary folks, and other queer folks. Plainly, Black queer and trans folks get it from all sides.

Back before dating apps and social media, I was often struck by how many white cis gay men in my life categorized those they desired, or did not, using terms that would otherwise be viewed as offensive. In evaluating their sexual tastes or those of others, they would describe other LGBTQ+ people with terms like "Bean Queen" (a white cis gay man who prefers to date and/or have sex only with Latinx men), "Rice Queen" (a white cis gay man who prefers to date and/or have sex only with Asian men), and "Snow Queen," (a Black cis gay man who prefers to date and/or have sex only with white men). These terms, meant to fetishize gay men based on their sexual choices, are also dehumanizing. Describing a person as a commodified good erases their subjectivity and limits them to the racist notions projected onto their bodies. These terms other interracial attraction and desire, categorizing attraction that does not center whiteness as a source of humor. In the case of a "Snow Queen," Black gay men's respective personhood and value are reduced to nothing more than what they desire, which are white men. Therefore, these terms and definitions police, stigmatize, and ridicule desirability in conjunction with race. The farther away one's desire veers from whiteness the more othered it becomes. This is another way white supremacy dictates the language and culture of white cis gay spaces, ultimately producing a rhetorical hierarchy of desirability that measures the degree of humanity in an individual through a racist lens.[14] It wasn't so much that I was surprised that cis gay white men racialized their carnal tastes. I was, however, surprised that this had continued for so long without anyone checking them about it. These terms and sentiments have been repeated loudly in public gay spaces; they seem to roll off people's tongues, and no one seems unsettled by it. While white cis gay men experience oppression based on their sexuality, they are still able to weaponize their whiteness, gender, and cisness, both consciously and unconsciously, to oppress others within queer communities. And because they possess privilege and power, both racially and through their gender identity, white cis gay men are able to take up space, remain silent, and cause harm to other LGBTQ+ people.[15]

Fatima Jamal, a writer, performance artist, graduate student, and model, noticed this trend on queer and trans dating apps. She decided to explore these harmful tensions in her documentary *No Fats, No Femmes*. In an interview with journalist Tre'vell Anderson for *Daily Xtra Magazine*, Fatima said she wanted to "consider how white supremacist, colonial gazes severely impact how we see ourselves and also how we see and understand others." She describes her documentary's title, which was "taken from the popular and problematic refrain often seen on gay dating apps, 'No fats. No femmes. No Blacks. No Asians,'" as an emblematic attempt to suppress the way trans folks can reimagine themselves. "This world hates trans people so much," she said, "because we dare, with audacity and courage, to reimagine ourselves." To Fatima, trans folks recognize early on how ridiculous narrow conceptions of gender are and discover that "it's all made up."[16]

Despite the resistance of people like Jamal and other Black trans and queer folks to this dehumanizing treatment on dating apps, racist and sexist tropes continue to inform queer and trans sexual politics and desirability. This has allowed many white cis gays to exist in a space of safety and privilege, while forcing Black queer and trans folks, as well as other queer and trans folks of color, to remain in a realm of oppression. Writer and trans advocate Janet Mock explored the privilege of being perceived as pretty in her 2017 op-ed in *Allure* magazine, "Being Pretty Is a Privilege, but We Refuse to Acknowledge It." Mock contends that when it comes to queer and trans sexual politics, being perceived as pretty operates as a springboard to social, cultural, and financial privileges. Mock asserts that the measures and evaluations of what people think it means to be pretty are still tethered to systems of racial and gendered power. Although Mock acknowledges that "pretty is subjective and means different things for different groups of people," she also contends "that there are shared, agreed-upon commonalities" when it comes to designating someone as pretty. More often than not, she argues, to be deemed as pretty, one must also be "thin, white, able-bodied, and cis."[17] In other words, we are living within a society that dehumanizes bodies that do not conform to conventional notions of gender, race, size, or skin tone.

Continuing to detail her own personal struggles with her body and looks, Mock discusses how she saw this same internal battle reflected in other teen girls her age. She contends that most of her "despair was amplified by the expectations of cisnormativity and the gender binary," as well as the impossibly high beauty expectations that she and her peers measured themselves against.[18] Mock, like many people of various racial, ethnic, and gendered backgrounds, inescapably struggled with her own conceptions of desirability. Ideas around pretty privilege promote unreasonable body politics that negatively affects our own conceptions of self.

As Jamal's and Mock's stories show, racism, cisnormativity, ability, and fatness inform queer and trans folks' thoughts of what an ideal person looks like. Our desires are formulated and socialized with these ideals in mind, which is why, despite various apps' initiatives to eradicate online harassment, many users of queer and trans dating apps continue to encounter violence when they use them.

In 2017, the popular gay dating app Grindr was acquired by the Kunlun Group Limited, removing former CEO Joel Simkhai from its helm.[19] While the changing of the guard did not raise eyebrows, the new viral campaign "Kinder," initiated by the Kunlun Group Limited, did.[20] The taglines for the campaign were "It's time to play nice" and "Kindness is our preference." And with the addition of newly instituted modes of conduct, many hoped these changes to the app's community guidelines would mean the end of the racist, fatphobic, and transmisogynist trolling by users that had become ubiquitous on the site. According to their press release, "sexual racism, transphobia, fat-shaming and others forms of discrimination," would no longer be tolerated on their site, and if some users insisted on doing so, they may eventually face permanent bans from the app.[21] The Kunlun Group also released a video series where app users of diverse gender identities, sexualities, and races discussed how, before this initiative, they all had to deal with insults, racist trolling, femmephobia, and even threats of violence based on their racial identities.[22]

While a myriad of users were relieved by the changes to the community guidelines and excited about the new inclusive campaign, others rejected the app's new direction. Much of the resistance came from users who argued that they just had "personal preferences" when it came to dating, and no app or company could force them to be inclusive when it came to who they desired or sought to hook up with.[23] Other users who were initially excited about the new guidelines felt that the app still put the onus of reporting discrimination on those that were negatively impacted by the racist or sexist harassment—placing the victimized in positions to report any abuse that they were subjected to by other users instead of using AI to scan for toxic language.[24]

Whatever varied problems Grindr users voiced about the app's changes, one thing became expressly clear through the backlash. Many LGBTQ+ folks simply did not want to own the fact that what they saw as their "personal desires" had political consequences for the vulnerable groups in their communities. Instead, many still choose to believe that the physical attributes of those they desire are innate, natural, and instinctive, and not influenced by their exposure to problematic and trope-filled advertising, film, and television.

Many, if not most, LGBTQ+ children grow up and are socialized within the same cultural nexus as everyone else, so despite mainstream media's portrayal of LGBTQ+ people operating with higher levels of sophistication, enlightenment, conscientiousness, and inclusivity, when it comes to forming community and intimate connections, they too dehumanize and stereotype other queer and trans folks through their supposed "preferences." This is especially prevalent if those queer and trans folks are Black or people of color. The app users who contend that it's just their "personal preferences" exemplify an inability to recognize that desirability functions within a political culture defined by femmephobia, fatphobia, white supremacy, and misogyny.

Choosing to view desires as nothing more than "personal preferences" illuminates how entrenched and invisible the history of body policing is within LGBTQ+ culture, just as it is within mainstream culture. The pervasive politics of the body not only shapes our culture but also infiltrates our systems of power and influence our public policies.

For example, LGBTQ+ people are at a 3 percent higher risk for developing an eating disorder than the general population, and 15 percent of trans folks, specifically, suffer from some form of disordered eating, according to the National Eating Disorders Association (NEDA).[25] The NEDA's findings all conclude that this is mostly due to fatphobic, transphobic, and homophobic norms. An example of how racism and body normativity infect our public policies and systems of power can be found within the story of high school wrestler Andrew Johnson, who was made to cut his locs in order to compete in a wrestling match. More recently, Jimmy Hoffmeyer had to transfer his biracial daughter, Jurnee, out of her school after a school official and a classmate cut his daughter's hair without permission.[26] We even have obesity policies on some of our commercial airlines that make passengers of a certain size buy an extra seat, which creates not only lack of access to travel but also puts an unnecessary financial burden on many Americans.[27] Further, Black trans women suffer from housing and employment discrimination due to the perception that their identities and bodies are not viewed as normal and therefore are seen as unvaluable, according to our politics of the body.[28]

Our denial of these political dynamics ensures that people's bodies remain political battlegrounds, and that bodily autonomy is undermined by perceptions of race, size, and ability. As the Grindr backlash demonstrates, some bodies are more desirable than others, and some people are more humanized than others. Far from being "personal preferences," our choices about who to couple with, pursue, or fantasize about is deeply entwined with our politics.

Acts of rhetorical violence that are seen on dating apps and within social media have real-world consequences for folks who are raced and gendered in pejorative and oppressive ways. No form of escapism—even that offered by queer dating apps—should prevent one from recognizing the fact that Black trans women, Black nonbinary folks, and Black queer folks experience multipronged violence. One need only look to their daily news feeds to see all of the ways that these particular people are routinely violated, hounded, and murdered at the hands of their partners, institutions, or even strangers.[29] A consummate example of rhetorical violence turning into physical violence can be found in the case of CeCe McDonald.

In June 2011, CeCe McDonald and a group of her four friends were walking to a store in their Minneapolis neighborhood when they were verbally accosted by forty-seven-year-old white man Dean Schmitz and his forty-year-old white ex-girlfriend Molly Flaherty, who were standing outside of a motorcycle bar. In a *Rolling Stone* interview by Sabrina Rubin Erdely, McDonald recounted her and her friends' experience that night, stating that at first McDonald and her group tried to ignore the racist and transphobic onslaught directed at them, but Schmitz and Flaherty's rants were so unrelenting that McDonald felt compelled to respond. McDonald told Flaherty and Schmitz, "We're just trying to walk to the store." Erdely writes that McDonald's had to raise "her voice over the blare of Schmitz and Flaherty's free-associating invective: 'bitches with dicks,' 'faggot-lovers,' 'niggers,' 'rapists.'" Even after McDonald's boyfriend, Larry Thomas, told the pair to have a good night, the couple still continued to holler at the group, with Flaherty now yelling, "I'll take all of you bitches on!" McDonald and her group's clapbacks, as well as their unbothered brush-off of the verbal assaults, seemed to enrage Flaherty in particular, who had now begun to pursue the group on foot. Flaherty then attacked McDonald while other patrons of the motorcycle bar watched intently, yelling derogatory slurs at McDonald and her friends. Their initial brawl left McDonald bloodied from being stabbed in the jaw with a beer bottle that Flaherty had flung at her, while Flaherty was laid out on the ground amid broken glass. As McDonald walked away, Schmitz then lunged toward her, leaving McDonald only moments to react. She quickly grabbed her school sewing scissors out of her purse, and as their bodies collided

Schmitz was stabbed. It was not until police arrived on the scene and promptly handcuffed and arrested McDonald that she found out Schmitz had died.[30]

Even though McDonald explained to police that she was defending herself and did not intend to kill anyone, the police still arrested her and charged her with second-degree murder, despite the many witnesses corroborating McDonald's innocence.[31] Subsequently, a judge in McDonald's case confined her to a male prison and then put her in solitary confinement, locking her away from the general population and keeping her confined to her cell for up to twenty-three hours a day for her "protection" as she awaited trial.[32] The judge did not recognize that confining McDonald to a male prison and therefore denying her womanhood directly endangered McDonald. McDonald would not be in need of protection if the judge had only honored McDonald's identity in the first place.[33] The judge's decision to then place McDonald in solitary confinement, despite its negative effects on people's mental health, further exacerbated this harm.[34] In the aftermath of Flaherty and Schmitz's racist and transphobic attack, McDonald had to endure the racist and transphobic criminal justice system, in which keeping her safe meant treating her as both a victim and an aggressor.

Ultimately, McDonald accepted a deal, pleading guilty to second-degree manslaughter, for which the judge sentenced her to serve a forty-one-month sentence in a men's prison.[35] However, due to the protests, activism, and intervention from McDonald's community, she was released early from prison after serving nineteen months plus the 275 days that she was incarcerated while awaiting trial.[36] In an interview with *Vulture* by Dee Lockett after her release, McDonald said that her time in solitary confinement made it hard for her to "maintain [her] sanity" and that while there she "couldn't think or concentrate," and that she "dealt with a lot of depression and anxiety."[37]

Experiencing prison and solitary confinement compelled McDonald to become a prison abolitionist, directing her activism toward a better understanding of the injustices that are deeply embedded within our criminal justice system. CeCe McDonald is now known as a community hero and trans activist. McDonald's story of empowered survival is a rare one that most often doesn't attract media attention. Although McDonald's story exists alongside numerous others that detail how transmisogyny and racism took the life of yet another Black trans person, mainstream media does not often publish stories about Black trans women who utilize their own ingenuity and self-love to navigate a racist, sexist, and transphobic world.[38] The state's decision to prosecute McDonald for murder is a clear example of why so many Black activists, intellectuals, and community care workers continue to organize and protest. The United States judicial system is not invested in protecting its most vulnerable groups.

Throughout McDonald's case, the state did not intervene in her best interest, nor did it acknowledge that McDonald was defending herself. An ironic comparison can be made to the decision made in Florida when an almost all-white jury acquitted George Zimmerman of killing Black teenager Trayvon Martin when he attempted to walk back from the store to his dad's house.[39] The state also did not recognize how rhetorical violence can lead to physical violence, undermining McDonald's claims of innocence from the beginning of her trial and throughout. Verbal abuse or rhetorical violence, which is rooted in the dehumanization of others based on their identities, can often lead to physical violence due to the resulting cognitive objectification—the perception that particular people or groups are not in fact human beings but rather objects that exist only for the approval or disapproval of others.[40] Doing harm or bringing harm to said group or person becomes that much easier because those doing the harm don't associate themselves or ones they love with the people they bring harm against.[41] In the case of McDonald, neither Flaherty nor Schmitz viewed McDonald and her group of friends as people they knew or wanted to know, and as a result didn't see anything wrong at all with accosting McDonald and her group. McDonald's early release from prison was the result of community action and her own determined response to the state's malign neglect of her life and freedom. Her case represents a contemporary reckoning between the criminal justice system and Black and trans communities.

Black queer maverick and visionary writer James Baldwin warned America that a formal reckoning would eventually come if our country did not embrace the folks who have continually existed at its margins. The outliers who are the focus of Baldwin's essay "Freaks and the American Ideal of Manhood," which he penned for a 1985 issue of *Playboy Magazine*, only exist on the margins of our society as misfits because their lives complicate and disrupt the rigid binaries that America forces us to acculturate to. Baldwin argued that America's insistence on viewing sexuality only through a lens of white supremacist masculinity had produced racial anxieties that had begun to intersect with issues concerning sexuality, power, and gender. While linguistically reclaiming the term *freak*, asserting that freaks are in fact just human beings that have only been labeled as such "because they . . . cause to echo, deep within us, our most profound terrors and desires," Baldwin contends that these folks are the ones who will eventually bring this social and cultural eruption to light. To Baldwin, the pervading binaries of Black/white and gay/straight have not only been harmful to the American psyche, producing false myths, racist and sexist narratives, and problematic popular representations of people and communities that already exist on the fringes, but these restrictive strangleholds also stifle the human imagination, limiting all of us to only conceive of our identities and those of others through a white supremacist, sexist, and homophobic lens.[42]

Even though Baldwin doesn't mention them by name, one can only imagine that if Black trans women were as culturally visible in 1985 as they are today, he would include them in his thesis. Black trans women live directly between the multiple binaries Baldwin mentions in his essay, and their identities as such are often distorted by both racialized and gendered myths. At the personal, intimate, institutional, and state levels, Black trans women are constantly made to explain who and why they are themselves, and to apologize for both. In 2019, Laverne Cox went on *BuzzFeed*'s Twitter morning show *AM to DM* to not only address "the epidemic of Black trans women being murdered in the United States" but also to dispel the many mythologies that are attached to Black trans women.[43] Cox said, "Your attraction to me as a trans woman is not a reason to kill me. . . . There's this whole sort of myth that trans women are out there tricking people, that they deserve to be murdered, and that's not the case."[44] The racist, sexist, and transphobic myths surrounding Black trans women were definitely at work at the personal level when it came to the way that Molly Flaherty and Dean Schmitz viewed CeCe McDonald and her group. These myths were also at work at the state level when it came to how police and the judge in McDonald's case viewed her, unable to wrap their minds around McDonald being a legitimate victim just because she was a Black trans woman.

These distorted projections and myths about Black trans women also extend to the people who desire, love, and form partnerships with them. In 2019, Maurice "Reese Him Daddie" Willoughby took to his Facebook page to talk about how much he loved his girlfriend Faith Palmer, a Black trans woman whom he had been dating for a long period of time. Posting a picture of himself with Palmer in the background kissing him, Willoughby commented under the post: "Y'all can say whatever about faith. I really don't care if she's not passable. I don't care if she wasn't born a woman. She is a woman to me. . . . I'm happy you should be happy for me."[45] Willoughby's post generated a lot of traffic, and subsequently he was relentlessly cyberbullied about his relationship with Faith. Willoughby was even confronted outside a convenience store, where several men hurled homophobic and transphobic abuse at him.[46] After attempting to defend himself against the taunts, Willoughby eventually walked away from the group, but this did not stop the video of the incident from going viral, adding to his already vulnerable state of mind due to the continued online harassment.[47]

One of Willoughby's friends, who chose to remain anonymous, told *The Advocate*, "He was getting picked on and joked on all the time," and that this drove him to depression.[48] The same friend went on to say that even though Willoughby and Faith were happy in their relationship and there were some folks who did support their union, the community of which Willoughby was part just couldn't accept their relationship as "normal." The friend continued, "Where we come from, if you like trans women, and you black, the streets will talk about you, fight you, even try to kill you."[49]

Inspired by Willoughby's story, actor Malik Yoba felt compelled to publicly share that he, like Willoughby, was also "trans attracted."[50] This term, *trans attracted*, has not only been controversial but also a term that many trans folks outright reject, seeing it as oppressive and derogatory. In a 2019 op-ed for *Out* magazine titled "The Problem with Identifying as 'Trans Attracted,'" Serena Sonoma argues that the term itself is not only dehumanizing, but that it actually "others" trans people. Sonoma writes, "whether the label is trans-attracted, transamorous, or the outdated and slur-based term 'tranny chaser,' the truth of the matter is that these types of people are often attracted to us due to our genitalia." Sonoma further asserts that these same folks often have "little to no regard for the person they are actually preying on. We become merely objects for their pleasure." Therefore, to Sonoma, these terms actually do the opposite of what those who use them think they do.[51] Yoba, who used the term to articulate his specific attraction to Black trans women, actually further othered them by using a term that many trans people themselves abhor.

Yoba took to social media to share the video of Willoughby being harassed with a caption that reads, "This is another heartbreaking example of the homophobia, transphobic hatred and hypocrisy WE as black folks, BLACK MEN in particular have to NAME, FACE and CALL OUT and do the work to heal!!!"[52] Yoba argued that

Willoughby's confidence about whom he loved was inspiring, and that the real shame should be directed to members of Willoughby's own Black community who chose to ridicule him instead of embracing him and the person he loved. Yoba continued, "I love ALL women AND count MYSELF among those that find themselves trans attracted and I too have felt the self-imposed shame that comes with that truth but it's time to speak up."[53] Though he faced harsh criticism for his use of the term *trans attracted*, Yoba also received praise from many social media users and fellow actors, including actress Trace Lysette, who commended him for speaking on his attraction to trans women as a high-profile man.[54]

However, in both Willoughby's and Yoba's stories, new details emerged about their treatment of Black trans women. Willoughby's and Palmer's relationship was fraught with incidents of domestic violence complicated by Willoughby's drug addiction.[55] Palmer had gone so far as to file a restraining order against Willoughby in the hopes that it would "pressure Willoughby to get help with his addiction," but after going back and forth not only with police but also "victim service organizations," Palmer was unable to obtain such an order against him.[56] In addition, after Yoba made his announcement, an allegation immediately emerged from Mariah Ebony Lopez, a longtime trans activist and former sex worker, who wrote in a Facebook post that Yoba frequently paid her for services at a time when she was both underage and housing insecure. Sharing her story with the hashtag #SurvivingMalikYoba (inspired by the movement for sexual assault victims of singer R. Kelly), Lopez wrote that even though "he was cute and polite . . . I'm sure he knew what he was doing was wrong."[57]

Even though both men were subjected to scrutiny and bullying due to their attraction to Black trans women, they were also commended by the general public for publicly voicing their attraction. *Them*, an LGBTQ+ alternative media site, even called Willoughby "a beacon of hope," applauding his bravery and confidence about being open about his attraction to Black trans women, and many other news outlets did the same with regard to Yoba.[58] Yet, based on the allegations brought against both Yoba and Willoughby, this is a much more complicated story.

The coverage of both of these stories shows that mainstream media continues to use a masculinist lens through which to view the lives of Black trans women, measuring the worth of Black trans women by their proximity to Black cis straight men. This thought process and practice is similar to how Black cis women's worth is measured. Both Black trans women and Black cis women are valued by their ability to obtain and maintain an intimate relationship with a man. This can be extremely harmful to both cis and trans women because it places their value in relation to their romantic partners. Black trans women and the men who desire them, pursue them, and love them exist at the intersection of public hate and private desire. In the cases of Yoba and Willoughby, two men who felt confident enough to declare their desires publicly, even among the praise they were met with backlash and ridicule for not remaining silent.[59] People from various racial and economic backgrounds put immense pressure on both men to reject Black trans women as "real" women and instead treat them as a threat to heteronormativity. For their very existence signifies, as Baldwin wrote, "deep within us, our most profound terrors and desires."[60] While cis men are certainly the primary propagators of the violence that Black trans women face, many cis women also participate in anti-trans practices, ranging from acts of verbal violence to physical assault.[61] When discussing the harm caused by toxic masculinity, cisnormativity, transphobia, and cis men, it is equally important to understand and eradicate the ways that cis women police womanhood and the politics of desirability when it comes to trans women. A common way cis women reinforce mythologies about attraction and desire is through harmful statements such as "Men who are attracted to or date trans women are secretly gay or not real men." Statements like this police desire, lean into fears that legitimize homophobia and transphobia, and conflate sexuality and gender, which creates harmful confusion and misguidance. The assertion that the men who desire trans women are secretly gay insinuates that trans women do not possess "real" womanhood. Both homophobia and transphobia are at play when the validity of these relationships is questioned, when a woman's transness is used to undermine her womanhood, and when a man's attraction to a trans woman is seen as indictive of his sexuality. The results are harmful, even if the words were subtly stated. These kinds of statements can also conflate sexuality with gender by rhetorically asserting transness with queerness. A trans identity is a gender identity, not a sexuality, and should not be understood as such. Additionally, cis men who are attracted to and romantically involved with trans women may or may not identify as straight in terms of their sexuality. One's gender does not dictate their sexuality and vice versa. Many cis women's inability to embrace and protect trans women is connected to a fear they must contend with, whether that fear is viewing trans women as competition for cis straight men's affection, fear of attraction existing beyond a constrained binary, or a general fear of "otherness" that one isn't willing to understand.

Molly Flaherty, a cis white woman who wielded cis antagonism, racism, and body policing to inflict harm on CeCe McDonald and her friends, repeatedly stated in her initial interview with police that McDonald was "really pretty." At the same time, she also admitted that she pursued the group, verbally harassed them, and tried to brutalize McDonald.[62] After reading Flaherty's statement about McDonald's prettiness, I was struck by how it was simultaneously affirming and dehumanizing of McDonald. For Flaherty, the idea of McDonald's prettiness was threatening, and McDonald's confidence and unbothered response to Flaherty's feeble attempt to undermine her womanhood somehow registered as hostile to Flaherty. Not only was McDonald "pretty," but she had the nerve to value her pretty self, despite public perception about who she was. Perhaps Flaherty was no stranger to struggling with her own conceptions of desirability. That night, it was a Black trans woman who made Flaherty feel self-conscious and insecure, just because she existed and had the nerve to walk her own path.[63] Of course, this is my own interpretation of Flaherty's actions based on the information from the case and her targeted treatment of McDonald. I am not arguing that this is how Flaherty actually felt but think it's important to expand our thinking when it comes to the violence that is directed specifically at Black trans women. While Flaherty may have tried to use racism and cisnormativity to repress her internal battle with her own insecurities, it was still not enough to keep them buried. Instead, she may have felt that physical violence was the only way to rid herself of the insecurities that McDonald's presence was making her confront.

Flaherty is not alone in being a cis- and straight-identified woman who has a problem with trans women existing as women. Author and self-defined feminist J. K. Rowling made world-famous for "penning fantastical worlds that shaped the childhoods for people across the globe," has been recently revealed to be a trans-exclusionary radical feminist (TERF), a term used to describe self-identified feminist cis women who exhibit various forms of transphobia through their politics, writing, and/or activism.[64] Rowling published her anti-trans views through a series of tweets where she argued that real women are "people who menstruate," and that "trans activism harms women."[65] Despite the overwhelming criticism of her anti-trans stance, Rowling has not backed down. In fact, one of her recent books, *Troubled Blood*, is a story about a cishet detective who kidnaps, rapes, tortures, and kills women by beheading his victims or boiling their flesh.[66] Rowling's protagonist commits these crimes all while cross-dressing as a woman.[67]

Although Rowling's new book is fiction, one cannot separate her anti-trans beliefs from her new fantasy novel, which characterizes the protagonist as someone living within the trans spectrum of identity only to harm and brutalize women. In June of 2020, Rowling tweeted a number of anti-trans statements. She also published a brief essay on her website that, according to TV critic Kelly Lawler, "conflated sex with gender and defended ideas suggesting that changing one's biological sex threatens her own gender identity and even her safety."[68] Although it might seem as if Rowling is just one feminist who believes that she can be both a feminist and anti-trans, the TERF movement is a growing one. TERFs have created reproductive justice movements that exclude trans folks from dialogue and activism, and universities across the country are witnessing an increasing number of young feminists who hold anti-trans views.[69]

In an interview with the *New Statesman*, queer theorist Judith Butler argues that Rowling's and other TERFs' distorted views about their own feminist ideals, and their anti-trans stances, are reflective neither of feminism nor of what the majority of feminists believe.[70] "There are trans-affirmative feminists, and many trans people are also committed feminists. . . . Trans activism is linked to queer activism and to feminist legacies," they state. Further, Butler articulates that "feminism has always been committed to the proposition that the social meaning of what it is to be a man or a woman are not yet settled."[71] Therefore, Butler asserts, "the trans-exclusionary radical feminist position attacks the dignity of trans people."[72] As Butler argues, Rowling and other prominent TERFs who utilize their platforms to propagate their anti-trans beliefs while maintaining that they are feminists contradict the very definition of feminism. When someone with such large platform frames anti-trans views as a form of feminism and gender liberation, they further legitimize transphobia. And when we consider that only 8 percent of Americans have a personal relationship with someone who identifies as trans, misinformation, inaccuracies, and rhetorical acts of violence continue to manifest, which promote harmful anti-trans narratives.[73]

Another example of cis women participating in anti-trans thought and action is the violence that Iyanna Dior, a young Black trans woman, faced. In June 2020, in Saint Paul, Minnesota, Dior feared for her life one night when she was confronted by a mob and severely beaten.[74] At the time, Dior was trying to move a friend's car when she accidently hit several other cars in the process. The owners of the cars confronted Dior and demanded money, and when she was unable to pay, she sought refuge in a nearby convenience store. However, once Dior was inside the store, the owners refused to call the police or intervene on Dior's behalf. Dior recalled the store owner telling her, "You're causing too much drama," and then seconds later she was sucker-punched in the face by a woman who was a part of the mob.[75] The mob, made up of cis women and men, yelled gay and transphobic slurs at Dior while they continued to beat her. In this instance, the neoliberal staple of valuing property over people came into play, with the community mob valuing their vehicles over the life of a young Black trans woman. This mob berated her, battered her, and yelled violent and aggressive slurs at her all because she dented a couple of cars, and just as in the case of CeCe McDonald, the first punch was thrown by a cis woman.[76]

Though Black cis women and Black trans women may share similar experiences, Black cis women are capable of dehumanizing Black trans women and weaponizing their privilege as cis people. This is largely due to the prevalence of our country's anti-trans cultural milieu that socializes Black cis women to adopt an anti-trans stance even though that politic might bring harm to another Black person, specifically another Black woman. Because of this socialization, many Black cis women are often unable to recognize how they participate in anti-trans thought and action. Our neoliberal culture's rigid definitions of gender identity are exacerbated by heteronormativity, which works both to excuse and justify any form of violence against Black trans women. Black cis women's participation in ritualized violence against Black trans women is a symptom of the larger collective issue that we as a country must reckon with.

In another incident, in March 2021, rapper Azealia Banks, who identifies as a Black bisexual cis woman and is widely known for her internet trolling antics, took to her Instagram account to announce her upcoming nuptials to Ryder Ripps. She also shared that she now identifies as Jewish.[77] Fans responded by pointing out that Banks needed to convert to Judaism—that simply being engaged to a Jewish man did not make her Jewish. Instead of taking the opportunity to learn something, Banks zeroed in on one particular Instagram user and launched into a transphobic tirade, writing, "I try to tell transgirls that getting castrated doesn't automatically make them a female but if society can do the mental gymnastics to lie and tell them an eggless person who still produces semen is a woman and let them rock, you all are going to bend the rules to accept this newly black jewish coochie."[78] This is not the first time Banks has verbally assaulted trans women, either. Sadly, Banks's transphobic rants have been so common that many expect them to surface every couple of months.[79] Banks is herself a queer woman and may have experienced monosexism, a biphobic notion that identifying as either straight or gay is superior to, and therefore a more legitimate form of desire than, identifying as bisexual. Yet she is still somehow unable to see how her transphobia is harmful to Black trans women and Black trans communities.[80] By consistently dehumanizing and objectifying trans women through her social networks and celebrity platforms, Banks exacerbates the precarity and vulnerability of Black trans women who are forced to contend with societal anti-Black and anti-trans culture.

Transphobic thought and action are even further amplified by a neoliberal socioeconomic order that directs citizens to devalue specific racial and gender identities. A culture that tells us to cater only to a respective group's buying power inevitably erodes the potential of oppressed groups to form political coalitions. In addition, neoliberal assimilationist politics and its resulting gendered and heterosexist product-pushing practices also reinforce the narrow, restrictive boundaries of heteronormativity and cisnormativity. As I've discussed, neoliberal politics tells its populace to purchase baby dolls, kitchen sets, kid vacuum cleaners, and the color pink for girls, and action figures, toy guns, wrestling mats, and the color blue for boys. This effectively socializes our tiny human population into fixed, static genders that can only exist within a binary, in order for them to grow up to be adults who are beholden to these restrictive sex/gender designations and performative expectations, all in the interest of ever-greater consumerism.[81] This happens even though most human identities cannot fit neatly or easily within these restrictive gendered and sexual roles.

What many of us need to understand is that criticizing people for voicing pro-trans views also limits the ability of cishet people to explore their own nuances ideologically or emotionally when it comes to the ways that they view their own sexuality and gender identity. The boundaries of heteronormativity have prevented many straight folks from discovering their own radical notions of sexuality, desire, and lust. The boundaries of cisnormativity function in a similar way in that only some gender identities within our culture should be valued, and as a result many cis people police and regulate their own gender identities.

This is the inherent damage that results from living within a neoliberal country, especially when that country is also anti-Black and transphobic. Neoliberalism hurts everyone, including cis people. We cis folks need to be intentional in creating a better world for our trans kin to live on their own terms, because this will also free us.[82] This is especially true of cis women, who experience gendered violence at some of the same epidemic levels as Black trans women.[83] Black trans women are harmed and made vulnerable to intimate, state, and institutional forms of violence. The police, the criminal justice system, and prisons, for example, also harm Black cis women. It is only our misogynist, transphobic, and heteronormative culture that prevents many Black cis women from recognizing this connection.

Since 1999, the United States has held annual Trans Day of Remembrance ceremonies across the country. These events recognize all of the trans lives that have been lost over the past year. Originally conceived as a vigil by trans advocate Gwendolyn Ann Smith "to honor the memory of Rita Hester, a transgender woman who was killed in 1998," over time it evolved into an annual tradition.[84] In the years since then, the rates of intimate partner violence as well as racialized and gendered violence leading to the deaths of Black trans women have continued to rise, reaching epidemic proportions since the first trans vigil was held.[85] In the *2015 U.S. Transgender Survey: Report on the Experiences of Black Respondents* by Sandy E. James, Carter Brown, and Isaiah Wilson, which was published in 2017, the authors determined that 56 percent of respondents "experienced some form of intimate partner violence, including acts of coercive control and physical violence," and 58 percent of Black trans women in particular reported experiencing some form of intimate partner violence.[86] Black nonbinary individuals reported that they too have experienced some form of intimate partner violence, reporting at forty-nine percent.[87] These statistics are even more alarming when we consider that they are based only on reported cases.

Similarly, the Centers for Disease Control and Prevention's *2017 Morbidity and Mortality Report* found that "homicide is one of the leading causes of death for women aged 44 years . . . and nearly half of victims are killed by a current or former male intimate partner." The report also concluded that "non-Hispanic black and American Indian/Alaska Native women experienced the highest rates of homicide (4.4 and 4.3 per 100,000 population, respectively)," and that over half of those were related to intimate partner violence. What these shocking statistics concerning both groups make clear is that both Black cis women and Black trans women share a relationship to epidemic levels of violence and even death at the hands of their intimate partners and lovers. Black cis women are vulnerable to the very same life outcomes and circumstances as Black trans women. The plight of Black cis women is inherently tied to the plight of Black trans women. Just as there have been public cases of Black trans women being brutalized or even murdered by their partners or strangers, there have also been public cases of Black cis women whose lives have either been ended or adversely affected by intimate partner violence.

Although Rihanna's career is long past the night in 2009 when R&B singer Chris Brown brutally assaulted the singer turned businesswoman, her public life as an artist and woman was forever altered.[88] When the story hit social media, many users, Black cis men and women alike, scrutinized Rihanna instead of believing what had happened to her.[89] They made excuses for Brown, saying that he was young, that she probably started the fight, or, even worse, that she gave him an STI and that was the reason he beat her.[90] Even though Rhianna survived her attack and moved forward with her life and career, the same was not the case for Islan Nettles. Nettles, a twenty-one-year-old Black trans woman, was beaten to death by twenty-five-year-old James Dixon, a Black cis man who had been flirting with Nettles in Harlem until he discovered that she was trans, and subsequently began beating her.[91] Nettles died as a result of her injuries, and Dixon was only sentenced to twelve years in prison for causing her death.[92]

While Rhianna's wealth, public persona, and fame aided in her ability to recover from the effects and public stigma of being a survivor of intimate-partner violence, Nettles was not able to benefit from the same type of interventions or support. Intimate-partner violence, domestic violence, and violence against vulnerable racialized and gendered groups continues to be a crisis due to our culture's institutional and systemic neglect when it comes to addressing the various harms that affect the lives of Black trans and cis women. Such community plagues continue to go unaddressed and unresolved at the structural level. As a result, the burden of eradicating these social ills falls on the shoulders of those who happen to survive such atrocities: Black trans and cis women.

Recently, a thirty-one-year-old Black woman who has chosen to remain anonymous was brutally and publicly assaulted on camera after refusing to purchase alcohol for three young men in Harlem, New York.[93] The woman said that she "was punched, kicked and her face bitten," just because she refused the young men's request.[94] The woman told NBC News that the group also spat on her and that her cell phone was stolen during the attack. However, in this instance, many members of the Harlem community rallied together on the woman's behalf, not only protesting her public beating but also marching through the New York streets chanting "protect Black women."[95] While there are many more instances of this specific racial and gendered harm that Black cis women and Black trans women have been subjected to, either by partners or strangers, at least the community response to the Harlem incident shows that some of our communities are changing their minds when it comes to the treatment of Black women. Black trans and cis women now unite under the same hashtags whose calls to action are rooted in resisting the racist and cisnormative hegemonies that continue to frame their lives. The hashtags #TrustBlackWomen, #TrustBlackTransWomen, #SayHerName, and #BlackTransLivesMatter show that many folks out there in various communities are actively combatting the violence wielded against Black trans women and Black cis women. We still need more to join in the struggle. When Black trans women's voices, experiences, and causes are lifted communally, everyone wins. If Black cis women collaborate not only with organizations and initiatives that support Black trans women but also with Black trans women personally, we as a culture have nowhere to go but up.

The shared hashtags used by some activists, artists, and educators have turned into shared goals, with many Black trans women, men, and nonbinary folks organizing their activism, scholarship, and art around building coalitions to eradicate the shared harm that both groups face. For example, the late Black trans woman blogger Monica Roberts, known throughout the world as the Transgriot, spent her entire writing career correcting journalists and media commentators about the ways in which they discussed Black trans women. Roberts highlighted how, even in death, Black trans women were still not given full humanity by the media because of journalists' propensity to deadname, misgender, and sensationalize the brutal and routine murdering of Black trans women.[96] Roberts did an exceptional job teaching the world how to name and treat Black trans women. But this should not have been her work. She should not have had to spend her life fighting to bring attention to the dignity, humanity, and three-dimensionality of Black trans women's lives.

The Black and LGBTQ+ led organization BEAM (Black Emotional and Mental Health) is an organization composed of Black and marginalized folks that offers trainings on grant making and movement building and is dedicated to the wellness, healing, and liberation of Black and marginalized communities. BEAM offers trainings and programs that aim to imagine Black masculinities differently, removing the confines of unemotionality, toxicity, abuse, and violence.[97] BEAM also uses dialogue to teach its participants new ways to envision masculinities that dispel myths about mental, physical, and sexual health.[98] Black trans activists Janet Mock and Laverne Cox's social media campaign and network, #GirlsLikeUS, which curates an intersectional "counterpublic" online, not only legitimizes and celebrates trans identities but also pushes back against the racialized, sexualized, and gendered myths that continue to haunt Black trans women and Black nonbinary folks, helping to correct the misrepresentation and dehumanization that frame their lives.[99]

In the realm of academic scholarship, *Black on Both Sides: A Racial History of Trans Identity*, by Dr. C. Riley Snorton, not only centers Black trans lives but also rebuilds a historical Black trans genealogy. The book aims to "eschew binaristic logic that might reify a distinction between transgender and cisgender, black and white, disabled and abled, and so on, in an effort to think expansively about how blackness and black studies, and transness and trans studies, yield insights that surpass an additive logic."[100] Dr. Moya Bailey, in her book *Misogynoir Transformed: Black Women's Digital Resistance*, brings to light how Black women, both trans and cis, systematically resist the hegemonic master tropes of racialized and gendered identity by using social media platforms and networks to combat misogynoir, and the racist and sexist hatred of Black women.[101] Bailey, whose book focuses on Black queer and trans women, argues that when Black women make their presence known through social media, they are in fact carving out their own spaces away from the precarity of the digitized world, allowing others to actively reimagine a world where no harms come to Black women.

Through grassroots organizing, social media campaigns, and scholarship, these Black trans educators, activists, media makers, and nonprofit creators are all working diligently to counteract the harmful reality of LGBTQ+ dating apps, cyberbullying, street harassment, intimate partner violence, and the racist, sexist, and cisnormative myths that continue to harm the lives of Black trans women. However, they cannot do it by themselves. They need the support of others. Due to our cultural understanding of gender, sex roles, and race, Black trans women still exist in a space of extreme vulnerability, and their survival, liberation, and freedom is a struggle that we must all fight for. The stakes are too high not to.

CHAPTER FIVE

OUR FIRST PRIDE WAS A RIOT

Despite the myriad of strides made by gay and lesbian organizations during the 1950s, regular raids by law enforcement on gay bars and nightclubs was common practice.[1] By the late 1960s, the Stonewall Inn and other gay venues were operating legally throughout New York City; however, law enforcement justified raiding these spaces by citing the anti-cross-dressing ordinance. By this point, anti-cross-dressing ordinances were nationwide, forcing citizens to wear at least three articles of clothing that correlated to their assigned sex at birth.[2] The police raid at the Stonewall Inn on June 28, 1969, began like previous raids on LGBTQ+ establishments. But it was on this night that the mostly Black and Latinx LGBTQ+ patrons had had enough. Stormé DeLarverie, commonly known as "the Black butch lesbian," is thought by many to have thrown the first brick at law enforcement.[3] This sparked a three-day-long violent confrontation between an estimated two thousand LGBTQ+ citizens and four hundred New York City police.[4]

The aftermath of the uprisings resulted in deaths, arrests, and immense damage to the bar. Today, it is known as igniting the beginning of the LGBTQ+ liberation movement. It was this direct action made possible by years of multiracial queer and trans organizing that took a mostly coastal movement to a national stage.[5] In order to understand why and how contemporary Pride festivals have strayed so far away from their original impetus, we have to look at this specific night in LGBTQ+ history and the work of multiracial trans and queer coalitions. The racist and sexist practices propagated by white LGBTQ+ Pride attendees, as well as the huge police presence at today's festivals, are both stark indicators that Pride festivals have lost their way. Additionally, the mostly white and cis queer leadership in national LGBTQ+ organizations, who presumably prioritized same-sex marriage and military access for LGBTQ+ communities as the only necessary avenues to freedom, also had a hand in reshaping and reinventing the premise of Pride festivals. Mainstream media has shifted Pride festivals from advocacy-based and activist-oriented celebrations into whitewashed, consumerist, and apolitical parties void of the same social and political consciousness that led to the Stonewall reckoning and to the first Pride.

I lost my enthusiasm for attending Pride festivals and events in October 2007. I was in New Orleans during Halloween that year and ended up at the Bourbon Street Pub. Chuck Knipp was performing as his drag persona, Shirley Q. Liquor. Knipp's performance of Shirley was "a welfare mother with nineteen kids who guzzles malt liquor, drives a Caddy and [speaks] in an 'ignunt' Gulf Coast black dialect."[6] That night, Knipp caked his face in a deep brown shade of makeup to make his skin appear Black, while sporting a rainbow afro wig. The mostly white, cis, and gay male audience burst out in raucous laughter when Shirley listed the names of her children, turning Black naming practices into a joke.[7]

While drag queens, often cis gay men who don feminine artifice and perform as their alter-egos, have been known to transgress racial, sexual, and gendered boundaries, Knipp's drag was nothing more than contemporary blackface made queer. In my experience, white people, regardless of their sexual orientation or gender identity, have a challenging time unlearning racism and racist practices. This has made it nearly impossible for many white LGBTQ+ people to see racism in their everyday lives, and especially so in exclusively LGBTQ+ spaces.[8] Knipp's performance and the audience's knee-slapping laughter reminded me that being queer does not negate racism or whiteness. As I watched this audience of mostly white, presumably cis gay men find pleasure in blackface, I knew that regardless of a public space being designated for queer and trans folks, race still remains an issue. For me personally, my identity as a Black woman was something for them to laugh at.

Knipp's performance is not an anomaly. During my first year in Louisville, I ventured out to the Connection, the biggest LGBTQ+ nightclub in the city.[9] There was a weekly drag show and most of the attendees that night were white cis gay men. When the show began, the music that started playing was the theme song to the popular Black television program *The Jeffersons*. The show's host, white drag queen Hurricane Summers, came onstage donning brown stockings and deep brown makeup, pretending to be the Black pop singer and icon Tina Turner. As she moved across the stage, attempting to imitate Turner's stage presence, the audience began cheering and laughing. After the music ended, Hurricane proceeded to tell a slew of racist and sexist jokes, which the attendees seemed to find wildly entertaining. I was disgusted. Although Knipp's shows had long been protested by many Black queer and trans folks across the country, there wasn't much resistance to Hurricane's Tina Turner performance.[10]

While Knipp's drag persona exemplified misogynoir, Summers's impression seemed to be interpreted as a tribute to Turner and a celebration of Black popular culture.[11] However, when a white drag queen uses the queer art form of drag to perpetuate harmful white supremacist and sexist notions of Blackness, it is no longer drag. Drag was created as a way for individuals and respective entertainers to destabilize the fixed boundaries of race, gender, and sexuality. It was not designed to further mock Black people or other people of color. When white drag queens do this, they are removing the transgressive potential of drag, by un-queering it. True, neither entertainer used burnt cork or bugged their eyes out like historical blackface performers, but both Knipp's and Summers's incorporation of the racist pastime of blackface made their drag typical of the racist practices that Black people and other racially marginalized folks constantly face in our country.

Conversely, queerness should always be seen as atypical, subversive, special if you will, and so when a white drag queen inserts racism, especially blackface, within their performances, they separate themselves from the subversive nature of drag, and instead reproduce derogatory notions of personhood that are already reflected within mainstream culture. Dehumanizing depictions of Black people began to emerge within American material culture after the Civil War. These stereotypes were formed from the white supremacist imagination. They were cemented through racist advertising and films with the attempt to pigeonhole Black people as deviant, libidinous, even dangerous. In Knipp's performance of Shirley Q. Liquor and Summers's performance of Turner, I saw nothing more than a remixing of the mammy and jezebel archetypes. To me, this showed that many white and trans queer folks are no more enlightened about race than their straight and cis counterparts. Summers's and Knipp's audiences' warm reception of their performances reveal that in white LGBTQ+ communities, mocking Black identity lives on as an acceptable pastime.

In July 2020 the popular DC gay bar Number Nine came under fire for one of its bartenders wearing a blackface mask.[12] In 2021, Scarlet Adams, a contestant on *RuPaul's Drag Race Down Under*, apologized for her use of blackface as well as for her past racist performances, after Felicia Foxx, an Indigenous Australian drag queen, called out Adams for her past displays of racial mockery.[13] These instances of queer folks using blackface are a troubling mirror of the larger culture's acceptance of the practice. For example, in 2019 the Pew Research Center found that 34 percent of Americans think that donning blackface, whatever the occasion, "is always or sometimes acceptable," with only 37 percent of Americans saying blackface is never acceptable.[14]

The refusal of many white LGBTQ+ folks to recognize the power and dehumanization of racism and sexism enables a deliberate ignorance of how systems of privilege and oppression continue to benefit them financially and socially. While some white queer and trans folks definitely hold racist and sexist views, some are just so fixated on their status as sexual and gendered minorities that it prevents them from being open to learning anything new, especially if it is about racism, sexism, or their own homonormative politics.[15]

This deliberate avoidance of unlearning racist and sexist practices transforms white LGBTQ+ folks into what Black queer theorist Roderick Ferguson calls a "one-dimensional queer."[16] Meaning that white LGBTQ+ people have had a deep investment in viewing the Stonewall uprisings and the resulting LGBTQ+ liberation movement as a one-time, standalone incident that only had one central goal. This goal, of course, was to free white LGBTQ+ people from sexual and gendered tyranny—and not to include racial and economic strategies for racialized and poor LGBTQ+ folks. Ferguson asserts that all folks must understand the aim of Stonewall, and the subsequent LGBTQ+ liberation movement, as one that was intersectional, not only dedicated to the liberation of all LGBTQ+ people but especially of those who were racially diverse. To Ferguson, white LGBTQ+ people who deliberately deny this history and understanding of our queer and trans past create their own mental metamorphosis, transforming themselves into one-dimensional queers. Taking the time to teach white queer and trans people about racism and its impact on the lives of Black LGBTQ+ people is exhausting. In my own experience, I've found it often puts me in a position to be further harmed. These exchanges usually escalate to shouting matches, where white queer or trans folks argue with me about how their queer or trans identity absolves them of any racial animus, giving them a pass to be racist. I've found that even when "well-meaning" white queer and trans folks seek out my counsel to unlearn racism, they have done so out of fear of financial or social backlash for their racist behavior, not because they are actually interested in removing racist and sexist biases from their own consciousness.

Pride, a celebration of the entire LGBTQ+ community, began as an inclusive tradition from the multiracial organizing and civil disobedience by Black and Latinx trans and queer activists. However, mainstream Pride festivals and queer nightclubs are often the places where I've experienced the most racial harm. Sometimes it's the white lesbians who come up to me at the bar, and before saying "hello," immediately ask me how to do their biracial child's hair, because Black hair is "wild" and "confusing." Or, it's been the white gay men who run up terribly excited to give me their best Black girl imitation from what they've seen on television. Or it is the white LGBTQ+ friend groups who ask my friends and me to show them the latest Black dances, as if we were only at Pride festivals to give Black dance tutorials. More often than not, my friends and I have consistently confronted racism or sexism from white LGBTQ+ Pride attendees. Instead of enjoying ourselves, we have often left these celebratory queer spaces feeling deflated, bruised, or antagonized. These experiences have taken their toll and made me avoid these types of gatherings altogether.

The disconnect between early conceptions of LGBTQ+ liberation and the social erasure of the multiracial activism that ignited Pride is not limited to overt acts of racism and sexism at festivals, either. The large police presence at Pride festivals signifies a deviation from their original conception. Law enforcement's looming presence at Pride indicates the social and political divisions between white LGBTQ+ folks and Black and Latinx LGBTQ+ people. While white LGBTQ+ people are able to view law enforcement as a protective force against homophobia and transphobia, Black and Latinx LGBTQ+ folks often see police as a violent and harmful organization. For this reason, it is important to look at LGBTQ+ communities' historical relationship to law enforcement, both before and after Stonewall, as that night in June of 1969 was not an unprecedented or isolated incident.

A couple of years prior to Stonewall, there were several altercations between queer and trans citizens of color and the police. One of the most famous incidents took place in August 1966 in San

Francisco.[17] The Compton's Cafeteria riot, led primarily by Black trans women and other drag queens of color, was a direct response to decades of scrutiny, brutality, and harassment by police against queer and trans people who lived in the area. San Francisco police justified their treatment of LGBTQ+ people by pointing to the many national anti-cross-dressing ordinances that forced citizens to wear at least three articles of clothing that correlated to their assigned sex.[18] Additionally, LGBTQ+ sex workers' presence on the street at night made them especially vulnerable to harassment and humiliating arrests by San Francisco law enforcement. Fed up with the police's gender terrorism, a reckoning ensued in which the Compton's Cafeteria's owner, Gene Compton, "banned trans women and drag queens" from the establishment.[19]

Another confrontation between LGBTQ+ folks and the police took place on New Year's Eve in Los Angeles in 1966. Queer and trans club goers partying at the Black Cat Tavern, a popular gay nightclub, were interrupted by a police raid. Undercover police officers masked themselves as patrons in the hopes that would be able to arrest the club goers for breaking "sexual perversion," and "public indecency" laws, which were in place in LA at the time.[20] Onstage, the Black drag queen trio known as the Rhythm Queens finished singing their number. That's when one of the plainclothes officers "yanked the plug from the jukebox, tore down the Christmas decorations, and turned the lights up," informing the festive crowd that if they did not disperse, they would be arrested.[21] Pandemonium ensued as the LGBTQ+ patrons tried their best to escape the bar swiftly, only to be met by uniformed police blocking all of the exit doors.

Bar goers at the Black Cat Tavern, like those at the Compton Cafeteria, were fatigued by the violent and terroristic ways law enforcement chose to carry out arrests in LGBTQ+ communities, and they fought back accordingly.[22] As with the aftermath of Stonewall, many Black Cat Tavern patrons were beaten, arrested, and humiliated that night. Queer and trans militancy, which had been growing nationwide in the 1960s, was a direct result of LGBTQ+ citizens connecting the injustice they faced at the hands of the police and society to their identities as racialized queer and trans people. Many of the civil disobedience strategies that were being utilized by civil rights and feminist activists in the United States, in response to racial and gender injustice, were adopted by Black and Latinx LGBTQ+ activists. These activists utilized these strategies to address the racial, gendered, and sexual terrorism they faced at the hands of the police. This cross pollination of justice strategies by some Black and Latinx LGBTQ+ activists was familiar to them because they were already a part of at least one or both movements for social and legal change. [23]

One such instance where Black and Latinx LGBTQ+ citizens incorporated civil disobedience strategies in the hopes of justice, for example, occurred at Dewey's, a popular LGBTQ+ hangout and burger joint in Philadelphia, in 1965.[24] Lunch counter resistances were a common practice employed by civil rights leaders in various cities across the country at popular eateries where Black customers were consistently denied service because of their race. Seeing the effectiveness of this strategy, LGBTQ+ citizens held two sit-ins on April 25 and May 2 in response to an anti-queer and anti-trans policy that began to deny service to anyone who was interpreted to be LGBTQ+. The dehumanizing policy was put into place after the restaurant denied service to a group of teenagers whom Dewey's management saw as queer because of the way that they were dressed. Since the establishment was already viewed by locals as a queer and trans eatery, the new policy ended up denying service to an estimated 150 people, all in one day.[25] Enraged by the discriminatory policy and the disrespectful treatment, LGBTQ+ patrons, joined by the homophile organization the Janus Society "proceeded to demonstrate outside of the restaurant, and handed out over 1,500 leaflets throughout the next five days," in addition to their organized two day sit-in.[26] Their collective action resulted in Dewey's putting an end to its policy.

LGBTQ+ communities' historically tumultuous relationship to law enforcement is an important part of LGBTQ+ history and activism that should be viewed as integral to the stories about the Stonewall uprisings. It should also be considered integral to other acts of civil disobedience that were carried out by various LGBTQ+ communities across the country. Having droves of police present at Pride festivals represents a lack of consideration for this sordid history between law enforcement and LGBTQ+ communities, particularly Black and Latinx LGBTQ+ people. The police presence serves to erase this complicated and violent history, instead creating an ahistorical and whitewashed narrative of LGBTQ+ activism. Even after the uprisings in New York, organized protests in response to police violence continued to take place across the country, as Stonewall alone did not stop police terrorism.[27] LGBTQ+ communities' dehumanizing subjugation at the hands of law enforcement in many ways mirrored the longstanding relationship that other marginalized communities have had with police. Our country's most vulnerable populations—Black, Latinx, queer, trans, and poor communities—have had, at best, a contentious relationship with police, and, at worse, one that is characterized by violence and brutality.

When modern Pride festivals hire police officers to maintain "safety" at their celebrations, they erase the history of the vibrant informal safety networks that were in place before and during the Stonewall uprisings. Stormé DeLarverie, the Black butch lesbian, along with other masculine lesbians of color, created informal safety networks through night patrols at the Stonewall Inn and other venues to keep patrons safe not only from outsiders but also from police harassment. However, today this form of community protection is not thought of as an alternative to police at Pride.[28] In a 2014 article about DeLarverie's life, activism, and her patrol work in Greenwich Village in the 1980s, DeLarverie details how her patrol work changed the ways that Black and Latinx LGBTQ+ folks conceived of protection at their gatherings.[29] DeLarverie continued to patrol the lower Seventh and Eighth Avenues decades after Stonewall to prevent, as she put it, "any form of intolerance, bullying or abuse of her baby girls."[30] The tradition of informal security networks like the one DeLarverie speaks of have continued. This has been especially the case when it comes to current Black LGBTQ+ party organizers who have hired private security companies made up of other Black LGBTQ+ people to maintain safety at their parties and festivals in lieu of police.[31] Black LGBTQ+ people have long recognized that the relationship between law enforcement and marginalized communities has been one fraught with violence, racial bias, and terror.[32] If we consider, then, that most if not all of our country's organized protest against racial, gendered, class, or sexual inequity has, at one point or another, directly responded to police violence, then we can understand why some Black LGBTQ+ party promoters and organizers have sought alternative networks of safety instead of hiring police to maintain safety at their events. This is especially true when we also consider that when law enforcement has shown up in any Black community, regardless of the sexualities or gender identities of community members, they have done nothing but further subject these communities to more scrutiny, humiliation, and violence.

Fifty-one years later, it is no wonder, then, that some white cis gay men have become increasingly incensed at the presence of various Black Lives Matter (BLM) chapters showing up at Pride festivals to demand, both here and abroad, that this revisionist history regarding Stonewall and the beginnings of Pride come to an end.[33] In an op-ed for the *Los Angeles Times*, James Kirchick, a white cis gay man, condemns the organized protest by the Toronto chapter of BLM by asserting that the protestors' interruption of the festival was "counterproductive," and was only a way for Black Lives Matter activists to "further their own anti-cop agendas." Kirchick asserts, "Condemning the police as an inherently racist, homophobic institution is not only false and counterproductive, but it also denigrates the many LGBT officers whose participation in these festivities would be annulled if the activists got their way." Kirchick goes on to contend that any LGBTQ+ citizen who supports BLM protestors because they "insist that the gay rights movement was birthed in protest against police harassment at Stonewall," should recognize that "similar episodes of historic police abuse only [show] how far . . . our country has come." Kirchick ends his inaccurate and racially absurd rant by stating, "In so many places around the world—Russia, and most recently Turkey—the police attack pride parades and arrest gay rights activists. In North America, police protect them."[34]

What's so troubling about Kirchick's last assertion is that, as a white man, his relationship to law enforcement has clearly been a benevolent and protective experience, so much so that he quotes a gay police officer to bolster his argument against BLM activists. Kirchick does not, however, extend this same form of grace to BLM activists, not taking into consideration how their relationship to the police as Black LGBTQ+ people has been one of terror and consistent harassment, not one of protection. Kirchick's refusal to see law enforcement in any other way but his own shows not only how limited his worldview is, but it also shows how whiteness, when it is not interrogated by white people themselves, reveals the arrogance and narcissism that bolster racial inequity. Kirchick's argument also erases the fact that some Black citizens are simultaneously LGBTQ+ citizens, and that these dual identities have a double function, which complicates their viewpoint of law enforcement. It erases BLM activists' LGBTQ+ identities, subsuming them under Blackness in order to characterize them as menaces who were only interested in showcasing their police abolitionist politics, and not in creating a Pride festival that was inclusive of Pride's beginnings and Black and Latinx LGBTQ+ people.

In an additional twist of irony, law enforcement in New York city in 2021 did the very opposite of what Kirchick argues they do. Instead of protecting LGBTQ+ citizens who were celebrating Pride in Washington Square Park that day, they pepper-sprayed and arrested them. NYPD made eight arrests and issued four summonses to people with charges ranging from disorderly conduct and resisting arrest, to criminal possession of a weapon and obstructing administration.[35] While NYPD claimed that the activists were blocking a police barricade that had been put up in order to control the crowd's movements, many activists in attendance that day assert that several folks who were asked to move did so, but that these acts of compliance were still met with hostility and brutality. According to one protestor, Janus Rose, "everything was peaceful before the cops showed up."[36] Rose's statement highlights how even today the police continue to function as a harmful force against Black and Latinx queer and trans communities. Outrage at the thought of police abolition or divestment shows how willfully ignorant some white queer and trans folks are and reveals their inability to even consider the historical and present-day relationship that Black and Latinx LGBTQ+ citizens have to policing systems. However, it has not just been the inclusion of police at current Pride festivals that has helped to sustain whitewashed and exclusionary practices at Pride. The mostly white and cis leadership of many national LGBTQ+ organizations that emerged across the nation after the Stonewall uprisings has also shaped what Pride festivals look like today.

The Human Rights Campaign (HRC), the National LGBTQ Task Force (NLTF), and the National Center for Lesbian Rights (NCLR) all placed white and cis queer folks at the helm of leadership in their organizations for several decades after Stonewall. This act alone ultimately shut out many of the concerns and priorities of Black and Latinx LGBTQ+ citizens post-Stonewall. These priorities included but were not limited to reducing LGBTQ+ youth houselessness, organizing for sex workers' rights, and establishing more racial and ethnic equality. None of these inclusive objectives were included within the agendas of these national organizations. Additionally, the HRC's decision to frame queer and trans freedom only around advocacy for same-sex marriage and military access further alienated LGBTQ+ folks of color. If we consider these actions, in addition to the National LGBTQ Task Force's reluctance to see how queer and trans issues are deeply tied to issues of race and religion, we can understand why these actions have led to a strong aversion to celebrating Pride in public ways by many Black and Latinx LGBTQ+ people.

Before the civil unrest at Stonewall there were only fifty gay and lesbian organizations in the US, and only four years after these uprisings, there were over eight hundred.[37] One of the first national LGBTQ+ organizations, the National LGBTQ Task Force, was formed in 1973. Initially, the organization went by the name the National Gay Task Force, and then changed its name in 1985 to the National Gay and Lesbian Task Force; it was not until 2014 that the organization adopted its present name. Howard Brown, Marin Duberman, Barbara Gittings, Ron Gold, Frank Kameny, Nathalie Rockhill, and Bruce Voeller were the founding members of the task force, and they all held out the hope that gay and lesbian politics would one day be at the forefront of national issues that sought to address inequity.[38] The NCLR was founded by Donna Hitchens in 1977, and was one of the few national LGBTQ+ organizations that was founded exclusively by lesbian women in the interest of pushing lesbian rights to forefront of popular political discourse.[39] The HRC, which was founded in 1984 by Steve Endean, a white cis gay man and AIDS activist, over time came to be regarded as the flagship LGBTQ+ organization, due to its funding sources and political influence.[40]

All three organizations initially claimed that their formulation and advocacy were in the interest of freedom for all LGBTQ+ communities. However, after each organization became an established 501(c)(3), none of them put the concerns of Black and Latinx LGBTQ+ citizens at the center of their activism or focus. Nor did any of these organizations appoint any Black or Latinx LGBTQ+ folks in positions of leadership within their organizations.[41] All three organizations would spend the next twenty years myopically focusing on gaining access to two of the most heteronormative institutions in our nation, the military and legal marriage, to the exclusion of all other issues affecting LGBTQ+ communities. Keith Boykin, a Black gay journalist and political commentator, wrote in his book *Where Rhetoric Meets Reality: The Role of Black Lesbians and Gays in "Queer" Politics* that even by the year 2000, "the dream of racial inclusion and sensitivity within the movement today still has not been realized."[42] Boykin argued that despite Black gay and lesbian membership within multiracial organizations immediately following Stonewall, such as Queer Nation, the Lesbian Avengers, and Q2L, white cis gay and lesbian leadership was still reluctant to put issues that affected Black and Latinx LGBTQ+ people at the forefront of their organizations.[43]

For example, after Stonewall, Sylvia Rivera and Marsha P. Johnson founded the Street Transvestite Action Revolutionaries (STAR), and Rivera then went on to become a member of the Gay Liberation Front (GLF) as well as the Gay Activist Alliance (GAA), which by the 1970s was working on behalf of all folks within LGBTQ+ communities in New York City.[44] However, to Rivera, the more mainstream credibility that was bestowed on these organizations by mainstream culture, the more they shifted their politics from a multipronged political stance into a narrow and assimilationist one. Plainly, once GLF became solidified as an organization, the more the needs of Black and Latinx trans women, poor LGBTQ+ citizens, sex workers, and any LGBTQ+ person with other racial or gendered identities were pushed to the side or not discussed at all.[45] Rivera spoke about these changes in an interview for Arthur Dong's PBS series *The Question of Equality*, stating, "When things started getting more mainstream, it was like, 'we don't need you no more.'"[46] For Rivera, the issues that were central to a multiracial queer and trans past, like LGBTQ+ houselessness, the criminalization of sex work, and racial injustice at the hands of white LGBTQ+ people and larger society, were continuously evaded in favor of issues—marriage specifically—that would directly benefit white cis gays and lesbians. Myrl Beam, in her book, *Gay, Inc.: The Nonprofitization of Queer Politics*, contends that even though marriage equality was not the central goal of the queer left, it became the most mainstream articulation of a faux queer politic due to the select few, mostly cis white gays and lesbians, who wielded "incredible power to determine the agenda of the movement with their money, through donations to the nonprofit organizations through which the LGBT movement largely operates."[47]

By the early 2000s, the National LGBTQ Task Force, NCLR, and HRC had already established themselves as formidable collectives that were sought out by mainstream journalists and news outlets to articulate what queer and trans freedoms looked like.[48] So, for these organizations to have only white cis gays and lesbians in positions of leadership, and for the HRC specifically to say that LGBTQ+ liberation equated to marriage equality and military access, meant that the public voice of LGBTQ+ rights was dominated by a only small subset of LGBTQ+ communities, namely white cis gays and lesbians with wealth. This public stance inevitably transformed the popular understanding of LGBTQ+ advocacy, which was once understood, shortly after Stonewall, as fighting against racial inequity, LGBTQ+ homelessness, the criminalization of sex work, and the like, into a single-axis type of activism that did not challenge the various systems of domination that have framed the lives of many Black and Latinx LGBTQ+ people.[49] By making queer and trans advocacy non-intersectional, these organizations further cemented the idea that queer and trans identity should be seen as synonymous with whiteness, wealth, and only include access to institutions that have been traditionally linked to citizenship. This practice inevitably shaped popular public discourse when it came to thinking about what LGBTQ+ equality looks like or should be.

To make matters worse, a 2015 internal report on diversity within the HRC illuminated just how awful it was to work for a national LGBTQ+ organization as a Black or Latinx LGBTQ+ person.[50] The report was conducted by the Pipeline Project, a now-defunct organization established in 2015 to ensure that LGBTQ+ people of color advanced in program development and board service within LGBTQ+ organizations.[51] The Pipeline Project's results indicated that the HRC was fraught with racism, transphobia, and sexism. Many respondents stated that the HRC was a white man's club whose exclusionary practices had been going on for years.[52] One respondent stated that "as a woman I feel excluded every day," and another stated that trans employees were tokenized, and indicated that there was a lack of safety within the work environment, with one respondent stating "the company dress code lists only male and female attire options, leaving genderqueer or nonbinary staffers without guidance."[53] Even worse, the same respondent also stated that they were "offended when they heard coworkers using the phrase tranny," and another respondent indicated that there was rampant "femophobia where feminine men and women [were] not considered as important as masculine staffers."[54]

The National LGBTQ Task Force has also received criticism, despite its annual Creating Change conference, which is viewed by many white LGBTQ+ people as a widely diverse gathering of LGBTQ+ people.[55] The task force's annual educational and activist conference has been happening since 1988 and has grown in participation by 1,000 percent. In 2016, however, its annual gathering was the target of protest. The conference that year originally scheduled "a session with Immigration and Customs Enforcement officials," which brought intense scrutiny to the National LGBTQ Task Force. While conference officials cancelled the session, it did not stop the backlash they faced from participants who saw the session as racially and culturally insensitive, as well as violent due to the conference being applauded as a safe space for the undocumented.[56] In 2019, the National LGBTQ Task Force had to deal with protestors once again because conference organizers decided to hold a reception for the pro-Israel and LGBTQ+ organization A Wider Bridge.[57] Protesters saw this reception, which was allegedly created by conference organizers in the interests of highlighting Israel as a country that was inclusive and accepting of LGBTQ+ people, as a deflection from the human rights violations that Israel has committed against Palestinians for years. The trans and nonbinary protestors, who were also Black and Brown, beat on drums and crowded the hallways to block attendees from entering the pro-Israel reception, and many white LGBTQ+ conference goers were outraged about the protestors' message.

In an op-ed for *The Advocate*, white trans activist Hannah Elyse Simpson expressed her outrage about the protestors, writing that "these particular demonstrators were ineffective at anything beyond taking up space—they were more fixated by documenting themselves with selfies and complaining about police being called, than by offering any actual message."[58] Simpson also stated that the protest and demonstrators made her "fear [for her] life," but she was still not able to comprehend the fear that demonstrators might have had about the police being called on them. Simpson was also not able to clearly see the racism that abounds in Israel, which demonstrators saw specifically directed at Palestinians. Her assessment that the protestors were just loud and seemingly violent agitators with no real agenda (just because their protest centered on racial inequality) speaks to the shortsightedness of many white LGBTQ+ people when it comes to Black and Latinx LGBTQ+ people advocating for racial justice alongside LGBTQ+ liberation.[59]

While the NCLR has not had to endure protests like those faced by the National LGBTQ Task Force and the HRC, the organization only appointed its first Black director, Imani Rupert-Gordon, in 2019, despite its founding commitments to racial equality.[60] At the time of her new appointment, Rupert-Gordon served as the executive director of a Chicago-based organization, Affinity Community Services, that focused on Black LGBTQ+ people, and specifically on Black LGBTQ+ women. In speaking with *The Advocate* about her new appointment, Rupert-Gordon stated that she would bring a unique perspective to the organization, as a Black lesbian cisgender woman, while also being mindful about working as a team. Although Rupert-Gordon stated that the "NCLR has long been intersectional," she still went on to say that "if anti-LGBTQ+ discrimination becomes a thing of the past, it [still] won't help those who can't take advantage of opportunities because of poverty, racial bias, and other barriers."

Rupert-Gordon also said that her aim was to change the focus of the organization from legal and legislative gains for white LGBTQ+ people to issues that affect the daily lives of all LGBTQ+ people, specifically Black LGBTQ+ people that have to navigate those racial and economic barriers more so than their white counterparts.[61] Rupert-Gordon, clearly not interested in bashing an organization she is now at the helm of, still pointed out that racial and economic inclusion has not been a focus of the organization for some time.

The limiting of the national conversation around LGBTQ+ freedoms to military access and marriage equality, the lack of Black leadership in the NCLR until recently, the terrorizing of HRC staffers because of their intersectional differences, and the protests at Creating Change all show just how resistant wealthy white LGBTQ+ folks have been to intersectional thinking and activist praxis post Stonewall. Once these organizations became institutionalized, the concerns of Black and Latinx LGBTQ+ people fell to the margins of their advocacy.

Black feminist and queer political scientist Cathy Cohen spoke to this very issue in her essay "Punks, Bulldaggers, and Welfare Queens: The Radical Potential of Queer Politics," arguing that once aspects of queer liberation became institutionalized through organizations and non-profits they began to stop challenging systems of domination on multiple levels.[62] Instead of national LGBTQ+ organizations challenging heteronormativity, racism, or poverty alongside calling for an end to gender and sexual tyranny, they instead began "to prioritize sexuality as the primary frame through which they [pursued] their politics."[63] The exclusionary advocacy of national LGBTQ+ organizations neglects the many ways that harmful systems of inequity and violence interact with and regulate the lives of Black and Latinx LGBTQ+ people. For example, it was reported by the Movement Advancement Project and the Center for American Progress in 2015 that many Black, Asian, Latinx and Native American LGBTQ+ people must deal with disproportionate levels of poverty, unemployment, police violence, and racial and class barriers to healthcare, in addition to having to combat homophobia or transphobia daily.[64] Queer and trans identities need to be understood as intersectional identities, simply because oppressive systems and institutions regard them this way, manifesting racist, classist, sexist, and ableist subjugation within their daily lives.

Before and after the uprisings at Stonewall, Black and Latinx LGBTQ+ citizens have known that queer and trans freedom dreams must be tied to other larger movements of struggle to ensure that freedom is gained by everyone, and not just a select few. For national LGBTQ+ organizations to transform this radical activist insight into a narrow, whitewashed, and exclusionary advocacy framework only produces additional harm to many Black, Latinx, Asian, and Native American LGBTQ+ people. This one-dimensional advocacy and limited view of LGBTQ+ communities also give many Americans who are not LGBTQ+ the perception that ending racial, gendered, or economic inequality isn't related to queer or trans freedoms, when in fact, the opposite is true. This uncritical view deradicalizes LGBTQ+ activism and identities, producing a homonormative LGBTQ+ citizenry, one that is socially compliant and uninterested in combatting heteronormativity, racism, or economic inequity.[65]

In this instance, white cis gay and lesbian leadership within the HRC, specifically, solidified the notion for the general public that the best way for LGBTQ+ people to achieve mainstream acceptance was to access one of the most heteronormative and racist institutions we have as a country. Though the institution of marriage is considered a staple of American life, white cis and straight Americans have historically been the only citizens able to access it, and therefore benefit from it. The benefits of generational wealth, the consequential framing of marriage as a representation of sexual respectability, and the framing of this normativity as white do double duty here when it comes to sustaining white queers' economic and racial privilege over Black and Latinx LGBTQ+ folks. Because marriage as an institution has been historically codified as a means by which to exchange property—whether that property be women or actual material goods—it denies access to many Black and Latinx LGBTQ+ citizens, as both groups have struggled to benefit from economic stability or wealth.

Inevitably, the HRC effectually erased any of the political and social concerns of queer and trans people of color. The white face of marriage-equality campaigns by the HRC solidified the notion that the only "legitimate" gay identity is a white one; the HRC's marriage-equality campaigning privileged marriage over desire, gay and lesbian identity over bisexual and transgender identity, and white queer middle-class men over poor and working-class queer people of color. The HRC's leadership's focus on sexuality as the only category of oppression, as Cohen argued, ignored the ways in which queer people of color have been disempowered by the very institution of marriage.

Compounding matters, mainstream media takes its representational cues about queer and trans identities from these national LGBTQ+ organizations. Mainstream television also aids in this fictitious creation of "legitimate" (white) gay identity. As a medium it has always had a problem presenting marginalized groups in three-dimensional ways, often presenting its audiences with sanitized, homonormative queer subjects, and consequently framing queer and trans identities as white, middle-class, or wealthy and as individuals committed to the permissibility to date and marry without ridicule. These representational practices of erasure, by both mainstream media and national LGBTQ+ organizations, construct apolitical and apathetic white and cis queer archetypes that are presented as the consummate representations of queer identity. Since we still live in such a segregated society where most folks don't lead diverse lives, most straight and cis Americans are exposed to queer and trans identities through media representations instead of personal interactions. As a result, many major corporations that extend financial support to Pride festivals inevitably turn these once radical celebrations against white imperialism, racism, and poverty into politically void dance parties that emphasize consumerism, wealth, and whiteness.

According to a recent study conducted by YouGov, which was commissioned by *Gay Times* and Karmarama, "72% of the LGBTQ+ community think that the way they are presented in advertising is tokenistic."[66] And typically, only a small segment of the LGBTQ+ community is represented, namely cis white gay and lesbians.[67] The same holds true regarding television portrayals of LGBTQ+ citizens. In 2015, the GLAAD (formerly the Gay and Lesbian Alliance Against Defamation) organization conducted a study of LGBTQ+ representation on cable, broadcast, and streaming television as part of its twentieth annual report. They found that, "on broadcast networks, 69% of gay characters were white, 19% were black, 7% were Latino and 6% Asian."[68] The study also discovered that in terms of streaming and cable platforms, "71% and 73% of gay characters were white."[69] Further, the findings of the study also reported that " fewer than half of these LGBT characters were women," accounting for only 43 percent of television representation.[70] This limited, mostly white, male, wealthy, and cis representation of queer identities is yet another way that the true meaning behind the creation of Pride festivals is erased, as it restricts our perceptions of what queer liberation has meant historically. This is also how media and national LGBTQ+ organizations bring perpetual harm to racialized members of LGBTQ+ communities.

In a piece for Vox News titled "How LGBTQ Pride Month became a branded holiday," Alex Abad-Santos argues that "as the general support for LGBTQ rights [grew], so [did] the corporate incentive for brands and companies to position themselves in sync with that growing sentiment."[71] While financial support for Pride events and festivals from big businesses gave many the perception that mainstream sentiments towards queer and trans identities were changing for the better, the participation of corporate sponsors commodifies LGBTQ+ politics, making their Pride month media campaigns about palatable awareness. For example, Abad-Santos points out that in

2016, Los Angeles Pride was referred to by the *New York Times* as a "gay Coachella," and LA Pride organizers got into some hot water because they had to turn hundreds away from the festival due to their overselling of tickets.[72] Additionally, the Pride Island celebration in New York in 2018, which was sponsored by Skyy vodka and featured several big musical acts, also thought it wise to sell a $3,000 cabana package, making the uncritical assumption that possible Pride attendees would easily be able to afford such a high-priced party package.[73] Yet probably the worst example of how corporate financial support can turn harmful was at the 2018 New York City Pride, which was sponsored by the pharmaceutical company Gilead. Gilead, which manufactures the pill Truvada for PrEP, that "when taken daily, can reduce the risk of HIV from sex by over 90 percent," inevitably denied the most vulnerable populations of the LGBTQ+ community access to the drug, due to its cost.[74] The cost of PrEP without insurance is "$2,110.99 per month; with insurance and a coupon card from Gilead, that costs goes down to zero."[75] So, even though "gay and bisexual black men have a higher HIV rate in the US than in any country in the world," the preventative drug's financial barrier has made it nearly impossible to access, resulting in the majority of PrEP users being "white men who are 25 and older."[76]

This consumerist and apolitical practice of sanitizing Pride's beginnings is also known as *pinkwashing*. This term describes the appropriation of LGBTQ+ activism, movements, and identities in order to push products and make companies appear queer- and trans-friendly. Pinkwashing is a very recent phenomenon that began during the Obama administration, when same-sex marriage acceptance became part of public discourse.[77] Prior to its current use, the term *pinkwashing* originated in 2002, coined by breast cancer advocates and activists who were tired of corporations using the fight against breast cancer as a way to strategically sell their carcinogenic products while simultaneously positioning themselves as corporations that cared about breast cancer survivors and their families.[78] Pinkwashing, of course, is a riff on the term *whitewashing*, which is the historical practice of turning movements for social and cultural change into palpable sound bites, mixed with white-faced imagery, giving "brands and consumers alike a low-effort way to support social and political causes."[79] To Abad-Santos, when companies use pinkwashing tactics to elicit donations from the mainstream public, it creates a "consumerist donation structure," which inevitably positions LGBTQ+ communities as a monolith interested only in being tolerated and accepted by the mainstream culture.[80]

Before the pinkwashing of Pride became ubiquitous, Pride festivals were financially backed by small businesses and neighborhood bars or nightclubs that were already invested in maintaining their LGBTQ+ clientele. Post-Stonewall, most of the small businesses that supported early Pride festivals did so because many of the business owners either identified as LGBTQ+ themselves or were former participants in LGBTQ+ activism.[81] However, this grassroots support only lasted a few years before mainstream companies intervened, sponsoring mainstream Pride festivals to push their products under the guise of LGBTQ+ inclusivity.[82]

Instead of continuing to deal with racism, sexism, and a deep sense of alienation at modern day Pride festivals, Black and Latinx LGBTQ+ Pride organizers decided to create their own spaces that made them feel safe to celebrate their queer and trans identities in tandem with their racial and ethnic identities.[83] These racially and ethnically specific Pride celebrations have also sought to honor the legacies of Black and Latinx LGBTQ+ forepersons who were invested in multipronged LGBTQ+ politics that sought an end to white supremacy and imperialism as much as it did homophobia and transphobia.[84] Currently, many Black and Latinx LGBTQ+ folks who see right through the hollow forms of activism that have become synonymous with current Pride festivals have begun to resist these festivals by either choosing not to attend or by using their platforms to point out the harmful nature of these mainstream celebrations.

Black and gay writer Aundaray Guess, for example, lists five reasons why he feels contemporary Pride festivals are no longer places for someone like him.[85] He states, "I don't feel, especially knowing how Stonewall started and the movement it helped create, that Pride helps us retain the reason why we fight."[86] He further asserts that current Pride festivals' dependence on corporate sponsorships silences the urgent issues affecting LGBTQ+ communities—issues like the ongoing violence against Black trans women, the increasing cases of HIV/AIDS in rural and southern parts of the country, and LGBTQ+ youth homelessness. All of these issues, to Guess, have been erased in favor of the consumerism that is ever present at these festivals. These willful obliterations are the reason he now says that he has a "love/hate relationship with Pride," and that this relationship will not change unless current Pride festivals change their ways of celebrating.[87]

In an interview for *Cassius Life*, Black trans actress and tech entrepreneur Angelica Ross spoke to the importance of Pride. "When it comes to Pride it's important to me that we finally understand that Black and Brown queer and trans people have been modeling a form of Pride that is the key to Black liberation. And, obviously, we can't be free until Black trans women are free."[88] Ross's words reflect a history of queer, racial, and gendered liberation movements that seem forgotten by contemporary organizers of the festivals. National LGBTQ+ organizations, mainstream media, and the consumerism that has become a staple of Pride festivals together create an exclusionary environment that reflects the social mores of mainstream society, reiterating the false social and political narrative that queer and trans identities should be synonymous with whiteness. Despite the pervasiveness of inaccurate narratives that are mistaken for the history of Stonewall and Pride, Black and Latinx LGBTQ+ grassroots organizers, academics, and creatives continue to push for the importance of correctly naming how radical and strategically diverse LGBTQ+ liberation once was.[89] Eventually, I hope, this pushback will result in a collective understanding that our first Pride was a riot.

CHAPTER SIX

›››››››››››››››››

#WEALLWEGOT

Post-Stonewall, police violence against LGBTQ+ communities has continued to grow. During Pride month in 2021, a group of queer and trans activists stood in front of the Stonewall Inn trying to call attention to the perpetual violence directed at Black trans women. They were met with police brutality.[1] On June 3, these LGBTQ+ protestors were beaten, taunted, and shoved aggressively into police cars just for exercising their right to protest in the name of justice. Unfortunately, this incident isn't an isolated one. According to *The 2015 U.S. Transgender Survey*, researchers found that "58 percent of trans respondents who said they interacted with police in the previous year alleged they had been harassed by law enforcement."[2] That same survey also found that "57 percent of respondents said they were uncomfortable contacting police for help."[3] Here we are fifty-two years post-Stonewall and police departments nationwide are still harming LGBTQ+ communities. The startling reality, as so many have come to realize in the past several years, is also true when it comes to police interacting with any racially marginalized community. White supremacist, homophobic, and transphobic biases continue to pervade law enforcement nationwide, and it is not the only system that continues to harm Black and Latinx LGBTQ+ communities.

The year 2021 also saw a rise in anti-LGBTQ+ legislative bills. According to the *Daily Beast*, "There have been more than 250 anti-LGBTQ bills introduced in 33 state legislatures."[4] The ACLU reported that in 2023 there were at least 508 bills targeting LGBTQ+ communities nationwide.[5] These bills range from restricting healthcare access for trans folks to denying trans kids the right to play sports in their schools. One of the newest bills even seeks to deny all children access to a school curriculum that is LGBTQ+ inclusive.[6] In Kentucky, for example, the state I live in, a number of anti-LGBTQ+ bills were proposed during the 2024 Kentucky General Assembly session. According to *Queer Kentucky*, there are fourteen anti-LGBTQ+ and three anti-DEI (diversity, equity, and inclusion) bills specifically directed at public education at the K to12 and college levels. Senate Bills 6 and 93, and House Bill 9 would "limit what it refers to as 'divisive concepts,' a subjective term that broadly covers evidence-based viewpoints such as anti-racist or LGBTQ+ affirming policies, beliefs or trainings."[7] The anti-LGBTQ+ bills include, but are not limited to, Senate Bill 147, which aimed to limit or ban drag performances in our state, and House Bill 47, which would allow business owners or property owners to refuse to rent to LGBTQ+ constituents or serve them in eateries because of how they identify.[8] Luckily, for us in Kentucky, none of the anti-LGBTQ+ or anti-DEI bills became laws during the 2024 session due in part to the relentless activism of students, activists, and constituents.[9] During the 2023 legislative session, Kentucky passed a law banning gender-affirming care for Kentucky youth.[10] In 2021, Kentucky legislators introduced a bill that "would ban critical race theory and teaching about LGBTQ+ identities," as well as another bill that would "allow any worker in a healthcare setting to deny service to anyone for any reason."[11] While these bills did not pass, conversion therapy for LGBTQ+ youth is still legal in Kentucky, despite experts' contentions that it has no scientific basis. [12]

Yet, in the face of this consistent adversity, violence, and intolerance, Black and Latinx LGBTQ+ communities, creatives, activists, and academics continue to advocate for a better world for themselves and their communities. In response to their unrelenting work, many racially, economically, and otherwise privileged folks who exist outside of Black and Latinx LGBTQ+ communities have tried to apply the term *resilient* to these oppressed groups. In 2021, however, oppressed communities resoundingly shouted that they were tired of being called resilient by mainstream privileged communities; they wanted, instead, for the world to change. They wanted the world to join them in their fight for justice.

On March 31, 2021, trauma specialist Dr. Dee Knight tweeted, "Stop calling people resilient without calling out the systems that force them to be resilient or die."[13] On May 18, 2021, writer and director, Zandashé Brown, who goes by the Twitter handle @zandase, said, "I dream of never being called resilient again in my life. I'm exhausted by strength. I want support. I want softness. I want ease. I want to be amongst kin. Not patted on the back for how well I take a hit. Or for how many."[14] On August 1, 2021, Twitter user and self-identified intersectional feminist @DandyCommie tweeted, "Cis people stop calling trans people 'brave,' and 'resilient,' . . . this shit is exhausting."[15] On April 12, 2021, Writer and filmmaker Danielle DeLoatch, who goes by the Twitter handle @Freckle&Tea, said, "Stop calling Black people resilient as a compliment because 9/10 we shouldn't even have to be in the circumstances to yield resilience."[16]

To these activists, calling folks resilient is an empty action, and an excuse to not place blame on harmful systems, people, and communities. To be resilient, one must have "the capacity to recover quickly from difficulties" and be able to operate throughout their lives with a certain "toughness," and the ability to "spring back into shape."[17] The projection of the term onto oppressed communities is a fundamentally individualistic assertion that implies that it is up to each individual to "bounce back" from struggle, which completely overlooks the importance of communal uplift and action. However, to Black and Latinx LGBTQ+ change agents, it has not been resiliency that has lifted Black and Latinx LGBTQ+ people up, and it is not resiliency that will free them. Rather, it is their collective and fundamental belief that who they are is not wrong. They recognize that it is only through their own social and political interventions they can free themselves from the confines of oppressive systems.

Black and Latinx LGBTQ+ folks recognize that inequality has a dual function. While inequality oppresses communities based on race, gender, and sexuality, it also has the potential to oppress privileged communities as well. It does this by keeping privileged communities ignorant of how racial, gendered, and sexual diversity can enrich their lives. By not being inclusive of human difference, they are effectually narrowing their worlds and limiting their worldviews. For example, before we as a country benefitted from widespread media visibility of LGBTQ+ people and communities, many cis and straight people had to continually deal with the social and cultural pressure to get married and have children as a requisite of adulthood. The more the public has been introduced to LGBTQ+ identities through media, the more these rigid notions have begun to loosen as LGBTQ+ folks have presented society with new and different ways to conceive of adulthood that do not require marriage or children. This is but one example of how eradicating homophobia and transphobia can effectually free cis and straight communities too.

Black and Latinx LGBTQ+ communities want justice, equity, and accountability for the suffering that they endure under oppressive systems. Instead of waiting on those doing the harm to change things, they're creating the change that they want to see for themselves. Through media creation, crowdsourced fundraising, mutual aid campaigns, academic expansion, and intersectional grassroots organizing, Black and Latinx LGBTQ+ activists, educators, and media makers have become their own advocates. Even though their work comes with a cost to their mental and physical well-being, they continue to fight for their lives in the name of sustainability, visibility, justice, freedom, and resistance for themselves and their communities.

During Barack Obama's first presidential bid in 2007, I, along with my friend Jaison, some colleagues, and students made our way to a local bar after several hours campaigning for the soon-to-be president. It was a mostly white gay bar, and we didn't feel especially welcomed, but we decided to relax, grab some drinks, and play pool. As we attempted to make ourselves comfortable, two large, unleashed dogs ran into the bar toward us. They weren't particularly friendly, and as someone who used to fear dogs, I instinctively hopped on the pool table to avoid their path. The dogs were followed by their owner, a gruff white man. When I asked him if he could leash the dogs, he bulged his eyes and said, "I don't like big girls on my pool tables."

An argument ensued as my friends jumped in to defend me, but the man, later revealed to be the owner of the bar, instead demanded that we leave his bar. As we were exiting, the disagreement escalated as the owner called my friend Jaison a "nigger" and my white student Lindsey a "cunt." But when I informed him that I was a professor at the University of Louisville and made sure he understood that I would be reporting him for racism and sexism, he changed his demeanor and began to apologize. Looking back on it, I think that he felt entitled and empowered by his gay racism and sexism that day, and I think in some ways, he honestly felt that his minoritized status as a gay man would ultimately excuse his racist and sexist behavior. The seat of privilege on which he sat as a cis white man wasn't interrupted or troubled by his other identity as a gay man.

After the incident, I decided that the most effective way to hold him accountable for his grotesque behavior was to take his bar. Accountability through his pockets was the only way I knew that he would understand what he did to us with his words and actions that day. When our group shared the incident with other LGBTQ+ folks, their responses ranged from insinuating that we were starting trouble to chastising us for seeking justice because it would jeopardize one of the only queer spaces in Louisville. I considered why both Black and white LGBTQ+ folks in Louisville were tolerating this type of behavior. Why hadn't anyone stood up to him? And what happened to those who had? The bar owner's display of gay racism and gender terror was something I was familiar with, but I had never experienced an instance of it that was this violent, or this indifferent. I knew that gay racism permeated LGBTQ+ bars, nightclubs, Pride parades, and other social spaces. I knew that it manifested on LGBTQ+ dating apps where users expressed in unabashed ways how they didn't want to date or be contacted by anybody who is femme, fat, or otherwise. Yet, when retelling this incident of hate I found that it underscored the complacency of even the most strident of my allies, who were either oblivious or intentional in their attempts to avoid combatting the harm that was brought to us. Despite these reactions, Jaison and I found support with Chris Hartman, the new director of the Fairness Campaign, Louisville's premier LGBTQ+ organization, and by 2010 both of the bars owned by this man had been taken away from him.

After the bars were shut down, Jaison and I felt that our direct confrontation with gay racism and queer misogyny was far too important to just be discussed among other Black and Latinx LGBTQ+ people, as this was already the reality for most of us. We decided to bring our discussions to social media in an effort to call out and confront gay racism and cis normativity in queer communities. We wanted to debunk the past and present myths of solidarity between Black, Latinx, and white LGBTQ+ people. We also wanted to create more visibility around Black and Latinx LGBTQ+ identities and people through engaging with them in our online discussions. We felt that Black and Latinx LGBTQ+ people needed to see us as queer people who were simultaneously, and unapologetically, Black as well as queer. It had been our experience that due to the prevalence of gay racism, many Black and Latinx LGBTQ+ folks often felt the need to amplify their queer or trans identities at the same time that they repressed their racial identities. Jaison and I both knew several Black and Latinx LGBTQ+ people who were so desperate to belong to a queer community that they would befriend white LGBTQ+ people knowing that they were also racist. We also knew Black and Latinx LGBTQ+ people who longed to be accepted within predominately white queer and trans public spaces so badly that they would often ignore or excuse things like racial microaggressions and racist exoticism, just to fit in those spaces, always chalking up the incidents to just queer and trans folks having fun. Jaison and I felt that these conversations framed our Black and queer adolescence and adulthood and needed to be amplified for larger audiences to weigh in on. Our cyber conversations and posts surrounding gay racism and cis gay transphobia were soon noticed by a local public radio producer, who then invited Jaison and me to create our own podcast, and in 2012, *Strange Fruit: Musings on Politics, Pop Culture, and Black Gay Life* was born.

Jaison and I turned back to social media to garner interest and gain listeners for the show, and it worked quickly, as social media had already become a main medium through which people and communities connected across economic, racial, and gendered lines. Social media also created new inroads for Black and Latinx LGBTQ+ visibility, connecting various Black, queer, trans, and nonbinary sibs together through various social networks.[18] Jaison and I recognized that social media allowed for Black and Latinx LGBTQ+ communities to use a public space to articulate and develop their political consciousness, while asserting how their political beliefs differed from those of mainstream communities. Black and Latinx LGBTQ+ communities were already using social media to share their collective joy, showcase their racialized and gendered identities, and address any social media trolls that tried to bring them or their communities harm. Jaison and I only sought to amplify these practices, and we used our podcast as the medium with which to do so.

In "Youth Voice, Media, and Political Engagement," Henry Jenkins contends that marginalized groups claiming public space through social media can "expand the civic domain, even as elite groups seek to constrain the definition of what is 'legitimate' in the public sphere."[19] He also asserts that "for subordinate groups, these spaces of 'everyday talk' are crucial for the development of political consciousness, for reinforcing shared cultural norms, and for working out alternatives to the dominant culture's views of their identities and interests."[20] Consequently, social media continues to serve as a space of resistance and visibility for Black and Latinx LGBTQ+ people and communities, allowing them to control how they are seen by others, and inviting them to become the architects of their own experiences and identities. Podcasting, which is an outgrowth of social media, operates in similar ways. Podcasting elicits hosts to become the authorities of their own experiences, framing their identities and their communities in ways that are accessible and decipherable to mainstream and privileged communities. It teaches mainstream and privileged communities to learn about identities outside of their own, to facilitate authentic interaction with minoritized folks in ways that are less harmful.

In creating our podcast, my cohost Jaison and I sought to echo and amplify the message that everyday folks had expertise when it came to their individual and collective experiences. This sentiment mirrored a major idea from Black feminist theory and practice, known as "experiential knowledge."[21] Experiential knowledge is the notion that intelligence and authority are gained through one's lived experiences, and that through critically analyzing those experiences, one can become informed about the world around them. Many self-identified Black feminists see experiential knowledge as a pathway to empowerment because it asserts that the real experts about our lives are ourselves. Since both Jaison and I are Black, Southern, and gay feminists, this concept resonated with us, and we wanted to create a show that empowered our listeners to become the architects of their own stories, experiences, and lives. At the same time, we also wanted to have our podcast create more visibility for the communities we belonged to. Since 2012, several Black and Latinx LGBTQ+ podcasts have been created that use experiential knowledge as a frame for their shows.[22] Podcasts like *Translash*, hosted by Imara Jones; *Democracy-ish*, hosted by Danielle Moodie; *The Laverne Cox Show*, hosted by Laverne Cox; *Never Before*, hosted by Janet Mock; and *Affirmative Reaction*, hosted by Xorje Olivares, all highlight Black and Latinx LGBTQ+ lives alongside their conversations about justice, policy change, and societal transformation. After recording over three hundred episodes over the course of almost ten years, Jaison and I have finally begun to understand the transformative impact that our show has had on our listeners. Our listeners, whom we affectionately called our fruitcakes, have continuously reached out to both Jaison and me over the years, to tell us how much comfort our conversations brought them, or to tell us how our words made them feel seen within their bodies, their jobs, and their lives. Our podcast did what Jaison and I set out to do: create more visibility and dialogue about Black and Latinx LGBTQ+ lives.

Visibility in media for minoritized groups is vital and necessary. Visibility aids in changing mainstream and privileged communities' perspectives around identities that they might not come to know on their own. It also allows Black and Latinx LGBTQ+ folks to see their experiences reflected to them, giving them the assurance that their experiences do not exist in isolation. Researchers Phillip M. Ayoub and Jeremiah Garretson found that in 2016, global attitudes from non-LGBTQ+ people toward gay and lesbian people and relationships had changed drastically from the 1980s onward due to more media exposure of LGBTQ+ communities and lives within media.[23] Ayoub and Garretson contended that "tolerance toward lesbian and gay relationships has increased in almost every continent," and that this was largely due to increased representation of LGBTQ+ people in media.[24] Similarly, in a 2020 study conducted by the company Procter & Gamble and by the LGBTQ+ activist organization GLAAD (Gay and Lesbian Alliance Against Defamation), researchers found that non-LGBTQ American consumers looked "favorably on companies that [included] LGBTQ people in their advertising."[25] The study also found that "exposure to LGBTQ people in media increases non-LGBTQ consumers' comfortability with LGBTQ people in their daily lives."[26] Other studies have found that when media highlights marginalized racial identities, there is a change in implicit and explicit biases against marginalized racial groups.[27] Taken together, the more Black and Latinx LGBTQ+ people and communities are highlighted in media, the more it contributes to deeper cultural understandings of both groups. This also allows Black and Latinx LGBTQ+ youth to see their lives as important enough to be made visible through media.[28]

These were the realities we sought to amplify through *Strange Fruit*. We wanted our listeners to see themselves by hearing about their lives, and we wanted to foster a collective space that gave us and people like us the opportunity to feel empowered by our content, sharing in the same joys and struggles. Through our guests' testimonials, we sought to amplify the notion for our listeners that their stories were important enough to be discussed, while we also challenged the misconceptions of Black and Latinx LGBTQ+ identities. While our podcast has been immensely successful, and the labor behind it has come from our hearts and justice-oriented spirits, our almost decade worth of labor also came with personal costs to us both. Some of our guests who also identified as either Black or Latinx LGBTQ+ media makers echoed these experiences without knowing it. They would often express the personal costs of creating the Black and Latinx LGBTQ+ content that they wanted to see in the larger world.[29]

For myself, Jaison, and our Black and Latinx LGBTQ+ interviewees, creating media representation about our communities was integral to our collective striving for Black and Latinx LGBTQ+ freedom. Having grown up in a society that shrouded divergent sexualities in shame, tethering it to a moral compass that even the cishets found difficult to navigate, we all understood that increasing visibility of people like us was a necessary activist praxis.[30] We all learned early on that our culture sought to be both puritanical and pornographic, with sex and sexuality being everywhere we looked but existing as something we couldn't discuss out loud. We grew up never learning comprehensive sex education in our schools, and when and if we did, LGBTQ+ sexualities were never discussed. At the same time, we also grew up in a world where Black, Indigenous, Latinx, and Asian identities were maligned due to white supremacy. As discussed, film and television have a longstanding history of excluding the lives of racially marginalized and LGBTQ+ people.[31] For Black and Latinx LGBTQ+ media makers, the internal pressure of creating content where there has been an absence of it, and getting that content right in its portrayal, is at times mentally and emotionally taxing, especially when coupled with the overwhelming feeling that if one does not continue to produce Black and Latinx LGBTQ+ content, then a particular institution, audience, or listener will begin to devalue Black and Latinx LGBTQ+ media visibility. So, while this collective work around Black and Latinx LGBTQ+ visibility in media has the potential to change minds, liberate communities, and create a better understanding of Black and Latinx LGBTQ+ lives for our own communities and others, the work comes with personal costs to those who create it.

While media visibility is vital to Black and Latinx LGBTQ+ survival, it is not the only avenue to freedom for Black and Latinx LGBTQ+ communities. No matter how many representations of ourselves we see on television or hear on the airwaves, we continue to read more and more tragic headlines.[32] Media visibility also does nothing for those Black and Latinx LGBTQ+ people who don't have free time to consume media or who do not have access to the internet due to their economic instability. As systems of oppression, white supremacy, homophobia, and transphobia have all ensured that many Black and Latinx LGBTQ+ people consistently struggle with keeping themselves and their families afloat financially.[33] Media visibility is one tool, one pathway that allows Black and Latinx LGBTQ+ folks freedom to dream about the possibility of a better world. However, to ensure financial and emotional sustainability for Black and Latinx LGBTQ+ communities, many activists create mutual-aid initiatives and crowd-source funding campaigns aimed at Black and Latinx LGBTQ+ families and individuals who could benefit from more community, more economic stability, and more communal support.

>>>>>>>>>>>>>>

While crowd-sourced funding campaigns are relatively new, ushered in during the 1990s, mutual aid initiatives have a longstanding history within racially colonized communities.[34] Indigenous peoples as well as Black American populations have relied on the cultural tradition of mutual aid for their communities' collective survival, using it to resist past and present colonizing and racially oppressive efforts that sought the annihilation of their communities.[35] Before the construction of white supremacist institutions such as colonization and enslavement, other cultures throughout the world practiced communal living and sustainable solidarity as well, relying on one another for economic stability and social support.[36] While mutual aid functions as a politicized form of care for oneself and one's communities through the creation of a local community network that is invested in meeting an individual's or family's material needs, crowdsourced funding's goal centers on raising small amounts of money from a large group of people to fund a project or community program, or to provide financial assurance to individuals and families in a time of crisis.[37] Mutual aid initiatives were birthed out of the notion that there are more social and communal ways for society to be organized and sustained, while crowdsourced funding helps to sustain communities through quick and recurring campaigns.

Both, however, differ tremendously from the notion of charity in that charitable organizations rely on tax deductibles to increase donations. As a result, charity is selective in choosing aid recipients because of tax-law restrictions that often stipulate criteria for aid to be given to communities.[38] The framework of most charities has also been contingent on a giver/receiver relationship with communities that can only continue if those receiver communities stay in perpetual need. After decades of charitable intervention, poor communities are no better off than they were before aid from charities was given.[39] The charity model framework can potentially become a toxic one, not a transformative one, due to its top-down model of giving, keeping the rich givers at the top and poor communities at the bottom.

This model also doesn't allow room for community members to give their own input or provide their expertise to the charity or donors. This type of funding arrangement inherently implies that rich donors and established 501(c)(3)s know better than the communities in need about what type of aid would benefit them most. Charity is also fraught with classism and paternalistic ideas about giving, as it puts a group of individuals who are financially stable in a position to give to other groups who are not but who are deemed "worthy" by them. This leaves many communities with temporary financial and material relief but does not provide those same communities with the sustainable finances that could potentially transform their communities.[40] So, while charity does help communities in need, its structure does not transform structural realities in the ways that mutual aid and crowdsourced funding campaigns are able to do. The giving models of mutual aid and crowdsourced funding campaigns have assisted these vulnerable communities when legislation, the government, and other policies have failed.

Mutual aid initiatives and crowdfunding campaigns allow individuals to see how their own well-being depends on the well-being of others, making it a mutually beneficial, inherently political form of care in a way that charity is not. Alternatively, crowdsourced funding and mutual aid are efforts organized around solidarity: the idea that communal, emotional, and financial support of individuals and families ultimately can benefit all of society. Organizers of mutual aid and crowdfunding campaigns recognize that everyone benefits when our most vulnerable communities are no longer silenced or forgotten. Such initiatives are yet another tool that Black and Latinx LGBTQ+ activists use in tandem with the tool of media visibility to create dialogue and financial advocacy for these communities.[41] Rising housing and food costs, police violence, and inaccessibility to the internet were all exacerbated by the global COVID-19 pandemic, and instead of Black and Latinx LGBTQ+ activists waiting on their state and local governments to bring relief that might never come, they engaged with their own communities to meet their needs.[42]

Recognizing that Black trans folks were suffering from housing and food insecurity, Asanni Armon, founder of the mutual aid initiative For the Gworls, threw a Fourth of July party in 2019 to raise funds "for two friends who needed help paying rent."[43] After Armon's party was a success, they decided to continue to use their party model to help more people. Armon, a Black genderqueer artist, realized that due to anti-Blackness, misogyny, and transphobia, Black trans citizens were not having their material and emotional needs met through legislation and public policy, and in this absence, For the Gworls was able to place "over six figures of money directly to Black trans people . . . directly into their hands, not through another person or anything like that."[44] To Armon, their mutual aid initiative was a real way to show up for people, materially, and to counter the saviorism that is so often the basis of a charity framework. In a 2020 interview with *Forbes*, Armon states that For the Gworls is "not telling them how to use their money but letting them tell you what they need in order to survive and then making sure that need is met."[45] By 2021, For the Gworls had raised over $1 million for Black trans communities, directly placing necessary funds in the hands of actual Black trans people to ensure their housing stability and gender-affirming surgeries. When the pandemic hit and the face-to-face parties had to stop, Armon switched gears to crowdsourced funding to make sure that Black trans communities did not suffer further just because they could no longer gather in person.[46]

Similarly, Organización Latina Trans en Texas, a bilingual community-based organization created by Latinx trans women, also uses mutual aid to frame its organizational practices and initiatives.[47] Organización Latina Trans en Texas raises funds for subsidized housing, groceries, and rent, and provides Latinx trans communities with their necessary medications.[48] During the COVID-19 pandemic, the organization began to provide meals for people who couldn't afford them and also started covering the cost of a stay in Casa Anandrea, the only shelter in Texas created for the LGBTQ+ Latinx community.[49] Organización Latina Trans en Texas recognized the continual financial need for food, housing, and medications, and realized that a charity framework simply would not serve as their organizational principle. While charity might provide temporary relief, it cannot ensure the continued assistance and reliability that Latinx trans communities need to survive and thrive in a country that still stigmatizes Latinx, LGBTQ+, and immigrant identities.[50] As the pandemic intensified, the material, emotional, and communal needs of Black and Latinx LGBTQ+ communities became more acute. In response, Black and Latinx LGBTQ+ activists sought to ease the stress, pain, and poverty for themselves and their communities through establishing a huge number of mutual aid and crowdfunding initiatives, organized by people like them, who live in community with them, and who wanted to ensure that Black and Latinx LGBTQ+ folks survived the devastating effects brought on by racism, police violence, homophobia, and transphobia.[51]

Alongside these vital efforts, Black and Latinx LGBTQ+ activists' direct actions against the police, white queer racism, and cis normativity also serve as necessary social and political interventions for Black and Latinx LGBTQ+ communities. Intersectional activists' protests and demonstrations, organized with the aim of bringing justice, accountability, and in their most optimistic view, freedom to Black and Latinx LGBTQ+ communities in the face of white supremacist, homophobic, and transphobic patriarchy, are another example of how Black and Latinx LGBTQ+ folks are becoming their own intervention. While media campaigns bring visibility to these communities, and mutual aid and crowdsourced funding campaigns bring sustenance, Black and Latinx LGBTQ+ activists understand that justice and accountability are another necessary path to chart in order for Black and Latinx LGBTQ+ communities to achieve their freedom.

Building on the traditions of Black and Latinx LGBTQ+ activists before them, current direct actions are demanding that the courts, the police, and policy makers recognize the humanity of marginalized communities. Black and Latinx LGBTQ+ activists use direct actions to call for an undoing of the oppressive structures that define Black and Latinx communities as inherently criminal, backward, or in need of supervision by law enforcement. A direct action involves a group of activists protesting, boycotting, or holding a public demonstration, in person or even online, to call out the racist, sexist, homophobic, classist, and transphobic behaviors of communities and institutions. Just as Latinx and Black trans activists Sylvia Rivera and Marsha P. Johnson viewed direct action spaces as having the potential to transform public discourse, the architects of Black Lives Matter continue to amplify Rivera and Johnson's sentiments by specifically calling out gay racism and cis gay normativity alongside police violence and systemic poverty. Building upon the legacies of the past, the Black Lives Matter founders sought to create an organization whose praxis was steeped in an intersectional framework, and one which would expand and challenge the discursive limits of direct-action spaces, allowing them to become more inclusive spaces.[52]

In 2013, three Black women community organizers and activists, Alicia Garza, Patrisse Cullors, and Opal Tometi, cofounded the hashtag and political network #BlackLivesMatter.[53] They did so in response to the 2012 acquittal of racist neighborhood vigilante George Zimmerman, who murdered Trayvon Martin, a young Black teenager who was on his way to visit his father. All three women, and Garza and Cullors specifically, who are both unapologetically queer identified, created an intersectional movement in the spirit of the many Black and Latinx queer and trans educators and activists before them. Their national-turned-international movement illuminated the transgressive potential of vocalizing intracultural differences and intersectional identity to serve as catalysts for change. The cofounders, who were already working for change within their own respective communities prior to the 2012 verdict, were foregrounding their intersectional identities and experiences to serve as springboards for transformative action, changing their communities for the better. After all their collective years of activism, the cofounders recognized that past movement spaces had been fraught with misogyny, transphobia, and homophobia, even while those spaces were advocating for racial or feminist justice. All three of them sought to create a movement that centered the voices of Black queer women and Black trans folks specifically. They understood that multiple identities existed within the overarching racial identity of "Black," and that in past movement spaces the concerns of Black queer women and Black trans women weren't addressed. The founders also realized that in a racist country, gendered and sexual specificity was often erased where Blackness as an identity was considered. Oppressive realities, such as transmisogyny and misogynoir, which exist alongside racism, needed to be discussed in tandem with Black freedom.[54]

Taking movement strategies from Black and Latinx LGBTQ+ activists before them, the cofounders continued the past work of expanding the possible uses of direct-action spaces to include the myriad of issues that bring harm into Black and Latinx communities. Black Lives Matter began to show the nation and larger world that all these issues were connected to one another, and that Black and LGBTQ+ folks achieved many of our country's past social justice wins, and therefore should be at the table, and at the forefront of our country's future. This is not to say that the cofounders of the current Black Lives Matter movement, which has now expanded to a global member-run movement with forty chapters across the world, gave Black and Latinx LGBTQ+ activists a voice to articulate their intersectional injustices to the world; many in their own respective communities had already been doing this. But this is to say that before the Black Lives Matter movement, many folks outside of Black and Latinx LGBTQ+ communities did not automatically connect racial injustices to other intersectional injustices until the Black Lives Matter movement took the world stage.[55]

The cofounders made visible to even the most mainstream of communities that white supremacist violence often worked in tandem with homophobia, transphobia, and sexism. Even if a particular direct action's focus centered around accountability for racist actions against Black and Latinx communities at the hands of the police, those direct-action spaces should also be ones that ushered in actions that were intersectional, multigendered, and trans inclusive. Cullors, Garza, and Tometi were tired of seeing their respective communities suffer at the hands of the police, but they were just as frustrated with other folks who weaponized race to deem Black bodies as suspicious, dangerous, and in many cases, criminal. So, when the killings of Breonna Taylor and George Floyd at the hand of the police happened, many Black and Latinx LGBTQ+ activists seized these demonstrations as opportunities to advocate for accountability for police injustices, and simultaneously to call out other harms that were present within white LGBTQ+ communities.

For longtime activists, the killings of Breonna Taylor and George Floyd by the police during the spring and summer months of 2020 proved that law enforcement was still unaccountable, and these murders radicalized even the most complacent of folks.[56] Even the COVID-19 pandemic did not halt protests and demonstrations from Black and Latinx LGBTQ+ activists, who wanted all officers involved in the killings to be held accountable for their racism and recklessness. Although the protests that summer did not stop police violence against racially marginalized communities, these direct actions did create the possibility for issues of racial injustice, poverty, and police violence to be discussed on mainstream news platforms and social media. The protests during the summer of 2020 were not just about police violence, either. While most direct actions that summer emphasized the Black lives that had been snuffed out by law enforcement in previous and current generations, Black and Latinx LGBTQ+ activists also sought to use these movement spaces as public forums where they could call out the other harmful practices of gay racism, cisnormativity, violence against immigrants, and the like. Black and Latinx LGBTQ+ activists saw the parallels that existed between the white supremacist violence involved in the killings of Taylor and Floyd with the practices of transmisogyny and queer racism within white LGBTQ+ communities. They recognized that these practices were direct outgrowths of white supremacist biases and understood that racism and misogyny were just as much LGBTQ+ issues as they were for any other community. So, they used that summer's protests as an opportunity to address racialized state violence and systemic police violence, engaging in direct actions across the country.

In June 2020 in Baltimore, Black LGBTQ+ activists took to the streets on International Pride Day to call out the police responsible for George Floyd's murder and call attention to gay racism and transphobia within and outside of LGBTQ+ communities.[57] A collective of Black LGBTQ+ activists, Queers for Black Lives Matter, held the demonstration with hundreds of participants, calling to defund the police, calling out LGBTQ+ organizations they accused of lacking diversity and being racist and transphobic, calling for the decriminalization of sex work, and highlighting the housing instability Black trans women face.[58] Queers for Black Lives Matter recognized that these issues needed to be addressed alongside calls for police accountability, as all of them were interrelated; they saw a direct link between the criminalization of sex workers, housing instability, police violence, and the vulnerability that these three forces created in the lives of Black trans women. Queers for Black Lives Matter also saw it as necessary to use this direct action to call attention to the racist and transphobic exclusionary practices that had been established by LGBTQ+ organizations. They saw these exclusionary practices as aiding in the oppression of Black queer and trans folks because these biases mirrored the harmful practices of law enforcement within our larger society. If Black queer and trans people weren't at the table to conceptualize what LGBTQ+ freedom would look like, how were these organizations intervening in the lives of Black LGBTQ+ people in any real way?

Similarly, in 2020 in Louisville, Kentucky, Black LGBTQ+ activists continued to meet in Jefferson Square Park, adjacent to the jail and across the street from the courthouse, with the aim of holding the officers who killed Breonna Taylor accountable. They also sought to make visible for the larger Louisville community that police accountability, reimagining community safety, and police abolition were priorities that specifically affected Black queer and trans lives too.[59] Merging their 2020 Pride celebrations with the international Black Lives Matter movement, Louisville Black LGBTQ+ activists called out the police, the court systems, and the white and cis silence of many gay and lesbian folks who did not see racial justice tethered to queer and trans justice. The silence from white LGBTQ+ communities regarding police brutality served as complicity. If white LGBTQ+ folks weren't standing in solidarity with Black LGBTQ+ folks, demanding accountability and justice in Breonna Taylor's murder, then they were also part of the problem, and a reflection of the expansive reach of white supremacist biases. To Black Louisville LGBTQ+ activists, the killing of Breonna Taylor was indicative of the systematic ways that the police and our country's criminal justice system devalued Black lives.[60]

Latinx LGBTQ+ activists worked tirelessly in 2020 to bring justice and accountability to their own communities. In Phoenix, Arizona, Latinx LGBTQ+ activists held a protest at the Arizona State Capital in tandem with their local Black Lives Matter chapter to call out police brutality, the over-policing of their neighborhoods, and to reiterate for the general public that Latinx LGBTQ+ folks share commonalities of injustice with Black LGBTQ+ folks.[61] Like Black LGBTQ+ folks, Latinx LGBTQ+ people consistently deal with the harms of racism, exoticism, and white supremacist policing and surveillance, as well as having to suffer with the added stigma around immigration status and citizenship. These harms for both groups show up within and outside of LGBTQ+ communities, and because of this, Latinx LGBTQ+ protesters in 2020 chose to use their direct actions to shed light on the inhumane treatment they faced at the hands of ICE and other deportation bodies, and pointed out the dehumanizing practices of the Trump-Pence administration toward their communities. To the Latinx LGBTQ+ demonstrators, the white supremacist scrutiny and regulation by ICE and local police directly related to the same racist injustices that Black LGBTQ+ communities faced in the larger society and inside of white LGBTQ+ communities. This particular protest was the perfect setting for having simultaneous discussions and calls to action against racist and immigrant-phobic policing, as well as the racism, exorcism, immigrant phobia, and cisnormativity that was frequently encountered within white LGBTQ+ public spaces and communities. They wanted to let white cis gay and lesbian folks know that it was time for them to show up for racial freedom and to begin to call out these racial injustices. The Latinx LGBTQ+ protestors expressed how tired they were of seeing white cis gays and lesbians hide behind their whiteness to avoid direct confrontation with state and federal bodies. They also called out their profound physical absence at the protest that day, declaring their absence as a form of complicity in racial harm.[62] Just like their Black and Latinx LGBTQ+ activist predecessors, they knew that racial, gendered, or any identity-focused biases were outgrowths on a tree that stemmed from the same root, white supremacy. They also recognized that they could simultaneously address a multitude of issues in direct actions. The myriad of issues enriched the protest space, making plain that true freedom can only be achieved if multiple identities and communities are at the table. The COVID-19 pandemic swelled experiences with inequity, injustices, and material needs within Latinx LGBTQ+ communities, as it did within Black LGBTQ+ communities. From New York to Los Angeles to Phoenix, Latinx LGBTQ+ activists sought to bring accountability to their communities through these direct actions nationwide.[63]

Black and Latinx LGBTQ+ activists' use of direct actions before and during the spring and summer months of 2020 served as necessary interventions and another pathway for actualizing freedom for their communities. Highlighting Black and Latinx LGBTQ+ identity within television, film, podcasting, and social media creates more visibility for these communities, while mutual aid campaigns and crowdsourced funding help to give these communities sustainability through advocating for their community members' material and emotional needs. Direct actions led by Black and Latinx LGBTQ+ grassroots activists serve as an additional prong to the multipronged efforts by Black and Latinx LGBTQ+ changemakers to bring justice to their communities. All these efforts work together to facilitate powerful and sustainable changes in the lives of Black and Latinx LGBTQ+ folks.

Alongside liberation efforts lies yet another social and political intervention. Social and political change can stem from formalized education. Black and Latinx LGBTQ+ scholars empower their Black and Latinx LGBTQ+ students by using their scholarship and public platforms to politically and theoretically connect racial, gendered, queer, and trans histories. These scholars use their abolitionist scholarship, intersectional teaching, and public platforms to enact structural and institutional change in the realm of education. They recognize that when one has a true sense of their own histories, one can become empowered by those histories.[64] While media, mutual aid networks, and direct actions all work to counter the harms of invisibility, poverty, and injustice, Black and Latinx LGBTQ+ scholars are doing the work within the realm of education to empower marginalized communities through their teaching, service to underrepresented student populations, and through their social activism as academics within and outside of universities.

Black and Latinx LGBTQ+ academics have long used their classrooms to teach counter-hegemonic narratives about our country and its history. This scholarship seeks to recognize and reverse the harm that comes from anti-Black, misogynist, and anti-queer sentiments within our educational systems.[65] These educators, having at one point been students themselves, realize that the white supremacist, misogynist, capitalist patriarchy has infected higher education in similar ways as it has other historical institutions. Like the police and criminal justice systems that continue to disregard Black and Latinx LGBTQ+ lives, higher education has similar practices in only teaching and valuing histories that center white, male, and cisgender lives and identities, valorizing these histories to the exclusion of others, and producing a student populace that has been formally educated without being made aware of their own histories and their places in the world.

The political war over "critical race theory" that is being waged against public intellectuals and higher education shows that education has the potential to empower and liberate students.[66] One reason political conservatives are attacking critical race theory is their deep investment in sustaining our culture's racial, gendered, and sexual biases.[67] Yet, Black and Latinx LGBTQ+ academics continue to resist their efforts by using their scholarship, their teaching, and their social media handles to stand in solidarity with our most vulnerable student populations and bring about political, social, and economic change through education. These educators are expanding what has been historically taught, while also including the experiences and histories of Black and Latinx LGBTQ+ people, countering the politically conservative notion that marginalized groups' distinct and unique experiences in the world have nothing to do with their races, genders, sexualities, or gender identities. Black and Latinx LGBTQ+ academics are teaching their students that the very opposite is true: their experiences create expertise and insight, which allows them to navigate oppressive systems and actualize their own and their communities' collective power. By creating courses that reflect minoritized histories, mentoring Black and Latinx LGBTQ+ students, and participating in community-engaged scholarship, Black and Latinx LGBTQ+ educators teach their students that their racial, gender, and sexual identities were springboards for social and political change historically, and that these identities are integral to global social justice movements.[68]

"Nontraditional" disciplines like women's and gender studies, Pan-African studies, Black studies, Latinx studies, and LGBTQ+ studies have all aided Black and Latinx LGBTQ+ academics in these pursuits of using education as a form of empowerment. This is not to say that traditional disciplines such as history, English, political science, and the like have not empowered Black and Latinx LGBTQ+ students; they most definitely have. Many of the original architects of “nontraditional” disciplines have sprung from the minds and labor of traditional scholars. Traditional scholars recognized the intellectual, racial, gendered, and sexual gaps that were present in traditional disciplines, curricula and expressly saw the need to create departments that could serve as warehouses for change within higher education, both for students and faculty.[69] Presently, disciplines like women’s and gender studies, Pan-African studies, Black studies, Latinx studies, and LGBTQ+ studies all serve to correct what some traditional disciplines might miss when it comes to teaching and conducting research that highlights marginalized communities and students. These relatively new disciplines are also doing the work of correcting the historical inaccuracies that still exist within various traditional academic disciplines, ones that only valorize certain scholarship. These new disciplines are providing students, faculty, and staff with a historically accurate picture of communities that have consistently contributed to and attempted to change the social ills of society. These radical academic departments and programs also gave birth to what we now know as intersectional and intellectually transformative scholarship that has helped shape the intellectual, social, and political pursuits of current Black and Latinx LGBTQ+ educators, teaching them how education can be used as a tool of empowerment for themselves and their communities. From the edited volume *The Bridge Called My Back: Writings by Radical Women of Color* (1981), to *All the Women Are White, All the Blacks Are Men, but Some of Us Are Brave: Black Women’s Studies* (1982), to *Presumed Incompetent: The Intersections of Race and Class for Women in Academia* (2012), Black and Latinx feminist LGBTQ+ academic offerings have utilized higher education as a space to tell the truth about marginalized identities, experiences, and lives, empowering readers with the notion that who they are has never been wrong or something that needed to be corrected.[70]

The fact that these teachings have yet to be read, listened to, or implemented at most colleges and universities speaks to the willful neglect by many faculty to take the sage advice given to them by their institution's most enlightened—yet most vulnerable—academic community members. By making only white, cis, and male intellectual works canonical, faculty in higher education assert that those works are more valuable and integral to student educations. Using my educational experience as an example, once I began taking classes within non-traditional disciplines, I was assigned scholarship by Black feminist, Black queer and trans, and Latinx LGBTQ+ authors and researchers, whereas my general education required courses did not reflect the histories or contributions made by intellectuals who had been marginalized by their race and gender identities. Just as educational lies have emboldened and empowered mainstream and privileged communities, educational truths can do the same for Black and Latinx LGBTQ+ communities. The reluctance by institutions of higher education to implement the necessary financial and labor incentives to attract faculty in traditional disciplines to more diverse curricula is a disservice to a myriad of students, not just Black and Latinx LGBTQ+ students.

Black and Latinx LGBTQ+ media makers, mutual aid initiators, crowdsourced funding creators, activists, and academics are trying to save themselves and their communities. They continue to fight because they know that Black and Latinx LGBTQ+ communities need and desire more visibility in media. Black and Latinx queer and trans activists and educators continue to strive to have their communities' material needs met, and to bring justice, equity, and accountability to their people. Instead of waiting on white LGBTQ+ and cishet people to change things, they're creating the change that they want to see. By becoming their own social and political intervention, they are bringing the sustainability, visibility, justice, freedom, and resistance to their communities, and effectually themselves. After all, if the past is prologue, we all we got.

EPILOGUE

ON TRANSCENDING THE RAINBOW AND LIVING BEYOND THE NOW

So, I know y'all thought I was finished, but before I go, I just wanted to mention a couple more things for us to keep in mind as we head toward the future. First up, the Black and Latinx LGBTQ+ creative vanguard is ushering in everything that we have ever wanted when it comes to solid, robust, and consistent media representation.[1]

As I've talked about, I came of age during the *Beverly Hills 90210* and *Melrose Place* era, where all the LGBTQ+ folks were either closeted, sad, and/or white, and all the Black characters were either invisible, hyperbolic, or secondary.[2] It has been truly refreshing to see such thoughtful, authentic, and multifaceted characters that are both Black and Latinx as well as LGBTQ+. From shows like *P-Valley*, *Pose*, *Twenties*, *David Makes Man*, *Boomerang*, and *The Chi*, to *Good Trouble*, *The L Word* reboot *Generation Q*, and *Claws*, we seem to finally have access to media that takes us beyond the empty symbolism of the rainbow, landing us into new political spaces and innovative social directions.[3] These contemporary media representations compel us as viewers to think about the possibility of a future that is not shackled with the biases of white supremacy, anti-Blackness, and misogyny.

We are currently living in a time when Black artists like Queen Latifah, Tevin Campbell, and Da Brat are all living their truths in new, bold, and public ways.[4] Y'all, we even have streaming shows like *The Ms. Pat Show*, *Loot*, *The Fresh Prince of Bel Air* reboot, as well as the reboot of the iconic television show *Roseanne*, now *The Conners*, which all feature LGBTQ+ characters whose sexualities are showcased in a way that lets the audience know that LGBTQ+ folks live and thrive in all types of environments.[5] These shows make transparent that LGBTQ+ people come from, and are a part of, all types of families that truly accept and love them, letting their audiences know that it's okay to do the same. We even got a whole Black queer mixtape from Beyoncé, in honor of her godmother, Uncle Johnny.[6]

Look, when I was a little girl growing up in the 1980s, I told my dad that I wanted to be an actress. He smiled at what I know he thought was an unrealistic dream for a little Black girl like me, but in the most tender way, he said, "Well that's all well and good, Munchkin, but you simply won't make any money doing that." He recognized that the Black actresses we did have were few, and the majority of them at that time were always typecast.[7] Although his honesty about my childhood dream seemed harsh, his analysis was completely accurate and necessary for me to hear. Needless to say, this new era that we are currently entering, inhabited by so many multifaceted Black and Latinx LGBTQ+ characters, is a welcome and needed change. Black and Latinx LGBTQ+ creatives are showing us that if we harness our imaginations, we can think and eventually live beyond our current atmosphere. We have the potential to reach a more inclusive future. Despite their valiant efforts to expand and enlighten our social and political horizons, there are still so many others who are hell-bent on taking us back to the past to prevent us from accessing a more diverse future.

Even as our screens show us increasingly liberatory possibilities, much of the world continues on a retrograde path. The Supreme Court overturned *Roe v. Wade*, leaving it up to individual states to decide when and how a person can or cannot bring life into the world.[8] In Kentucky, for example, SCOTUS's decision to overturn *Roe v. Wade* allowed the state to enact draconian laws that effectively banned abortion.[9] While the ACLU of Kentucky challenged these laws and initially won, in August 2022, a Kentucky judge overturned the ACLU decision, stopping abortion procedures in our state, even in cases of rape and incest.[10] Meanwhile, Black lesbian basketball player Brittney Griner was sentenced to ten years in a Russian penal colony for possessing less than two ounces of marijuana.[11] Although Biden's deal with Russia ended up bringing Griner home, she has since published a book about all of the trauma she endured while incarcerated there.[12] The state of Florida is allowing former military personnel to teach public school children, with their military service being their only credential. And we have several states banning books that discuss Black LGBTQ+ people, talk about institutional racism and sexism, or challenge white supremacy as a normal ideological position.[13] Anti-trans and anti-queer legislation is also at an all-time high, while Black trans women continue to be brutally murdered.[14]

We got Bette Midler and Macy Gray spouting anti-trans views on their social media platforms and in interviews because both of them are so threatened by expanding our conceptions of womanhood.[15] Teachers can't say the word *gay* in the state of Florida, and rappers, celebrities, and preachers get to spew hate. The rapper Lil Duval wants a content warning to be placed at the top of each *P-Valley* episode because he can't take witnessing intimacy when it involves Black queer folks.[16] White cis gays and lesbians continue to uphold sexism, racism, and transphobia, and Black and Latinx LGBTQ+ bodies continue to be trolled and fetishized online and accosted in public.[17] We have one of the most famous Black comics of our time, Dave Chappelle, bemoaning the "alphabet people," who in his view are destroying his career, our society, and the art form of comedy altogether.[18] Black preacher T. D. Jakes thinks Black women should shut up and take orders from Black men in order to ensure the Black family remains intact.[19] We even have white folks protesting the new *Little Mermaid* film because Halle Bailey is playing Ariel.[20] Y'all, these anti-Black Americans can't even handle a fictional character to be made Black. These are just some of the happenings and some of the folks who are invested in returning us to a time when LGBTQ+ didn't exist, when women of all races knew "their place," and when the only books taught in schools highlighted cishet white folks. When they are challenged for their repugnant views, others salute them for "being honest" and "brave," for stating their opinions in this "hostile" climate of what those who want to roll back progress call "excessive wokeness."[21]

I know many of you reading this will say, "This is why we need more allies! To aid in the freedom fighting to help minoritized communities access more equality," and I totally get it. I am here to tell y'all, however, that is not what is needed. Let me explain. Although the word *allyship* was Dictionary.com's 2021 word of the year, in my work and leisure over the past eighteen years, educating Black and Latinx LGBTQ+ students, and supporting and amplifying those communities' voices through my podcast, *Strange Fruit*, I've come across a number of "allies" who think they are doing allyship correctly, but they're wrong.[22] Their behavior in minoritized spaces is anything but mutually supportive. For example, I've witnessed straight and cis folks, both Black and white, who have claimed to be allies but have chosen to show up in LGBTQ+ nightclubs in their wedding sashes that said, "bride to be," years before same-sex marriage was made law by the Supreme Court.[23] Not one of them understood how offensive it was to flaunt their upcoming nuptials in a space where the club goers were forbidden by law to marry one another. Some even sought to add insult to injury by coming up to random queer and trans folks to boast about how excited they were to tie the knot, not even sensing the dismay of their chosen audience. These "allies," lack of self-awareness and their sense of entitlement don't stop here.

I've seen these same folks jump onstage when drag entertainers were trying to put on a show for club goers. These alleged allies viewed the stage and drag entertainers as their own personal songstresses, and to them, the stage served as a platform where they could take part in their own personal concerts. I've seen these allies block the tip line because they don't understand the practice of tipping drag performers. I've also witnessed several drag emcees having to stop their shows altogether to give specific directives to these folks about how no one is allowed to jump on the stage, block the stage, or block the tip line. But this still hasn't stopped them. Instead of these "allies" doing their research about how drag shows work, how tipping functions in LGBTQ+ nightclubs, and about how they should conduct themselves as guests in these spaces, they continue to enter LGBTQ+ nightclubs with the entitled idea that LGBTQ+ club goers in queer and trans venues look forward to their presence, because they honestly believe that LGBTQ+ folks seek their personal affirmations about their identities.

I've witnessed "allies" who believe that they are committed to social justice and anti-racism continue to disassociate themselves from the people who raised them to be racist in the first place. I've been in protest spaces and heard white "allies" say things like, "Yeah my family is totally racist, and that's why I have nothing to do with them, because racism is gross to me." I've seen their anxious eyes swell with hope that their statement will engender Black and Latinx protestors to give them a pat on the back for doing racial justice work right. I've seen them show up in student organization meetings on campus and try to brag about how their "grandfather uses the N-word every chance he gets," but how they are different from him. I've seen them take over protest spaces or use direct action trainings to purge their feelings of white supremacist guilt, and they have the unmitigated gall to expect the students of color in these spaces to counsel them, teach them, and support them through those feelings.

As an educator, I've had white and cis gay and lesbian students who see themselves as freedom fighters take over discussions in my classroom, muting the voices of Black and Latinx LGBTQ+ students, and even after I have made plain to them that they are dominating the space, this hasn't stopped them from doing it over and over again, even if they know they will be met by pushback. I've witnessed these same kinds of "allies" tag all of their minoritized "friends" in social media posts that show grotesque "Karen" confrontations, violent displays of police brutality, or op-eds on racial trauma as a tokenized form of their allyship, never once thinking that their sharing of this information over and over again causes further harm to Black and Latinx social media users.[24] These "allies" consistently make the mistake of thinking that minoritized groups are seeking their individual favor and approval, while they never seem to understand that minoritized communities are actually seeking intentional and informed action in regard to dismantling the systems of white supremacy, misogyny, anti-queerness, and transphobia that force their communities to constantly navigate injustice, suffering, and dehumanization.

Minoritized communities do not need "allies" showing up in Black spaces, boasting about how much they love Black people and Black culture, while at the same time refusing to challenge their own families' racism. Black and Latinx LGBTQ+ communities do not need "allies" showing up in Black and Latinx queer and trans spaces, shouting from the rooftops about how much they live for LGBTQ+ folks, all the while refusing to challenge their heteronormative families, partners, or friends about why they should too. These "allies" might show up to a rally, or donate to a social justice cause, or brag about how they're nothing like others in their lives who hold repugnant views about human identity, but that's the extent of their "work."[25] In my experience, "allies" have never really been interested in challenging or endangering their relationships with problematic folks. It has also been my experience that these "allies" have not been willing to struggle through personal discomfort and confrontation or do the necessary work it takes to bring about institutional and structural change. Rather, they have seemed only to be interested in distinguishing themselves from others they see as problematic through empty rhetoric and unintentional action and deed. So, no, we don't need more allies. Black and Latinx LGBTQ+ communities, anti-racists, and social justice activists have been calling for "accomplices" and "coconspirators" to replace the empty actions of past allies. That's just what we need.

Hear me out. While I understand many might feel apprehensive about these words due to their definitions being tethered to criminal activity, the work of accomplices and coconspirators is abolitionist in nature. Accomplices are interested in doing away with any system that brings harm to vulnerable communities.[26] This work includes, but is not limited to, abolishing the policing system in our country, making our school curriculums more inclusive of marginalized identities, and directly challenging landlords who continually exploit and evict poor people. This kind of thoughtful and inclusive labor also involves accomplices sacrificing their personal comfort to use their privilege to challenge the institutional and structural anti-Blackness, anti-queerness, misogyny, and transphobia. Accomplices understand what mutual support actually means, and they uplift this kind of transformational work by challenging injustice at the root in the spirit of solidarity, liberation, and freedom.

While many social justice activists believe that allyship and accomplice-ship are similar and argue that both types of support are needed, I believe the very opposite.[27] These critical times need accomplices taking over for allies. While allyship denotes an individual who comes from a space of racial, gendered, or sexual privilege to stand with a minoritized group or an individual who is already engaging in either anti-racist or LGBTQ+ activism, an accomplice focuses their work on dismantling the systems of domination that are in place within our society that engender the dehumanization, harm, and discriminatory practices that minoritized communities are expected to navigate. Accomplices go beyond allyship because instead of using their privilege to take up and dominate Black and Latinx LGBTQ+ social justice spaces, accomplices "use their privilege to challenge existing conditions at the risk of their own comfort and well-being."[28] Unlike allies, accomplices know that fighting for Black and Latinx LGBTQ+ liberation, justice, and freedom is necessary to create a better world for all of us. Many allies commit themselves to social justice because it makes them feel better as individuals, and because they also think that it will absolve them from their own white supremacist, homophobic, and transphobic guilt. That's just not enough. Accomplices view any form of discriminatory behavior as a morally bankrupt practice that denies rights and freedom to minoritized communities, which gives mainstream communities a false sense of personal power over racially diverse and vulnerable groups. Being an accomplice is more about action, and as social justice leader and podcaster Dr. Jon Paul asserts, "This course of action is more often than not uncomfortable, challenging, and fraught with confrontation." Being an accomplice is a "commitment to disrupting the status quo."[29]

These frightening and demoralizing times call for something more than mere allyship from mainstream and privileged communities. Just showing up at protests, joining student organizations on college campuses, or appearing in spaces where privileged folks are the racial, sexual, or gendered minority, and then proceeding to tell Black and Latinx queer and trans communities that they are cool, interesting, or attractive, are not what is needed. This allyship was always insufficient, and it's surely insufficient in today's climate of crisis. Justice has been needed, equality has been needed, freedom has been needed, direct confrontation with white supremacist institutions, sexist familial structures, and anti-LGBTQ+ legislators has been needed. What has been, and still is, needed is for mainstream and privileged communities to go into the communities that raised them and taught them these pejorative views and to teach them differently. This is the work that allies simply haven't been willing to do, but it is work that accomplices are doing. Accomplices understand, unlike allies, that our racial, gendered, and sexual differences should always be understood as a source for collective change and intersectional celebration, because this acknowledgment and understanding allows all of us to dream bigger about freedom.

The time has come to stop narrow-minded reactionaries who insist on us returning to a bygone time, and the time has come to start building the future that we want to see. The time has come for privileged folks who claim to be committed to structural and institutional freedom to begin to do the work of being accomplices to the Black and Latinx LGBTQ+ communities that have already been working to abolish the systems and practices that harm us. The time is now!

ACKNOWLEDGMENTS

I would like to take this opportunity to thank those special individuals for their encouragement, expertise, love, and support throughout this process. To my exquisite editors, Maya Fernandez and Will Meyers, thank you so much for believing in my abilities as a scholar and thinker. There are no words that can express my immense gratitude for you both. To my confidant, comrade, and cohost, Jaison Ashley Gardner, thank you so much for always believing in me and encouraging me. Thank you for being a listening ear, a shoulder to cry on, and a supportive and loving friend. Together, as #TeamStrangeFruit we have transformed people's way of thinking and the city of Louisville for the better. I've always learned so much from you and I am so grateful that you were my first friend here in Louisville, and now my family.

To my sister and homegirl, Dr. Yaba Amgborale Blay, brilliant and beautiful scholar-warrior for the people. Thank you for always supporting, guiding, and loving me in so many ways. I can't even fathom words that are strong enough to explain the many ways I love you, or for how grateful I have been and am for you. I love every bit of you. Always, all ways. To Little (Rebecca Nussbaum), my best friend and sister of almost thirty years. My love for you knows no bounds. You are a spectacular human being, an incredible mom, and an out-of-this-world best friend. Through all of life's extraordinary changes we have always maintained our devoted connection, and I thank you, and the universe, for keeping you in my life and heart. Thank you for inspiring me, lifting me up, and always reminding me that no matter how cruel this world can be, people like you, generous, kind, thoughtful, and oh so loving, still do exist. I love you bigger than a thousand oceans and as big as the sky.

To the Pleasure Ninjas, Drs. Joan Morgan, Brittney Cooper, and Treva B. Lindsey, as well as Esther Armah, thank you all so much for traveling the world with me, supporting me, challenging me, and believing in my abilities as a writer, thinker, and scholar. Your love and encouragement have meant so very much to me. Joan, I am so honored and thankful to call you my friend, while you still remain a hero to me. Your words, vision, and intervention with your work, forever changed me and my feminism those many years ago. Your friendship over all of these years has continued to bless me in such beautiful and wondrous ways. Brittney, you are by far one of the most brilliant women I've ever come to know and love. I am honored to be your friend and fellow pleasure ninja. Your words, wisdom, and writing have continued to inspire me. Me and this world is so lucky to have you in it. Treva, you are one of the most brilliant professors and scholars in the game, and I am immensely proud to be your friend and fellow Pleasure. Thank you for your sweetness and positivity in my life; I am so very grateful for you. Esther, thank you for being such a great voice for all of us, the emotional us, the us that hides, and the us that needs to be heard. I am so grateful for you and your enlightening work.

To the incomparable Dr. E. Patrick Johnson, E, I am so incredibly grateful for you, your generosity, and your work, not only in my life but also in this world. You are literally the light that reflects the absolute best of us. This work, and all of my other work, wouldn't be possible without you and your extraordinary guidance and love. To all of the Black feminist and Black LGBTQ+ scholars, writers, activists, creatives, and professors, including but not limited to: Yolo Akili, Jafari S. Allen, Marlon M. Bailey, La Marr Jurelle Bruce, Cathy J. Cohen, Marshall M. Green, Alexis Pauline Gumbs, Heidi Renee Lewis, Tamura Lomax, Ian Patrick-Polk, Gwendolyn D. Pough, Jeffrey Q. McCune, Darnell L. Moore, Imani Perry, Josh Rivers, Francesca Royster, Beverly Guy-Sheftall, Mecca Jamilah Sullivan,

C. Riley Snorton, Omise'eke Natasha Tinsley, and Kortney Ziegler. Thank you all for your thoughts, art, activism, and work. I humbly hope this book adds to our brilliant and beautiful tradition of amplifying our communities' voices and lives. To my chairs, past and current, in the departments of women's, gender, and sexuality studies, and Pan-African studies, Drs. Michael Brandon McCormack, Dawn Heinecken, Ricky L. Jones, and Nancy Theriot, thank you for always supporting me in all ways, academic and otherwise. Your encouragement and cheerleading all these years has meant so absolutely much to me. To my colleagues in the departments of women's, gender, and sexuality studies, and Pan-African studies, Drs. Tyler Fleming, Shelby Pumphrey, Shirletta Kinchen, Mawuena Logan Kossi, Yvonne Jones, Cara Snyder, Ahmad Washington, and W. S. Tkweme, thank you for making coming to work a delight and a pleasure. Your support as colleagues and friends has meant so much to me. To all of my students that I have had the pleasure of teaching over the past twenty years, your continued faith and belief in me as a professor has, in so many ways, made me realize that I had a meaningful contribution to make. Thank you for supporting me, rooting for me, and for standing with me, always. Your love and insight continue to make me a better scholar and teacher.

To my partner, my wife, Missy Story-Jackson, you are my greatest love. You have opened up my whole world with your love, and I still give thanks to the universe for you every day. You have taught me patience, understanding, and what real love feels like. Thank you for holding me, cherishing me, supporting me, and loving me throughout all of our time together. You are truly an exceptional human being, and I am so proud to walk through this world with you. I love you in this life and the next. To my mom, Sylvia Rogers, you are an amazingly intelligent, loving, funny, and magical woman. I am so grateful that I have had the pleasure and honor of being your daughter and your friend. I thank the universe for you every single day, and I thank God for you every single second. You are my best friend and my angel on earth. Thank you for being a constant example of love, ambition, and resilience for me. I love you always, all ways, and forever. To my dad, Dr. Ralph DeWitt Story, who left this earth before this book was released into the world. Daddy, as deep and as wide as my grief is, I also feel incredibly grateful and honored to have been your daughter and friend for forty-two years. I cherish all of our memories, laughter, and love daily, and there are no words that can express how much you mean to me. Thank you for loving, guiding, and embracing all of me. Thank you for teaching me what justice and freedom were from the start. Thank you for nourishing and cultivating my love for Black people, books, music, and culture. You are everything that love feels like. You remain my forever hero. If I know nothing else in this life, I know love. Gratitude abounds.

NOTES

PREFACE: ON REMEMBERING AND HONORING THE RAINBOW

1. Nancy Coleman, "Why We're Capitalizing Black," *New York Times*, July 5, 2020, https://www.nytimes.com/2020/07/05/insider/capitalized-black.html.

2. Kaila Adia Story, "Fear of a Black Femme: The Existential Conundrum of Embodying a Black Femme Identity While Being a Professor of Black, Queer, and Feminist Studies," *Journal of Lesbian Studies* 21, no. 4 (2017): 407–19, DOI: 10.1080/10894160.2016.1165043.

3. Dr. Ibram X. Kendi and I were enrolled in the same African American studies graduate program at Temple University in Philadelphia. He talks extensively about our experiences together there in chapters 14 and 15 of his book, *How to Be an Antiracist*. Dr. Kendi states how both Dr. Yaba Blay and I profoundly impacted him to think intersectionally while in the program and challenged him to be more inclusive of Black women and Black LGBTQ+ people. For more, see *How to Be an Antiracist* (London: One World Press, 2019), 181–93. Dr. Kendi reiterates our influence on his current intersectional thinking in a 2019 interview with the *Washington Post* and on C-SPAN as well. For more, see David Montgomery, "The Anti-Racist Revelations of Ibram X. Kendi," *Washington Post*, October 14, 2019, https://www.washingtonpost.com/magazine/2019/10/14/anti-racist-revelations-ibram-x-kendi; C-SPAN, "After Words with Ibram X. Kendi and Imani Perry," September 7, 2019, https://www.c-span.org/video/?c4815618/user-clip-imani-perry-ibram-kendi.

4. Kendi, *How to Be an Antiracist*.

5. Pat Parker, *Movement in Black: The Collected Poetry of Pat Parker* (Baltimore: Diana Press, 1978).

6. Marlon Riggs, Essex Hemphill, Audre Lorde, Barbara Smith, Joseph Beam, and Marsha P. Johnson were all Black LGBTQ+ people who worked before and after the Stonewall uprisings to create vital public discourse via their filmmaking, poetry, prose, and activism for Black LGBTQ+ people to be fully seen, free from policing and scrutiny, and embraced for who they truly are.

7. See above.

8. Josh Milton, "White, Gay Trump Supporter Epically Schooled After Claiming Black Lives Matter Is Trying to 'Colonise' Pride Month," *Pink News*, June 22, 2020, https://www.pinknews.co.uk/2020/06/22/chadwick-moore-black-lives-matter-colonise-pride-month-gay-donald-trump-trinity-tuck.

9. Milton, "White, Gay Trump Supporter Epically Schooled After Claiming Black Lives Matter Is Trying to 'Colonise' Pride Month."

10. Adrian Moore, "Boosie Badazz's Transphobic Rant Against Dwyane Wade's Kid Has Twitter Revisiting His Problematic Parenting," *NewsOne*, February 18, 2020, https://newsone.com/playlist/boosie-badazz-transphobic-dwyane-wade-twitter.

11. Moore, "Boosie Badazz's Transphobic Rant Against Dwyane Wade's Kid Has Twitter Revisiting His Problematic Parenting."

12. *Complex* Staff, "Boosie Badazz Doubles Down on Comments Aimed at Dwyane Wade's Daughter Zaya," *Complex*, March 24, 2020, https://www.complex.com/music/2020/03/boosie-badazz-doubles-down-comments-aimed-dwyane-wade-zaya.

13. Louis Chilton, "Boosie Badazz: Outrage as Rapper Claims to Have Paid for Oral Sex for 12-Year-Old Son and Nephews," *The Independent*, May 14, 2020, https://www.independent.co.uk/arts-entertainment/music/news/boosie-badazz-son-nephews-sex-instagram-live-illegal-a9514271.html.

14. David Artavia, "Anti-LGBTQ+ Boosie Hired Sex Worker to 'Prepare' Pre-Teens," *Out*, May 13, 2020, https://www.out.com/music/2020/5/13/anti-lgbtq-boosie-hired-sex-worker-prepare-pre-teens.

15. Nick Duffy, "'Gender Critical' Activists with 'I Heart JK Rowling' Banner Mock Black Lives Matter Protesters in Ugly Confrontation," *Pink News*, August 31, 2020, https://www.pinknews.co.uk/2020/08/31/gender-critical-posie-parker-jk-rowling-banner-black-lives-matter-protesters-transphobia; Aja Ramona, "Harry Potter and the Author Who Failed Us," *Vox Magazine*, June 11, 2020, https://www.vox.com/culture/21285396/jk-rowling-transphobic-backlash-harry-potter.

16. Jorge Fitz-Gibbon, "Woman Fired After Yelling 'White Lives Are Better' at Black Lives Matter Rally," *New York Post*, July 7, 2020, https://nypost.com/2020/07/07/woman-fired-for-yelling-white-lives-are-better-at-black-lives-matter-rally.

INTRODUCTION: ON WHY THE RAINBOW AIN'T NEVER BEEN ENUF

1. Lauren Slagter, "BarStar Group Takes Over Ann Arbor's /aut/ BAR, Other Braun Court Properties," *MLive*, March 2, 2019, https://www.mlive.com/news/ann-arbor/2019/03/barstar-group-takes-over-ann-arbors-aut-bar-other-braun-court-properties.html.

2. Monique Harris, *Pushout: The Criminalization of Black Girls in Schools* (New York: The New Press, 2018).

3. Oliver Laughland and John Swain, "Officer Who Killed Tamir Rice Says He Believed 12-Year-Old Was in Fact 18," *The Guardian*, December 1,

2015, https://www.theguardian.com/us-news/2015/dec/01/tamir-rice-shooting-cleveland-police-timothy-loehmann-grand-jury.

4. Harris, *Pushout*. Georgetown Law completed a study that showed how white people see Black kids, which asserted that Black girls specifically are typically viewed as older and less innocent. The results can be found here: https://www.law.georgetown.edu/news/black-girls-viewed-as-less-innocent-than-white-girls-georgetown-law-research-finds-2.

5. *In Living Color* was a sketch comedy series that aired on the Fox television network 1990–1994.

6. The phrase *spilling the tea* was originally created within the Black and Latinx House Ball scene, and *Urban Dictionary* defines it as "the act of sharing juicy gossip between one or more people." See, for example, https://www.urbandictionary.com/define.php?term=spill%20the%20tea.

7. Jarrod Hayes, *Queer Nations: Marginal Sexualities in the Maghreb* (Chicago: University of Chicago Press, 2000), 24.

8. Sophie Saint Thomas, "What Does It Mean to Be Cisgender? Your Comprehensive Guide to One of Many Gender Identities," *Cosmopolitan*, March 20, 2019, https://www.cosmopolitan.com/sex-love/a25253578/cisgender-meaning-definition.

9. James Baldwin, *James Baldwin: The Last Interview and Other Conversations* (Jackson: University of Mississippi Press, 1989), 67.

10. John D'Emilio, *The World Turned: Essays on Gay History, Politics, and Culture* (Durham, NC: Duke University Press, 2002), 38.

11. Keith Boykin, *One More River to Cross: Black and Gay in America* (New York: Anchor Press, 1997).

12. In an NPR interview with Tavis Smiley in 2003 about her book *Twilight on Equality*, Lisa Duggan defined neoliberalism as "a set of policies that were put together by corporations based in the United States and Europe at a time when global competition was driving profit rates up." The immediate beneficiaries of neoliberal policies were global corporations and political elites. Duggan stated that "in the United States specifically, neoliberals initially made alliances with conservatives—moral conservatives, religious conservatives. They made electoral alliances through the Reagan administration and in company with, you know, corporate allies. And then with racial nationalists and anti-feminists and anti-gay forces within the moral conservative ranks in order to shore up the winners in a set of other sets of inequalities—racial inequalities, gender inequalities and sexual inequalities." However, Duggan asserts that "over about the past 10 years, there's been a slight shift away from that set of alliances and towards forwarding a kind of phony, multicultural, egalitarianism that promotes a very narrow form of equality politics that offers a limited kind of inclusion but that doesn't do any kind of redistribution." Tavis Smiley, "Lisa Duggan: How Neoliberalism Has Helped Undermine the New Deal and Great Society," History News Network, December 8, 2003, https://historynewsnetwork.org/article/2819.

13. Lisa Duggan, *The Twilight of Equality? Neoliberalism, Cultural Politics, and the Attack on Democracy* (Boston: Beacon Press, 2003), 50.

14. Duggan, *The Twilight of Equality?*

15. Duggan, *The Twilight of Equality?*

16. Cathy Cohen, "Punks, Bulldaggers and Welfare Queens: The Radical Potential of Queer Politics," *GLQ: A Journal of Lesbian & Gay Studies* 3, no. 4 (May 1997): 450.

17. Homonormativity "is a politic that does not contest dominant heteronormative assumptions and institutions but upholds and sustains them while promising the possibility of a demobilized gay constituency and a privatized, depoliticized gay culture anchored in domesticity and consumption." Lisa Duggan, "The New Homonormativity: The Sexual Politics of Neoliberalism," in *Materializing Democracy: Toward a Revitalized Cultural Politics*, ed. Russ Castonovo and Dana D. Nelson (Durham, NC: Duke University Press, 2002), 175–94.

18. Duggan, "The New Homonormativity," 175–94.

CHAPTER ONE: ON THE MYTH AND REALITY OF THE RAINBOW

1. Ntozake Shange, *For Colored Girls Who Have Considered Suicide When the Rainbow Is Enuf* (New York: Scribner Press, 1975).

2. Queer theory is an academic field of study that begins with theorist and historian Michel Foucault and uses gender and sexuality as its categories of analysis and inquiry. Most if not all queer theorists contend that gender and sexuality are not fixed or stable categories of identity but rather that both can change and evolve within individuals and within society. Michel Foucault, *The History of Sexuality: An Introduction, Volume 1* (New York: Vintage Books, 1978).

3. Urban Dictionary defines a *gayborhood* as any neighborhood with a high concentration of same-sex oriented individuals, https://www.urbandictionary.com/define.php?term=Gayborhood.

4. A *gayby* is a newly out gay/queer person; it is a combination of the words *gay* and *baby* to symbolize that the coming-out process is the beginning of a new life. A gayby's age is relative because the process of coming out and the subjective declaration of a sexual identity/orientation can happen at any time in one's life. For example, a *gayby* can be thirteen years or fifty-five years old.

5. Gilbert Baker, *Rainbow Warrior: My Life in Color* (Chicago: Chicago Review Press, 2019).

6. José Esteban Muñoz, *Disidentifications: Queers of Color and the Performance of Politics* (Minneapolis: University of Minnesota Press, 2013).

7. LoveTapesCollective, "Sylvia Rivera, Ya'll Betta Quite Down," *Vimeo*, September 18, 2017, https://vimeo.com/234353103.

8. Global Network of Sex Work Projects, "Street Transvestites Action Revolutionaries Found STAR House," 2014, https://www.nswp.org/timeline/event/street-transvestite-action-revolutionaries-found-star-house.

9. Global Network of Sex Work Projects, "Street Transvestites Action Revolutionaries Found STAR House."

10. Christina Maxouris, "Marsha P. Johnson, a Black Transgender Woman, Was a Central Figure in the Gay Liberation Movement," CNN, June 26, 2019, https://www.cnn.com/2019/06/26/us/marsha-p-johnson-biography/index.html.

11. Julia Jacobs, "Two Transgender Activists Are Getting a Monument in New York," *New York Times*, May 29, 2019, https://www.nytimes.com/2019/05/29/arts/transgender-monument-stonewall.html.

12. Alex Abad-Santos, "Philadelphia's New, Inclusive Gay Pride Flag Is Making Gay White Men Angry," *Vox*, June 20, 2017, https://www.vox.com/culture/2017/6/20/15821858/gay-pride-flag-philadelphia-fight-explained.

13. Abad-Santos, "Philadelphia's New, Inclusive Gay Pride Flag."

14. Abad-Santos, "Philadelphia's New, Inclusive Gay Pride Flag."

15. Michael J. Murphy, "We Don't Need a New Pride Flag: Gilbert Baker's Still Works Just Fine," *Medium*, June 27, 2018, https://medium.com/@emjaymurphee/we-dont-need-a-new-pride-flag-efc883e0817b.

16. Murphy, "We Don't Need a New Pride Flag."

17. Rainbow Noir, "Anger over Black and Brown Stripes on Pride Flag Shows Problem with Racism," *Gay Star News*, January 29, 2019, accessed June 28, 2024.

18. Rainbow Noir, "Anger over Black and Brown Stripes on Pride Flag."

19. Rainbow Noir, "Anger over Black and Brown Stripes on Pride Flag."

20. Stonewall Impact, "Racism Rife in LGBT Community Stonewall Research Reveals," *Stonewall*, June 27, 2018, https://www.stonewall.org.uk/sites/default/files/lgbt_in_britain_home_and_communities.pdf.

21. Stonewall Impact, "Racism Rife in LGBT Community."

22. *Cisnormativity* is the assumption that all human beings are cisgender, i.e., have a gender identity that matches their biological sex. *Homonormativity* is a politics that does not contest dominant heteronormative assumptions and institutions but upholds and sustains them while promising the possibility of a demobilized gay constituency and a privatized, depoliticized gay culture anchored in domesticity and consumption. See Lisa Duggan, "The New Homonormativity: The Sexual Politics of Neoliberalism," in *Materializing Democracy: Toward a Revitalized Cultural Politics*, ed. Russ Castonovo and Dana D. Nelson (Durham, NC: Duke University Press, 2002), 175–94.

CHAPTER TWO: YOUR BLACK AIN'T LIKE MINE

1. Adam Smith, "New App Let's You Put Your Face on GIFs—But Is It Safe?" *The Independent*, August 7, 2020, https://www.independent.co.uk/life-style/gadgets-and-tech/news/doublicat-gif-safe-app-deep-fake-celebrities-a9628906.html.

2. Carla Peterson, "Foreword: Eccentric Bodies," in *Recovering the Black Female Body: Self-Representations by African American Women*, ed. Michael

Bennett and Vanessa D. Dickerson (New Brunswick, NJ: Rutgers University Press, 2000), viii–xi.

3. Naomi Scheman, *Engenderings: Constructions of Knowledge, Authority, and Privilege* (New York: Routledge Press, 1993), 186.

4. Elizabeth Grosz, "Bodies and Knowledges: Feminism and the Crisis of Reason," in *Feminist Epistemologies*, ed. Linda Alcoff and Elizabeth Potter (New York: Routledge Press, 1994), 198.

5. Oyeronke Oyewumi, *The Invention of Women: Making Sense of Western Gender Discourses* (Minneapolis: University of Minnesota Press, 1997), 2.

6. Londa Schiebinger, *Nature's Body: Gender in the Making of Modern Science* (Boston: Beacon Press, 1993).

7. Oyewumi, *The Invention of Women*, 3.

8. Oyewumi, *The Invention of Women*, 3.

9. Oyewumi, *The Invention of Women*, 7.

10. Schiebinger, *Nature's Body*, 116.

11. See, for example, Sander Gilman, *Sexuality: An Illustrated History* (New York: John Wiley & Sons, 1989), 110; T. Denean Sharpley-Whiting, *Black Venus: Sexualized Savages, Primal Fears, and Primitive Narratives in French* (Durham, NC: Duke University Press, 1999), 22; Ann Stoler, "Carnal Knowledge and Imperial Power: Gender, Race, and Morality in Colonial Asia," in *The Gender/Sexuality Reader*, ed. Roger N. Lancaster et al. (New York: Routledge Press, 1997), 14; Deborah Willis and Carla Williams, *The Black Female Body: A Photographic History* (Philadelphia: Temple University Press, 2002), 1–2.

12. Judith Butler, *Bodies That Matter: On the Discursive Limitations of Sex* (New York: Routledge Press, 1993), 31.

13. Butler, *Bodies That Matter*, 32.

14. Deborah Willis and Carla Williams, *The Black Female Body: A Photographic History* (Philadelphia: Temple University Press, 2002), 1–2.

15. Sonya Renee Taylor, *The Body Is Not an Apology: The Power of Radical Self-Love* (Oakland, CA: Berrett-Koehler Publishers, 2018), 6.

16. Taylor, *The Body Is Not an Apology*, 7.

17. Lisa Duggan, *The Twilight of Equality? Neoliberalism, Cultural Politics, and the Attack on Democracy* (Boston: Beacon Press, 2003), 50.

18. Toni Morrison, *The Bluest Eye* (Visalia: Vintage Press, 1970).

19. John Huston, dir., *Annie*, Columbia Pictures, 1982; Michael Lehmann, dir., *Heathers*, New World Pictures, 1989; John Hughes, dir., *The Breakfast Club*, A&M Films, 1985; Steven Spielberg, dir., *The Color Purple*, Warner Brothers, 1989; Donna Deitch, dir., *The Women of Brewster Place*, Xeon Entertainment Group, 1989.

20. Maria Maggenti, dir., *The Incredibly True Adventures of Two Girls in Love*, Fine Line Pictures, 1995; Cheryl Dunye, dir., *The Watermelon Woman*, Peccadillo Pictures, 1996.

21. The Queer Resource Center of the Claremont Colleges defines a *butch* as "a person who identifies themselves as masculine, whether it be physically, mentally, or emotionally. 'Butch' is sometimes used as a derogatory term for lesbians, but it can also be claimed as an affirmative identity label." They define a *stud* as "an African American and/or Latina masculine lesbian. Also known as 'butch' or 'aggressive.'" I use both terms interchangeably throughout this book as in my experience the terms have been and are used interchangeably among various races of queer people to describe masculine-identified women. The Queer Resource Center, *Butch*, https://colleges.claremont.edu/qrc/education/lgbtq-glossary.

22. Merriam-Webster defines the term *microaggression* as "a comment or action that subtly and often unconsciously or unintentionally expresses a prejudiced attitude toward a member of a marginalized group (such as a racial minority)." See https://www.merriam-webster.com/dictionary/microaggression.

23. Hari Ziyad, "3 Reasons Dating, Attraction and Desire Are Always Political," *Everyday Feminism*, April 4, 2016, https://everydayfeminism.com/2016/04/attraction-desire-political.

24. Ziyad, "3 Reasons."

25. Rose Troche, dir., *Go Fish*, Samuel Goldwyn Company, 1994; Marita Giovanni, dir., *Bar Girls*, Avant Garde Cinema, 1994.

26. Patrik-Ian Polk, dir., *Punks*, Black Boy Productions, 2000; *Noah's Arc*, Patrik-Ian Polk, dir., Logo TV Productions/Viacom Production Company, 2005–2006; Patrik-Ian Polk, dir., *The Skinny*, Black Boy Productions, 2012.

27. *The L Word*, Ilene Chaiken, dir., Dufferin Gate Productions/Showtime, 2004–2009.

28. *Will & Grace*, James Burrows, dir., NBC Productions, 1998–2020; the US Supreme Court made same-sex marriage legal in all of the United States in 2015.

29. *The Ellen DeGeneres Show*, created by Ellen DeGeneres, Ellen TV Productions, 2003–2022.

30. Netflix streaming services became available to American audiences in 1997, with many Americans beginning to binge-watch through the service in 2003.

31. *The Fosters*, dir. Michael Medico, Freeform Productions Limited, 2013–2018; *Empire*, dir. Lee Daniels, Fox Broadcasting Company, 2015–2020; *Orange Is the New Black*, created by Jenji Kohan, Netflix, 2013–2019; *Huffington Post* was launched as alternative media outlet in 2005; NewNowNext was launched as queer alternative media outlet in 2008.

32. Tristan, "What Are the Politics of Desirability?" *Unite for Reproductive & Gender Equity*, April 8, 2015, https://urge.org/what-are-the-politics-of-desirability.

33. Rebecca Schiller, "Why the Mother Who Started Gender-Reveal Parties Regrets Them," *The Guardian*, October 20, 2019, https://www.the

guardian.com/lifeandstyle/2019/oct/20/why-the-mother-who-started-gender-reveal-parties-regrets-them.

34. Schiller, "Why the Mother Who Started Gender-Reveal Parties Regrets Them."

35. Feminist scientist and scholar Anne Fausto-Sterling argues in her essay "The Five Sexes, Revisited" that a two-sex system is based only upon a medical professional creating a sex assignment out of visibly viewing a child's genitals at birth, not on what sexes human beings might embody if their sexes were based on a chromosomal level. Therefore, Fausto-Sterling argues, the two-sex system was created not in the name of science but rather to reenforce a structure of power. See Anne Fausto-Sterling, "The Five Sexes, Revisited," *The Sciences* 40, no. 4 (May 2000).

36. Gabrielle Canon, "California Couple Whose Gender-Reveal Party Sparked a Wildfire Charged with 30 Crimes," *The Guardian*, July 21, 2021, https://www.theguardian.com/us-news/2021/jul/21/couple-gender-reveal-party-wildfire-charged.

37. GLAAD Transgender Media Program, 2020, https://www.glaad.org/transgender.

38. Laverne Cox, interview with Sam Feder, *Disclosure: Trans Lives on Screen*, Los Angeles: Bow and Arrow Entertainment, 2020.

39. Lauren Slagter, "BarStar Group Takes Over Ann Arbor's /aut/BAR, Other Braun Court Properties," *MLive*, March 2, 2019, https://www.mlive.com/news/ann-arbor/2019/03/barstar-group-takes-over-ann-arbors-aut-bar-other-braun-court-properties.html.

40. The phrase *spilling the tea*, or *the tea*, or *teas*, was originally created within the Black and Latinx ball house scene, and *Urban Dictionary* defines it as "the act of sharing juicy gossip between one or more people." For example, see https://www.urbandictionary.com/define.php?term=spill%20the%20tea.

41. Neil Jordan, dir., *The Crying Game*, Channel Four Films, 1992.

42. Sam Feder, dir., *Disclosure: Trans Lives on Screen*, Los Angeles: Bow and Arrow Entertainment, 2020.

43. Nick Adams, interview with Sam Feder, in *Disclosure*.

44. Michael D. Cohen, interview with Sam Feder, in *Disclosure*.

45. Cohen, interview with Sam Feder, in *Disclosure*.

46. J. Jack Halberstam, "Unlosing Brandon: Brandon Teena, Billy Tipton, and Transgender Biography," in *In a Queer Time & Place: Transgender Bodies, Subcultural Lives* (New York: New York University Press, 2005).

47. Halberstam, "Unlosing Brandon," 55.

48. Halberstam, "Unlosing Brandon," 54–55.

49. Halberstam, "Unlosing Brandon."

50. D. W. Griffith, *Judith of Bethulia*, Biograph Company, 1914; Roger Spottiswode, dir., *Terror Train*, Orion Pictures, 1980; Alfred Hitchcock, dir., *Psycho*, Hitchcock Productions, 1960; Brian De Palma, dir., *Dressed to Kill*,

Orion Pictures, 1980; Jonathan Demme, dir., *Silence of the Lambs*, Strong Heart Productions, 1991.

51. Joel Zwick, dir., *Bosom Buddies*, ABC Productions, 1980–1982; Sydney Pollack, dir., *Tootsie*, Columbia Pictures, 1982; Lisa Gottlieb, dir., *Just One of the Guys*, Columbia Pictures, 1985; Chris Columbus, dir., *Mrs. Doubtfire*, 20th Century Studios, 1993; Raja Gosnell, dir., *Big Mama's House*, 20th Century Studios, 2000.

52. Laverne Cox, interview with Sam Feder, *Disclosure*.

53. Halberstam, "Unlosing Brandon," 55.

54. Jack Smight, dir., *Fast Break*, Columbia Pictures, 1979; Frank Pierson, dir., *Soldier's Girl*, Bachrach/Gottlieb Productions, 2003; Duncan Tucker, dir., *TransAmerica*, Belladonna Productions, 2005; Jean-Marc Vallee, dir., *Dallas Buyer's Club*, Voltage Pictures, 2013.

55. *The L Word*, dir. Ilene Chaiken, Dufferin Gate Productions, Showtime, 2004–2009.

56. Zeke Smith, interview with Sam Feder, in *Disclosure*.

57. Brian Michael Smith, interview with Sam Feder, in *Disclosure*.

58. Zeke Smith, interview with Sam Feder, in *Disclosure*.

59. Smith, interview with Sam Feder, in *Disclosure*.

60. Alexandra Holden, "The Gay/Trans Panic Defense: What It Is, and How to End It," American Bar Association, April 1, 2020, https://www.americanbar.org/groups/crsj/publications/member-features/gay-trans-panic-defense.

61. Holden, "The Gay/Trans Panic Defense."

62. Sarah McBride, "HRC Releases Annual Report on Epidemic of Anti-Transgender of Violence," Human Rights Campaign, November 18, 2019, https://www.hrc.org/news/hrc-releases-annual-report-on-epidemic-of-anti-transgender-violence-2019.

63. National Center for Transgender Equality, "Murders of Transgender People in 2020 Surpasses Total for Last Year in Just Seven Months." August 7, 2020, https://transequality.org/blog/murders-of-transgender-people-in-2020-surpasses-total-for-last-year-in-just-seven-months.

64. Nick Adams, interview with Sam Feder, in *Disclosure*.

65. Emma Fraser, "In Praise of Angelica Ross in American Horror Story: 1984," *Primetimer*, October 16, 2019, https://www.primetimer.com/features/in-praise-of-angelica-ross-on-american-horror-story-1984#:~:text=As%20a%20sleepaway%20camp%20nurse,the%20blood%20is%20still%20fresh.

66. Tanya A. Christian, "Transgender Activist Raquel Willis Appointed Executive Editor at *Out* Magazine," *Essence*, December 10, 2018, https://www.essence.com/news/transgender-activist-raquel-willis-appointed-executive-editor-out-magazine.

67. Annie Martin, "Lena Waithe: 'The Chi' to Feature First Transgender Character," *Entertainment News*, June 23, 2020, https://www.upi.com

/Entertainment_News/TV/2020/06/23/Lena-Waithe-The-Chi-to-feature-first-transgender-character/2261592918124.

68. Nina Metz, "Meet Jasmine Davis, a Breakout Performer on 'The Chi,' and the Show's First Transgender Character," *Chicago Tribune*, July 22, 2020, https://www.chicagotribune.com/entertainment/tv/ct-mov-jasmine-davis-the-chi-0824–20200722-wkkzw7vlkjcynhzndk26icx5ty-story.html.

69. Will Throne, "Lena Waithe, Halle Berry Show 'Boomerang' Renewed for Season 2," *Variety*, April 2, 2019, https://variety.com/2019/tv/news/lena-waithe-halle-berry-show-boomerang-renewed-season-2-bet-1203178355.

70. Blue Telusma, "South Sudanese Model Aweng Chuol Gets Married to Fiancée," *The Grio*, December 17, 2019, https://thegrio.com/2019/12/17/south-sudanese-model-aweng-chuol-gets-married-to-fiancee.

71. Benjamin Lindsay, "Pose Isn't Just Giving an AIDS History Lesson," *Vulture*, June 18, 2019, https://www.vulture.com/2019/06/pose-season-2-hiv-aids-crisis.html.

72. Tessa Vikander, "The Etiquette of Whether to Say 'YAS Queen,'" *The Star*, February 28, 2019, https://www.thestar.com/vancouver/2019/02/28/the-etiquette-of-when-to-say-yaas-queen.html.

73. Jacob Bogage, "Dwyane Wade's perspective changed as he watched 'son . . . become into who she now is,'" *Washington Post*, December 20, 2019, https://www.washingtonpost.com/sports/2019/12/20/dwyane-wades-perspective-changed-he-watched-son-become-into-who-she-now-is.

74. Black Lives Matter Archived Mission Statement, Library of Congress Web Archive, https://www.loc.gov/item/lcwaN0016241.

75. Rashaad Ernesto Green, dir., *Gun Hill Road*, Motion Film Group, Sony Pictures, 2011; Alan Berliner, dir., *Ma vie En Rose (My Life in Pink)*, Canal+, 1997.

76. In Sian Ferguson's article "Cisgender and Straight Don't Mean the Same Thing—Here's Why," Ferguson defines the term *cishet* as: "someone is both cisgender and heterosexual. It could also mean both cisgender and heteroromantic. In other words, a cishet person identifies as the gender they were assigned at birth, and they're attracted to people of the opposite gender." For more information, see Sian Ferguson, "Cisgender and Straight Don't Mean the Same Thing—Here's Why," *Healthline*, September 23, 2019, https://www.healthline.com/health/cisgender-vs-straight#overview.

77. Yance Ford, interview with Sam Feder, in *Disclosure*.

CHAPTER THREE: WE AIN'T HAVING A BALL

1. *RuPaul's Drag Race*, dir. Nick Murray, Viacom CBS Domestic Media Networks, Logo TV, VH1, and MTV, 2009–2020.

2. The Black and Latinx ball scene has transmitted its language and phrasing through an oral tradition, and therefore the following terms have not been formally defined in different sources of inquiry. While I was able to find a definition of the term *shade*, I will use my own understandings of the

terms *werq*, *gag*, and *YAAAS*. *YAAAS* is a word used to express immeasurable excitement about an idea, outfit, stance, etc. *Werq* is a term bestowed on an individual who is deserving of praise or some kind of salute due to their outfit, attitude, or statements. Both *werq* and *YAAAS* should be understood as creative signifiers within ballroom culture. *Gag* is a term used when someone is surprised or shocked about another's statement, attire, or boldness. *What's the Tea? A Glossary of Queer Slang* defines the term *shade* as "an underhanded jab that's slightly insulting and usually an inside joke. Shade can also be an action, such as an eye-roll or even a smile." See https://yr.media/identity/whats-the-tea-a-glossary-of-queer-slang/.

3. *Lovecraft Country*, season 1, developed by Misha Green, HBO, August 8, 2020.

4. Even though the episode doesn't give a specific date, I added the time period the "1950s" because the official description on the show's website states that the show takes place then. See https://www.hbo.com/lovecraft-country.

5. *Lovecraft Country*, season 1, episode 5, "Strange Case," developed by Misha Green, dir. Cheryl Dunye, HBO, September 9, 2020. Although the episode doesn't specify an exact time period or date when Montrose attends the drag ball, the audience is able to contextualize the time period based on what is happening with the other characters in the episode. The character Ruby discovers that a Black woman has been hired at a major department store downtown, which leads the audience to believe that the time period in which Montrose attends the ball would have to be after the Civil Rights Act of 1964, which outlawed racial segregation in public accommodations. For more on this see Traci Parker, *Department Stores and the Black Freedom Movement: Workers, Consumers, and Civil Rights from the 1930s to the 1980s* (Chapel Hill: University of North Carolina Press, 2019).

6. Marlon Bailey, *Butch Queens Up in Pumps: Gender, Performance, and Ballroom Culture in Detroit* (Ann Arbor: University of Michigan Press, 2013).

7. Bailey, *Butch Queens Up in Pumps*.

8. Jennie Livingston, dir., *Paris Is Burning*, Academy Entertainment Off White Productions, 1991.

9. Livingston, dir., *Paris Is Burning*.

10. Frank Simon, dir., *The Queen*, Grove/Atlantic Productions, 1968.

11. *Your Ballroom Glossary* defines *reading* as "the art of insults. A good read should never be overtly bitchy. You find a flaw in your opponent and verbally exaggerate it." For the *What's the Tea? A Glossary of Queer Slang* definition of *reading*, see https://yr.media/identity/whats-the-tea-a-glossary-of-queer-slang/.

12. Crystal LaBeija, interview with Frank Simon, in Simon, *The Queen*.

13. Backstage white drag-queen heckler in Simon, *The Queen*.

14. Crystal LaBeija, interview with Frank Simon, in Simon, *The Queen*.

15. Backstage Black drag queen in Simon, *The Queen*.

16. Pardedos94501, "The Queen, 1967—Crystal LaBeija Fierce Reading Session," YouTube video, March 14, 2010, https://www.youtube.com/watch?v=rcMdNLe5xzo.

17. Matt Baume, "The Queen: NYC Drag Pageant Scene Before House LaBeija," YouTube video, May 26, 2020, https://www.youtube.com/watch?v=lNJjzlRsB40.

18. Allison B. Siegel, "The Oft-Overlooked 'Drag Balls' of Harlem," *Bowery Boogie*, June 28, 2019, https://www.boweryboogie.com/2019/06/the-oft-overlooked-drag-balls-of-harlem-history.

19. Matt Baume, "The Queen: NYC Drag Pageant Scene Before House LaBeija," YouTube video, May 26, 2020, https://www.youtube.com/watch?v=lNJjzlRsB40.

20. Matt Baume, "The Queen: NYC Drag Pageant Scene Before House LaBeija."

21. Elyssa Goodman, Crystal LaBeija Reinvented Ball Culture: A Short History," *Them*, March 23, 2018, https://www.them.us/story/how-crystal-labeija-reinvented-ball-culture.

22. Livingston, dir., *Paris Is Burning*; Sara Jordenö, dir., *Kiki*, Hard Working Movies, 2016; *What's the Tea? A Glossary of Queer Slang* defines *femme queen* as "a trans woman. Categories with this description are for trans women only," and therefore a drag queen is a cis gay man who competes at balls in drags wearing feminine artifice. See https://yr.media/identity/whats-the-tea-a-glossary-of-queer-slang/.

23. Frank Leon Roberts, "There's No Place Like Home: A History of House Ball Culture," in Monica Roberts, ed., *Transgriot*, February 18, 2008, https://transgriot.blogspot.com/2008/02/theres-no-place-like-home-history-of.html.

24. Roberts, "There's No Place Like Home."

25. Roberts, "There's No Place Like Home."

26. Dorian Corey, interview with Jennie Livingston, in Livingston, *Paris Is Burning*.

27. Esther Gould and Reijer Zwaan, dir., *Strike A Pose*, CTM Docs & The Other Room with Serendipity Films & NTR, 2016.

28. German Lopez, "The Reagan Administration's Unbelievable Response to the HIV/AIDS Epidemic, *Vox*, December 1, 2016, https://www.vox.com/2015/12/1/9828348/ronald-reagan-hiv-aids.

29. In the film *Paris Is Burning* Angie Xtravaganza in conversation with Jennie Livingston tells the audience that Venus was found murdered in a hotel. Dorian Corey and Pepper LaBeija died of natural causes. For more on Venus Xtravaganza's murder and Dorian Corey's and Pepper LaBeija's untimely deaths, see https://medium.com/th-ink/justice-for-venus-xtravaganza-1cbd45bc504a; https://www.atlasobscura.com/articles/a-famous-drag-queen-a-mummy-in-the-closet-and-a-baffling-mystery; https://www.nytimes

.com/2003/05/26/arts/pepper-labeija-queen-of-harlem-drag-balls-is-dead-at-53.html.

30. Carmen Xtravaganza, interview with Wolfgang Busch, in Wolfgang Busch, dir., *How Do I Look*, Art from The Heart Films, 2006.

31. Marcell LaBeija, interview with Wolfgang Busch, in Busch, *How Do I Look*.

32. Octavia St. Laurent, interview with Wolfgang Busch, in Busch, *How Do I Look*.

33. Busch, *How Do I Look*.

34. *America's Next Top Model*, season 13, episode 6, created by Tyra Banks, developed by Kenya Barris and Ken Mock, VH1, October 7, 2009. Benny Ninja from the house of Ninja had a recurring role on the show the entire thirteenth season.

35. Jordenö, *Kiki*.

36. *POSE*, created by Steven Canals, Brad Falchuk, and Ryan Murphy, Walt Disney Company, FX, 2018–2021.

37. Lisa Duggan, *The Twilight of Equality? Neoliberalism, Cultural Politics, and the Attack on Democracy* (Boston: Beacon Press, 2003).

38. Roland Emmerich, dir., *Stonewall*, Centropolis Entertainment, 2015.

39. Emmerich, dir., *Stonewall*.

40. Devon Ivie, "Stonewall Is Bad, but How Bad? What Critics Are Saying," *Vulture*, September 24, 2015, https://www.vulture.com/2015/09/what-critics-are-saying-about-stonewall.html.

41. *The Real Housewives of Atlanta*, created by Princess Banton-Lofters, True Entertainment, Bravo, 2008–.

42. *The Real Housewives of Atlanta*.

43. Brenda Salinas defines the term *Columbusing* in her op-ed "'Columbusing': The Art of Discovering Something That Is Not New," NPR, June 6, 2014, https://www.npr.org/sections/codeswitch/2014/07/06/328466757/columbusing-the-art-of-discovering-something-that-is-not-new.

44. Salinas, "Columbusing."

45. *Braxton Family Values*, WeTV (2011–2019).

46. Elizabeth Salton, "'The Real' Hosts Explain Tamar Braxton's Firing," Entertainment Tonight, October 12, 2018, https://www.etonline.com/the-real-hosts-explain-tamar-braxtons-firing-111527.

47. The House of Enigma. *The House of Naphtali: Ball Slang, Categories, and Everything About Vogue* defines *reading* as "the art of insults; finding a flaw in your opponent and verbally showcasing and exaggerating it; giving someone a 'piece of your mind.'" For the definition of *reading*, see https://houseofnaphtali.tripod.com/id3.html.

48. The Black and Latinx ball scene transmitted its language and phrasing through an oral tradition, and therefore the many phrases and terms have not been formally defined through different sources of inquiry. I use my own understanding of the phrase "Get life" in the text.

49. Sherronda J. Brown, "What Tamar Braxton's Comments About Men Not Wanting Sex Reveal About Compulsory (Hetero)Sexuality," Black Youth Project, November 19, 2019, http://blackyouthproject.com/what-tamar-braxtons-comments-about-men-not-wanting-sex-reveal-about-compulsory-heterosexuality.

50. Brown, "What Tamar Braxton's Comments about Men Not Wanting Sex Reveal."

51. Brown, "What Tamar Braxton's Comments about Men Not Wanting Sex Reveal."

52. Adam Howard, "Are Gay Men the New Mammies of Reality TV?" *The Grio*, June 2, 2012, https://thegrio.com/2012/07/02/are-gay-men-the-new-mammies-of-reality-tv/.

53. Robin M. Boylorn, "The Frustration of Watching the Kardashians as a Black Woman," *Slate*, September 30, 2020, https://slate.com/culture/2020/09/watching-keeping-up-with-the-kardashians-as-a-black-woman.html.

54. Sierra Mannie, "Dear White Gays: Stop Stealing Black Female Culture," *Time*, July 9, 2014, https://time.com/2969951/dear-white-gays-stop-stealing-black-female-culture.

55. Don Lemon, CNN interview with Sierra Mannie and H. Allen Scott, YouTube video, July 11, 2014, https://www.youtube.com/watch?v=o2wwRyarBfQ&list=FLwF7gQdLXerjN42E5XCE0Yw&index=1189.

56. Don Lemon, CNN interview with Sierra Mannie and H. Allen Scott.

57. William Friedkin, dir., *The Boys in the Band*, Cinema Center Films, 1970.

58. Sierra Mannie, "Dear White Gays: Stop Stealing Black Female Culture," *Time*, July 9, 2014, https://time.com/2969951/dear-white-gays-stop-stealing-black-female-culture.

CHAPTER FOUR: THE STAKES IS HIGH

1. Centers for Disease Control and Prevention, COVID Data Tracker, https://covid.cdc.gov/covid-data-tracker/#trends_totaldeaths_select_00, updated June 15, 2024.

2. Human Rights Campaign, *The Epidemic of Violence Against the Transgender and Gender Non-Conforming Community in the United States: The 2023 Report*, Human Rights Campaign Foundation, November 2023, https://reports.hrc.org/an-epidemic-of-violence-2023.

3. Hannah Yasharoff, "Laverne Cox Is 'in Shock' but OK After She and a Friend Were Targeted in Transphobic Attack," *USA Today*, November 29, 2020, https://www.usatoday.com/story/entertainment/celebrities/2020/11/29/laverne-cox-in-shock-but-ok-after-transphobic-attack-park/6455897002.

4. The Queer Dictionary defines the term *cisnormativity* as "the assumption that all, or almost all, individuals are cisgender. Although transgender-identified people comprise a fairly small percentage of the human population, many trans people and allies consider it to be offensive to presume

that everyone is cisgender unless otherwise specified." For more on the term *cisnormativity*, see http://queerdictionary.blogspot.com/2014/09/definition-of-cisnormativity.html. *Misogynoir* is a term that was coined by Black queer feminist activist and professor Dr. Moya Bailey, who defines it as the specific hatred of Black women. For more on the term *misogynoir*, see www.moyabailey.com.

5. Keaton Hare, "Transphobia Within LGBTQ+ Community," *North Texas Daily*, August 4, 2020, https://www.ntdaily.com/transphobia-within-lgbtq-community.

6. Bethany Ao, "Black Trans Communities Suffer a Greater Mental-Health Burden from Discrimination and Violence," *Philadelphia Inquirer*, June 25, 2020, https://www.inquirer.com/health/black-transgender-trans-mental-health-therapy-20200625.html.

7. Daniel Reynolds, "Milo Yiannopoulos Takes Transphobia on Tour," *The Advocate*, October 26, 2016, https://www.advocate.com/transgender/2016/10/26/milo-yiannopoulos-takes-transphobia-tour.

8. A Gender Agenda (AGA), according to its website, "is a unique community organization actively engaged in increasing public awareness and understanding of intersex, trans and gender diversity issues." *Sib* is defined as [gender] neutral, short for sibling." See https://genderrights.org.au/faq_type/language. GLAAD, "Transgender Day of Remembrance," https://www.glaad.org/tdor.

9. Jamal Hailey, Whitney Burton, and Joyell Arscott, "We Are Family: Chosen and Created Families as a Protective Factor Against Racialized Trauma and Anti-LGBTQ Oppression Among African American Sexual and Gender Minority Youth," *Journal of GLBT Family Studies* 16, no. 2 (2020): 176–91, DOI: 10.1080/1550428X.2020.1724133.

10. Jennie Livingston, dir., *Paris Is Burning*, Academy Entertainment Off White Productions, 1991.

11. Livingston, *Paris Is Burning*.

12. Rik Reinholdtsen, dir., *Legendary*, Scout Productions, 2020.

13. Hailey, Burton, and Arscott, "We Are Family."

14. Jarrod Hayes, *Queer Nations: Marginal Sexualities in the Maghreb* (Chicago: University of Chicago Press, 2000), 24.

15. Kaila Adia Story, "Racing Sex—Sexing Race: The Invention of the Black Feminine Body," in *Imagining the Black Female Body: Reconciling Image in Print and Visual Culture*, ed. Carol E. Henderson (London: Palgrave Macmillan Press, 2011), 23–43; Sander Gilman, *Sexuality: An Illustrated History* (New York: John Wiley & Sons, 1989); Stephen Jay Gould, *The Mismeasure of Man* (New York: W. W. Norton, 1996); Elizabeth Grosz, "Bodies and Knowledges: Feminism and the Crisis of Reason," in *Feminist Epistemologies*, ed. Linda Alcoff and Elizabeth Potter (New York: Routledge Press, 1994), 190–200; Oyeronke Oyewumi, *The Invention of Women: Making Sense of Western Gender Discourses* (Minneapolis: University of Minnesota Press,

1997); Carla Peterson, "Foreword: Eccentric Bodies," in *Recovering the Black Female Body: Self-Representations by African American Women*, ed. Michael Bennett and Vanessa D. Dickerson (New Brunswick, NJ: Rutgers University Press, 2000), viii–xi.

16. Tre'vell Anderson, "With 'No Fats, No Femmes,' Fatima Jamal Aims for More Than Just Visibility and Representation," *Daily Xtra Magazine*, April 3, 2020, https://xtramagazine.com/culture/fatima-jamal-trans-reckoning-169530-169530.

17. Janet Mock, "Being Pretty Is a Privilege, but We Refuse to Acknowledge It," *Allure*, June 28, 2017, https://www.allure.com/story/pretty-privilege.

18. Mock, "Being Pretty Is a Privilege, but We Refuse to Acknowledge It."

19. Lance Richardson, "Making Grindr Kinder," *Slate*, November 8, 2018, https://slate.com/human-interest/2018/11/kindr-grindr-hookup-apps-discrimination.html.

20. Richardson, "Making Grindr Kinder."

21. Richardson, "Making Grindr Kinder."

22. Kindr Grindr, "Kindness Is Our Preference," *Kindr Grindr*, 2018, https://www.kindr.grindr.com.

23. J. D. Shadel, "Grindr Was the First Big Dating App for Gay Men. Now It's Falling Out of Favor," *Washington Post*, December 6, 2018, https://www.washingtonpost.com/lifestyle/2018/12/06/grindr-was-first-big-dating-app-gay-men-now-its-falling-out-favor.

24. Richardson, "Making Grindr Kinder."

25. Veritas Collaborative, "Eating Disorders and the LGBTQ+ Community: A Disproportionate Impact," Veritas Collaborative, March 4, 2018, https://veritascollaborative.com/veritas-collaborative/eating-disorders-and-the-lgbtq-community-a-disproportionate-impact.

26. Jesse Washington, "The Untold Story of Wrestler Andrew Johnson's Dreadlocks," *The Undefeated*, September 18, 2019, https://theundefeated.com/features/the-untold-story-of-wrestler-andrew-johnsons-dreadlocks; Associated Press, "Michigan Father Angry After Teacher Cuts Biracial Daughter's Hair," NBC News, April 22, 2021, https://www.nbcnews.com/news/nbcblk/michigan-father-angry-after-teacher-cuts-biracial-daughter-s-hair-n1264930.

27. Ed Hewitt, "Airline Passenger of Size Policies: Will You Be Forced to Buy an Extra Seat?" *Smarter Travel*, April 16, 2019, https://www.smartertravel.com/airline-obesity-policies.

28. S. E. James, C. Brown, and I. Wilson, *2015 U.S. Transgender Survey: Report on the Experiences of Black Respondents* (Washington, DC: National Center for Transgender Equality, Black Trans Advocacy, & National Black Justice Coalition, 2017), www.USTransSurvey.org; E. Petrosky, J. M. Blair, C. J. Betz, K. A. Fowler, S. P. Jack, and B. H. Lyons, "Racial and Ethnic Differences in Homicides of Adult Women and the Role of Intimate Partner Violence—United States, 2003–2014," *Morbidity and Mortality Weekly Re-*

port (*MMWR*) 66 (2017): 741–46, DOI: http://dx.doi.org/10.15585/mmwr.mm6628a1.

29. Wyatt Ronan, "Pledge to End Violence Against Black and Brown Transgender Women," Human Rights Campaign, October 28, 2020, https://www.hrc.org/press-releases/pledge-to-end-violence-against-black-and-brown-transgender-women.

30. Sabrina Rubin Erdely, "The Transgender Crucible: How CeCe McDonald Became a Folk Hero," *Rolling Stone*, July 30, 2014, https://www.rollingstone.com/culture/culture-news/the-transgender-crucible-114095.

31. Erdely, "The Transgender Crucible."

32. Dee Lockett, "The Traumatic Reality of Getting Sent to Solitary Confinement for Being Trans That *Orange Is the New Black* Can't Show," *Vulture*, June 28, 2016, https://www.vulture.com/2016/06/cece-mcdonald-as-told-to-orange-is-the-new-black.html.

33. Lockett, "The Traumatic Reality of Getting Sent to Solitary Confinement for Being Trans."

34. Lockett, "The Traumatic Reality of Getting Sent to Solitary Confinement for Being Trans."

35. Lockett, "The Traumatic Reality of Getting Sent to Solitary Confinement for Being Trans."

36. Lockett, "The Traumatic Reality of Getting Sent to Solitary Confinement for Being Trans."

37. Lockett, "The Traumatic Reality of Getting Sent to Solitary Confinement for Being Trans."

38. *Transmisogyny* refers to the specific prejudice and hatred of trans women. For more on the term *transmisogyny*, see Julia Serano, "Transmisogyny Primer," https://www.juliaserano.com/av/TransmisogynyPrimer-Serano.pdf.

39. Kaila Adia Story, "Mama's Gon' Buy You a Mockingbird: Why #BlackMothersStillMatter: A Short Genealogy of Black Mothers' Maternal Activism and Politicized Care," in *M4BL and the Critical Matter of Black Lives*, special edition of *Biography* 41, no. 4 (Fall 2018).

40. Jean Kilbourne, *Deadly Persuasion: Why Women and Girls Must Fight the Addictive Power of Advertising* (New York: Free Press Publishers, 1999).

41. Kilbourne, *Deadly Persuasion*.

42. James Baldwin, "Freaks and the American Ideal of Manhood," *layboy*, 1985, https://www.cusd80.com/cms/lib/AZ01001175/Centricity/Domain/1073/Full%20Text%20Here-be-Dragons-James-Baldwin.pdf.

43. Michael Blackmon, "Laverne Cox Opened Up on the Epidemic of Black Trans Women Being Murdered in the US," *BuzzFeed*, June 28, 2019, https://www.buzzfeednews.com/article/michaelblackmon/laverne-cox-black-trans-women-murders.

44. Blackmon, "Laverne Cox Opened Up on the Epidemic of Black Trans Women Being Murdered in the US."

45. Matt Keeley, "Americans Make #RIPReese Trend by Mourning Alleged Suicide of Man Who Actually Died of an Overdose," *Newsweek,* August 21, 2019, https://www.newsweek.com/americans-make-ripreese-trend-mourning-alleged-suicide-man-who-actually-died-overdose-1455608.

46. Keeley, "Americans Make #RIPReese Trend by Mourning Alleged Suicide of Man Who Actually Died of an Overdose."

47. Keeley, "Americans Make #RIPReese Trend by Mourning Alleged Suicide of Man Who Actually Died of an Overdose."

48. Jacob Ogles, "Man Bullied for Being Open About Trans Relationship Dies by Suicide," *The Advocate*, August 21, 2019, https://www.advocate.com/news/2019/8/21/man-bullied-being-open-about-trans-relationship-dies-suicide.

49. Ogles, "Man Bullied for Being Open About Trans Relationship Dies by Suicide."

50. Helen Murphy, "Cool Runnings Actor Malik Yoba Says He Is Attracted to Transgender Women: 'It's Time to Speak,'" *People*, September 4, 2019, https://people.com/movies/malik-yoba-reveals-attraction-to-transgender-women.

51. Serena Sonoma, "The Problem with Identifying as 'Trans Attracted,'" op-ed, *Out*, September 14, 2019, https://www.out.com/transgender/2019/9/14/op-ed-problem-identifying-trans-attracted.

52. Serena Sonoma, "The Problem with Identifying as 'Trans Attracted.'"

53. Serena Sonoma, "The Problem with Identifying as 'Trans Attracted.'"

54. Serena Sonoma, "The Problem with Identifying as 'Trans Attracted.'"

55. Laura Smythe, "Trans Girlfriend of Deceased North Philadelphia Man Receives Harassment, Institutional Misgendering in Wake of His Death," *Philadelphia Gay News*, September 5, 2019, https://epgn.com/2019/09/05/trans-girlfriend-of-deceased-north-philadelphia-man-receives-harassment-institutional-misgendering-in-wake-of-his-death.

56. Smythe, "Trans Girlfriend of Deceased North Philadelphia Man Receives Harassment, Institutional Misgendering in Wake of His Death."

57. Terrell Jermaine Star, "Malik Yoba Storms Off Set After Being Pressed on Allegations of Soliciting Sex from a Minor," *The Root*, September 25, 2019, https://www.theroot.com/malik-yoba-storms-off-set-after-being-pressed-on-allega-1838377159.

58. Michael Cuby, "Maurice Willoughby's Death Unveils the Tragic Dangers of Toxic Masculinity," *Them.Us*, August 21, 2019, https://www.them.us/story/maurice-willoughby-faith-palmer.

59. Smythe, "Trans Girlfriend of Deceased North Philadelphia Man Receives Harassment, Institutional Misgendering in Wake of His Death."

60. Baldwin, "Freaks and the American Ideal of Manhood."

61. Baldwin, "Freaks and the American Ideal of Manhood."

62. Erdely, "The Transgender Crucible."

63. Erdely, "The Transgender Crucible."

64. Canela Lopez, "JK Rowling Wrote a Controversial Statement About Transgender People in Response to Being Called a 'TERF.' Here's What It Means," *Insider*, June 10, 2020, https://www.businessinsider.com/jk-rowling-what-is-a-terf-trans-exclusionary-radical-feminist-2020-6.

65. Lopez, "JK Rowling Wrote a Controversial Statement About Transgender People in Response to Being Called a 'TERF.'"

66. Kelly Lawler, "Do J. K. Rowling's Transphobic Comments Taint Her New Book, 'Troubled Blood'? For Me, They Do," *USA Today*, September 23, 2020, https://www.usatoday.com/story/entertainment/books/2020/09/15/jk-rowling-troubled-blood-transgender-comments-can-you-separate-art-artist/5760735002.

67. Lawler, "Do J. K. Rowling's Transphobic Comments Taint Her New Book?"

68. Lawler, "Do J. K. Rowling's Transphobic Comments Taint Her New Book?"

69. Katelyn Burns, "The Rise of Anti-Trans 'Radical' Feminists, Explained," *Vox*, September 5, 2019, https://www.vox.com/identities/2019/9/5/20840101/terfs-radical-feminists-gender-critical.

70. Alona Ferber, "Judith Butler on the Culture Wars, JK Rowling and Living in 'Anti-Intellectual Times,'" *New Statesman*, September 22, 2020, https://www.newstatesman.com/international/2020/09/judith-butler-culture-wars-jk-rowling-and-living-anti-intellectual-times.

71. Ferber, "Judith Butler on the Culture Wars, JK Rowling and Living in 'Anti-Intellectual Times.'"

72. Ferber, "Judith Butler on the Culture Wars, JK Rowling and Living in 'Anti-Intellectual Times.'"

73. GLAAD Transgender Media Program, https://www.glaad.org/transgender, accessed May 14, 2024.

74. Tim Fitzsimons, "Minnesota Trans Woman Said She Thought She Was Going to Die in Beating," NBC News, June 5, 2020, https://www.nbcnews.com/feature/nbc-out/minnesota-trans-woman-said-she-thought-she-was-going-die-n1226216.

75. Fitzsimons, "Minnesota Trans Woman Said She Thought She Was Going to Die in Beating."

76. Fitzsimons, "Minnesota Trans Woman Said She Thought She Was Going to Die in Beating."

77. John Riley, "Black Civil Rights Organization Urges Instagram to Suspend Azealia Banks over Transphobic Tirade," *Metroweekly*, March 2, 2021, https://www.metroweekly.com/2021/02/black-civil-rights-organization-calls-on-instagram-to-suspend-azealia-banks-account.

78. Riley, "Black Civil Rights Organization Urges Instagram to Suspend Azealia Banks over Transphobic Tirade."

79. Sa'iyda Shabazz, "Azealia Banks Is Spewing Transphobic Bullsh*t Again, and She's Also Confused About Judaism," *Scary Mommy*, February 25,

2021, https://www.scarymommy.com/azealia-banks-transphobic-rant-dangerous.

80. Shiri Eisner, *Bi: Notes for a Bisexual Revolution* (Seattle: Seal Press, 2013).

81. Lisa Duggan: *The Twilight of Equality? Neoliberalism, Cultural Politics, and the Attack on Democracy* (Boston: Beacon Press, 2003), 50.

82. A Gender Agenda (AGA), according to their website, "is a unique community organization actively engaged in increasing public awareness and understanding of intersex, trans and gender diversity issues." They define "sib" (located under the header "Sister/Brothers") as "[gender] neutral, short for sibling." See https://genderrights.org.au/faq_type/language.

83. Roberta K. Lee, Vetta L. Sanders Thompson, and Mindy B. Mechanic, "Intimate Partner Violence and Women of Color: A Call for Innovations," *US National Library of Medicine* 92, no. 4 (April 2002): 530–34, doi: 10.2105/ajph.92.4.530, https://www.ncbi.nlm.nih.gov/pmc/articles/PMC1447110.

84. GLAAD, "Transgender Day of Remembrance," https://www.glaad.org/tdor, accessed May 14, 2024.

85. James et al., *2015 U.S. Transgender Survey*; Petrosky et al., "Racial and Ethnic Differences in Homicides of Adult Women and the Role of Intimate Partner Violence," 741–46.

86. James et al., *2015 U.S. Transgender Survey*.

87. James et al., *2015 U.S. Transgender Survey*.

88. Louis Donovan, "Chris Brown's Response to the Night He Assaulted Rihanna Is Unconscionable," *Elle*, August 17, 2017, https://www.elle.com/uk/life-and-culture/culture/news/a37820/chris-brown-rihanna-domestic-violence.

89. BBC News Staff, "Rihanna Opens Up About Chris Brown Assault," BBC News, October 7, 2015, https://www.bbc.com/news/entertainment-arts-34463146.

90. BBC News Staff, "Rihanna Opens Up About Chris Brown Assault."

91. Yezmin Villarreal, "Man Who Beat Trans Woman to Death Sentenced to 12 Years," *The Advocate*, April 19, 2016, https://www.advocate.com/transgender/2016/4/19/man-who-beat-trans-woman-death-sentenced-12-years.

92. Villarreal, "Man Who Beat Trans Woman to Death Sentenced to 12 Years."

93. Matthew Allen, "Harlem Community Rallies in Defense of Black Women Attacked at Liquor Store," *The Grio*, January 24, 2021, https://thegrio.com/2021/01/24/harlem-protest-protect-black-women-liquor-store.

94. Allen, "Harlem Community Rallies in Defense of Black Women Attacked at Liquor Store."

95. Allen, "Harlem Community Rallies in Defense of Black Women Attacked at Liquor Store."

96. Steven Kurutz, "Monica Roberts, Transgender Advocate and Journalist, Dies at 58," *New York Times*, October 13, 2020, https://www.nytimes.com/2020/10/13/us/monica-roberts-dead.html.

97. Black Emotional and Mental Health Collective (BEAM), https://www.beam.community, accessed May 14, 2024.

98. Black Emotional and Mental Health Collective.

99. Sarah Jackson, "#GirlsLikeUs: Trans Advocacy and Community Building Online," *University of Pennsylvania Scholarly Commons*, 2018, https://repository.upenn.edu/cgi/viewcontent.cgi?article=1803&context=asc_papers; Michael T. Warner defines *counterpublic* on page 84 of his essay "Publics and Counterpublics." He states: "A counterpublic maintains at some level, conscious or not, an awareness of its subordinate status. The cultural horizon against which it marks itself is not just a general public or wider public, but a dominant one," *Public Culture* 14, no. 1 (2002): 49–90, https://muse.jhu.edu/article/26277.

100. C. Riley Snorton, *Black on Both Sides: A Racial History of Trans Identity* (Minneapolis: University of Minnesota Press, 2017), 7.

101. Moya Bailey, *Misogynoir Transformed: Black Women's Digital Resistance* (New York: New York University Press, 2021).

CHAPTER FIVE: OUR FIRST PRIDE WAS A RIOT

1. Martin Duberman, *Stonewall: The Definitive Story of the* LGBTQ *Rights Uprising That Changed America* (New York: Plume Press, 1993).

2. Hugh Ryan, "How Dressing in Drag Was Labeled a Crime in the 20th Century," The History Channel, June 28, 2019, https://www.history.com/news/stonewall-riots-lgbtq-drag-three-article-rule.

3. William Yardley, "Stormé DeLarverie, Early Leader in the Gay Rights Movement, Dies at 93," *New York Times*, May 29, 2014, https://www.nytimes.com/2014/05/30/nyregion/storme-delarverie-early-leader-in-the-gay-rights-movement-dies-at-93.html; Jodi-Ann Burey, "'It Wasn't No Damn Riot': Celebrating Stonewall Uprising Activist Stormé DeLarverie," *The Riveter*, n.d., https://theriveter.co/voice/it-wasnt-no-damn-riot-celebrating-stonewall-uprising-activist-storme-delarverie, accessed May 14, 2024.

4. Duberman, *Stonewall.*

5. James Greig and Omar Shweiki, "Gay Against Imperialism," *Jacobin*, June 30, 2021, https://jacobinmag.com/2021/06/gay-liberation-lgbtq-struggle-queer-revolt-imperialism.

6. David Holthouse, "Shirley Q. Liquor: The Most Dangerous Comedian in America," *Rolling Stone*, May 31, 2007, https://www.rollingstone.com/culture/culture-features/shirley-q-liquor-the-most-dangerous-comedian-in-america-188700.

7. When Knipp is in drag, I refer to Knipp as "she," and when Knipp is not, I refer to him as "he." These pronoun switches are common when

referring to drag queens. Mickey Hess, "A Funny Thing About Racism: Shirley Q. Liquor, Real Women, and Hot-and Cold-Running Strippers," Edge Media Network, May 10, 2008, https://www.edgemedianetwork.com/news.php?74290.

8. Historically, blackface and/or blackface minstrelsy have allowed white Americans to objectify African American life experiences, aesthetics, and spiritual traditions. As an American tradition, it has also engendered imagined histories of the "sexually aggressive" and "uneducated" nature of African American women and men, discursively writing them as hypersexual, vulgar, and primitive. Blackface is said to have started around the 1830s and continued to be a staple in the American theater tradition for the next hundred years. Its popularity in the United States carried the tradition overseas to Britain for a time, but by the twentieth century its presence in British theater was fleeting. However, by the late 1920s, blackface performance returned to United States radio with the creation of *Amos 'n' Andy*. For more on the tradition of blackface, see John Jeremiah Sullivan, "Shuffle Along and the Lost History of Black Performance in America," *New York Times*, March 24, 2016, https://www.nytimes.com/2016/03/27/magazine/shuffle-along-and-the-painful-history-of-black-performance-in-america.html.

9. The Connection nightclub in Louisville, Kentucky, opened in 1988 but had to close its doors in 2016 after twenty-eight years, following the opening of the Louisville LGBTQ+ nightclub Play Dance Bar in 2013. For more on this, see Sara Wagner, "The Connection Closes Its Doors with One Last Dance," WHAS11 News, August 7, 2016, https://www.whas11.com/article/news/local/the-connection-closes-its-doors-with-one-last-dance/289913593.

10. Tamara Lush, "Shirley Q. Liquor's Racist Scum," *Miami New Times*, April 17, 2008, https://www.miaminewtimes.com/news/shirley-q-liquors-racist-scum-6366942.

11. My podcast cohost, Louisville activist Jaison Gardiner, told me that he along with Black trans activists Monica Roberts, Dawn Wilson, and others were integral in stopping Shirley Q. Liquor's performance at Eastern Kentucky University during their Pride week in the early 2000s, and how after that success they all tried to protest Liquor's presence at a Christmas Party that the Louisville nightclub Fusion was having, but they were unsuccessful because of the racial climate in Louisville's gay community. They did, however, get *G3* magazine (a local Louisville publication that is now defunct) to pull their name, but not their money, off the promotion flyers.

12. Graham Gremore, "Popular DC Gay Bar Under Fire After Bartender Wears Blackface Mask to Work," *Queerty*, July 15, 2020, https://www.queerty.com/popular-dc-gay-bar-fire-bartender-wears-blackface-mask-work-20200715.

13. Sam Damshenas, "RuPaul's Drag Race Down Under Contestants Apologise for Racist Pasts," *Gay Times*, 2021, https://www.gaytimes.co.uk

/culture/rupauls-drag-race-down-under-contestants-apologise-for-racist-pasts.

14. Anna Brown, "About a Third of Americans Say Blackface in a Halloween Costume Is Acceptable at Least Sometimes," Pew Research Center, February 11, 2019, https://www.pewresearch.org/fact-tank/2019/02/11/about-a-third-of-americans-say-blackface-in-a-halloween-costume-is-acceptable-at-least-sometimes.

15. Queer theorist Lisa Duggan has defined a homonormative person as a queer person "who is politically neutered, socially compliant, and one who's politic does not contest dominant heteronormative assumptions and institutions, but upholds and sustains them, while promising the possibility of a demobilized gay constituency and a privatized, depoliticized gay culture anchored in domesticity and consumption." For more on homonormativity and homonormative politics, see Lisa Duggan, *The Twilight of Equality? Neoliberalism, Cultural Politics, and the Attack on Democracy* (Boston: Beacon Press, 2003).

16. Roderick A. Ferguson, *One-Dimensional Queer* (Cambridge: Polity Press, 2018).

17. Neal Broverman, "Don't Let History Forget About Compton's Cafeteria Riot," *The Advocate*, August 2, 2018, https://www.advocate.com/transgender/2018/8/02/dont-let-history-forget-about-comptons-cafeteria-riot.

18. Hugh Ryan, "How Dressing in Drag Was Labeled a Crime in the 20th Century," The History Channel, June 28, 2019, https://www.history.com/news/stonewall-riots-lgbtq-drag-three-article-rule.

19. Broverman, "Don't Let History Forget About Compton's Cafeteria Riot."

20. Jason McGahan, "Before Stonewall, the Queer Revolution Started Right Here in Los Angeles," *Los Angeles Magazine*, May 29, 2019, https://www.lamag.com/citythinkblog/before-stonewall-gay-pride-history.

21. McGahan, "Before Stonewall, the Queer Revolution Started Right Here in Los Angeles."

22. McGahan, "Before Stonewall, the Queer Revolution Started Right Here in Los Angeles."

23. "(1970) Huey P. Newton, the Women's Liberation and Gay Liberation Movements," *Blackpast*, April 17, 2018, https://www.blackpast.org/african-american-history/speeches-african-american-history/huey-p-newton-women-s-liberation-and-gay-liberation-movements; James Greig and Omar Shweiki, "Gay Against Imperialism," *Jacobin*, June 30, 2021, https://jacobinmag.com/2021/06/gay-liberation-lgbtq-struggle-queer-revolt-imperialism.

24. Lawrence D. Mass, "Dewey's Lunch Counter Sit-Ins," *World Queerstory*, June 15, 2017, https://worldqueerstory.org/2017/06/15/deweys-lunch-counter-sit-ins.

25. Mass, "Dewey's Lunch Counter Sit-Ins."

26. The US Library of Congress defines the homophile movement as follows: "the local, national and international social-political movement for gay and lesbian rights which emerged following World War II. Many consider the birth of the homophile movement to be sometime around 1950/1951, a date that corresponds to the founding of the Mattachine Society, and then eventually, to ONE, Inc., and the Daughters of Bilitis. U.S. gay rights organizations that pre-date the Mattachine Society include the Chicago Society for Human Rights, founded by Henry Gerber in 1924, the Sons of Hamidy (est. 1934 in the Midwest), and the Veterans Benevolent Association founded in New York in 1945. Before Stonewall, there were by conservative estimates at least 60 homophile or gay rights groups operating. According to NACHO, in 1970 there were 143 'homosexual or gay groups' operating in the United States and Canada. After Stonewall, the number of LGBTQIA+ groups proliferated so rapidly it becomes difficult to keep track. However, just a year after Stonewall, there were upwards of 1,500–2,000 LGBT+ liberation groups in the United States, and many more internationally." For more on the homophile gay rights movement and the Janus Society, see https://guides.loc.gov/lgbtq-studies/before-stonewall.

27. Other acts of resistance include, but are not limited to, the following: There was a police raid of Ansley's Mini-Cinema in Atlanta, and ACT UP also vocally denounced police brutality and persistent arrests at its actions during the AIDS crisis. The LGBTQ+ liberation movement also collaborated with the Black Panther Party to resist state violence. For more on these acts, see McGahan, "Before Stonewall, the Queer Revolution Started Right Here in Los Angeles."

28. Jodi-Ann Burey, "It Wasn't No Damn Riot": Celebrating Stonewall Uprising Activist Stormé DeLarverie," *The Riveter*, n.d., https://theriveter.co/voice/it-wasnt-no-damn-riot-celebrating-stonewall-uprising-activist-storme-delarverie.

29. William Yardley, "Stormé DeLarverie, Early Leader in the Gay Rights Movement, Dies at 93," *New York Times*, May 29, 2014, https://www.nytimes.com/2014/05/30/nyregion/storme-delarverie-early-leader-in-the-gay-rights-movement-dies-at-93.html.

30. Yardley, "Stormé DeLarverie, Early Leader in the Gay Rights Movement, Dies at 93."

31. While this interesting history of Black LGBTQ+ citizens hiring informal security firms or their comrades to maintain safety at their parties and festivals lacks specific documentation, I can personally attest to bearing witness to such realities, as I have attended many Black LGBTQ+ led festivals and parties where this was the case.

32. I am inferring here that this is the reason why Black LGBTQ+ party promoters have utilized these informal security networks instead of hiring traditional law enforcement to maintain safety at their events. However, I do

concede that they might also do this because these firms and comrades have more reasonable rates for these services and therefore might be cheaper to employ than traditional law enforcement.

33. Various chapters of Black Lives Matter have disrupted Pride festivals, demanding that Pride festival organizers recognize the harmful effects of racism and police violence in the lives of Black and Latinx LGBTQ+ communities. Some of these direct actions include, but are not limited to: In 2015, a group of LGBTQ+ activists of color stopped the city's Pride parade to issue a series of demands, including more diversity in leadership, WBUR reported. In 2020, a Boston Pride statement addressing police brutality after the deaths of George Floyd and Breonna Taylor reportedly removed any reference to Black Lives Matter, according to New England LGBTQ+ outlet *The Rainbow Times*, resulting in 80 percent of the group's volunteers quitting in protest. For more on these actions, see https://www.therainbowtimesmass.com/boston-pride-boycott-glad-joins and https://www.wbur.org/news/2020/10/09/boston-pride-clashes-with-boston-black-pride-and-pride-for-the-people-over-name.

34. James Kirchick, "Politics on Parade: How Black Lives Matter Halted a Gay Pride Parade in Toronto," *Los Angeles Times*, July 6, 2016, https://www.latimes.com/opinion/op-ed/la-oe-kirchick-gay-pride-black-lives-matter-20160705-snap-story.html.

35. Jo Yurcaba, "Pride Marchers Sprayed by NYPD Marchers Say," NBC News, June 28, 2021, https://www.nbcnews.com/nbc-out/out-news/pride-marchers-pepper-sprayed-nypd-witnesses-say-rcna1284.

36. Yurcaba, "Pride Marchers Sprayed by NYPD Marchers Say."

37. John D' Emilio, "Cycles of Change, Questions of Strategy: The Gay and Lesbian Movement After Fifty Years," in *The Politics of Gay Rights*, ed. Craig A. Rimmerman, Kenneth D. Wald, and Clyde Wilcox (Chicago: University of Chicago Press, 2000), 35–36.

38. National LGBTQ Task Force, "Our Mission & History," https://www.thetaskforce.org/about/mission-history.html.

39. The National Center for Lesbian Rights, "Mission & History," https://www.nclrights.org/about-us/mission-history, accessed May 14, 2024.

40. Steve Endean, *Bringing Lesbian and Gay Rights into the Mainstream: Twenty Years of Progress*, ed. Vicki L Eaklor (New York: Haworth Press, 2004).

41. Keith Boykin, "Where Rhetoric Meets Reality: The Role of Black Lesbians and Gays in 'Queer' Politics," in Rimmerman, Wald, and Wilcox, *The Politics of Gay Rights*, 79–96.

42. Boykin, "Where Rhetoric Meets Reality," 82.

43. Queer to the Left (Q2L), The Lesbian Avengers (TLA), and Queer Nation (QN), most of which were established in the 1990s, all focused their activism on addressing the multilayered inequity and oppression that continue to frame the lives of LGBTQ+ citizens post-Stonewall. Q2L was a Chicago-based activist group formed during the late 1990s, with the aim of

combatting homonormativity, racism, police brutality, the death penalty, and gentrification, as Q2L felt that LGBTQ+ injustice should address all these structural barriers that brought harm into LGBTQ+ citizens' lives. Q2L also felt that the mainstream gay rights movement largely began to ignore these issues after the more financially affluent members of LGBTQ+ movement deemed that the AIDS crisis was coming to an end after the introduction of antiviral drugs that only the wealthy could afford. In 1998, Q2L published *It's Time to End the Gay Rights Movement as We Know It*, a manifesto critiquing how the overwhelmingly white, rich, and cis mainstream gay movement had actively suppressed the multiracial collaborative tradition of LGBTQ+ activism, turning their advocacy for gay rights into a one-dimensional set of politics that only emphasized same-sex marriage and military access. See Queer to the Left, *It's Time to End the Gay Rights Movement as We Know It*, 2005, https://web.archive.org/web/20051018072839/http:/www.queertotheleft.org/propaganda%20archive/end%20of%20gays%20rights%20mvmnt%20as%20we%20know%20it%20page.html.

44. New York Public Library's Online Exhibition Archive, "Street Transvestites Action Revolutionaries (STAR)," http://web-static.nypl.org/exhibitions/1969/revolutionaries.html.

45. New York Public Library's Online Exhibition Archive, "Street Transvestites Action Revolutionaries (STAR)."

46. Arthur Dong, "The Question of Equality–Part 1–Out Rage '69," YouTube video, February 23, 2016, https://www.youtube.com/watch?v=uuTNXnQA-ww.

47. Myrl Beam, *Gay, Inc.: The Nonprofitization of Queer Politics* (Minneapolis: University of Minnesota Press, 2018), 5–6.

48. Beam, *Gay, Inc.*

49. Beam, *Gay, Inc.*

50. Yezmin Villarreal, "5 Most Disappointing Things We Learned About HRC's 'White Men's Club,'" *The Advocate*, June 4, 2015, https://www.advocate.com/human-rights-campaign-hrc/2015/06/04/5-most-disappointing-things-we-learned-about-hrcs-white-mens-cl.

51. The Pipeline Project, https://lgbtpipeline.org.

52. Villarreal, "5 Most Disappointing Things We Learned About HRC's 'White Men's Club.'"

53. Villarreal, "5 Most Disappointing Things We Learned About HRC's 'White Men's Club.'"

54. Villarreal, "5 Most Disappointing Things We Learned About HRC's 'White Men's Club.'"

55. Rea Carey, "Growing Pains, Opportunity for Nation's Most Influential Queer Gathering," *The Advocate*, December 14, 2016, https://www.advocate.com/commentary/2016/12/14/growing-pains-opportunity-nations-most-influential-queer-gathering.

56. Carey, "Growing Pains, Opportunity for Nation's Most Influential Queer Gathering."

57. Hannah Elyse Simpson, "Chicago's Creating Change Conference Was a Mess," *The Advocate*, February 5, 2016, https://www.advocate.com/commentary/2016/2/05/chicagos-creating-change-conference-was-mess.

58. Simpson, "Chicago's Creating Change Conference Was a Mess."

59. Simpson, "Chicago's Creating Change Conference Was a Mess."

60. Trudy Ring, "National Center for Lesbian Rights Leader on Making a Movement for All," *The Advocate*, December 17, 2019, https://www.advocate.com/news/2019/12/17/national-center-lesbian-rights-leader-making-movement-all.

61. Ring, "National Center for Lesbian Rights Leader on Making a Movement for All."

62. Cathy Cohen, "Punks, Bulldaggers and Welfare Queens: The Radical Potential of Queer Politics," *GLQ: A Journal of Lesbian & Gay Studies* 3, no. 4 (May 1997): 450.

63. Cohen, "Punks, Bulldaggers and Welfare Queens."

64. Marisa Taylor, "Report: LGBT People of Color at High Risk of Poverty," *Al Jazeera America*, August 23, 2015, http://america.aljazeera.com/articles/2015/4/23/lgbt-people-of-color-more-likely-to-face-poverty.html.

65. Lisa Duggan, *The Twilight of Equality? Neoliberalism, Cultural Politics, and the Attack on Democracy* (Boston: Beacon Press, 2003), 50.

66. Imogen Watson, "The 3 Pitfalls of LGBTQ+ Marketing: Failure to Represent Society Both Inside and Out," *The Drum*, June 21, 2019, https://www.thedrum.com/news/2019/06/21/the-3-pitfalls-lgbtq-marketing-failure-represent-society-both-inside-and-out.

67. Watson, "The 3 Pitfalls of LGBTQ+ Marketing."

68. Bryan Moylan, "Most LGBT Characters on US TV Are White and Male, Study Finds," *The Guardian*, October 27, 2015, https://www.theguardian.com/tv-and-radio/2015/oct/27/most-lgbt-characters-on-us-tv-are-white-and-male-study-finds.

69. Moylan, "Most LGBT Characters on US TV Are White and Male."

70. Moylan, "Most LGBT Characters on US TV Are White and Male."

71. Alex Abad-Santos, "How LGBTQ Pride Month Became a Branded Holiday. And Why That's a Problem," *Vox News*, June 25, 2018, https://www.vox.com/2018/6/25/17476850/pride-month-lgbtq-corporate-explained.

72. Kim Severson, "Gay Pride's Choice: March in Protest or Dance Worries Away," *New York Times*, June 19, 2017, https://www.nytimes.com/2017/06/19/us/gay-pride-lgbtq-protest-or-party.html.

73. Abad-Santos, "How LGBTQ Pride Month Became a Branded Holiday."

74. Abad-Santos, "How LGBTQ Pride Month Became a Branded Holiday."

75. Abad-Santos, "How LGBTQ Pride Month Became a Branded Holiday."

76. Abad-Santos, "How LGBTQ Pride Month Became a Branded Holiday."

77. Fem News Magazine Staff, "Feminism 101: What Is Pinkwashing?" *Fem News Magazine*, March 2, 2019, https://femmagazine.com/feminism-101-what-is-pinkwashing.

78. Fem News Magazine Staff, "Feminism 101."

79. Abad-Santos, "How LGBTQ Pride Month Became a Branded Holiday."

80. Abad-Santos, "How LGBTQ Pride Month Became a Branded Holiday."

81. Nils D'Aularire, "Rainbow Road: The Secret History of Advertising to LGBTQ+ Consumers," *SXM Media*, July 17, 2020, https://www.sxmmedia.com/insights/rainbow-road-the-secret-history-of-advertising-to-lgbtq-consumers.

82. Like Q2L, other organizations, such as the Lesbian Avengers and Queer Nation, have protested and organized to bring an end to mainstream gay movements that have chosen to excise the valiant efforts and forms of resistance by Black and Latinx trans women and racialized nonbinary folks. Activists in Q2L, the Lesbian Avengers, and Queer Nation all recognized that if it was not for the activist strategies employed before and during Stonewall by Black and Latinx LGBTQ+ people, queer and trans communities would have never garnered mainstream recognition and support for LGBTQ+ issues. These advocacy groups also adopted a multipronged societal intervention that called for an end to sexual and gendered tyranny, and at the same time, sought to undo and reform other systemic oppressions in order for queer liberation to operate in an inclusive way for the entire LGBTQ+ community. For more on this, see Queer to the Left, *It's Time to End The Gay Movement As We Know It*, 2005, https://web.archive.org/web/20051018072839/http:/www.queertotheleft.org/propaganda%20archive/end%20of%20gays%20rights%20mvmnt%20as%20we%20know%20it%20page.html; Annie Howard, "Queer to the Left Came to Raise Hell," *Chicago Reader*, June 9, 2021, https://chicagoreader.com/news-politics/queer-to-the-left-came-to-raise-hell; Michael Specter, "How Act Up Changed America," *New Yorker*, June 7, 2021, https://www.newyorker.com/magazine/2021/06/14/how-act-up-changed-america.

83. These organizations include but are not limited to the Center for Black Equity, La Marcha de la Diversidad, and the Latino Pride Alliance. For more on these organizations, please see https://centerforblackequity.org/black-lgbtq-prides; Emma Specter, "Thousands Rallied to Protect the Safety and Joy of Trans Youth at This Weekend's Brooklyn Liberation March," *Vogue*, June 14, 2021, https://www.vogue.com/slideshow/brooklyn-liberation-march-for-trans-youth-2021; https://www.brooklynliberation.com; Dani Elli, "Pride Celebrations Are Happening Around the World and the Biggest Ones Are Taking Place in Latin America," Mitú, June 17, 2019, https://wearemitu.com/wearemitu/culture/latin-america-pride-celebrations; Julian Alberto Hernandez, "'We're Making History Today': Phoenix Celebrates 1st Latino Pride Festival, Largest LGBT Gathering in Arizona," *Republic AZ Central News*, December 1, 2018, https://www.azcentral.com/story/news/local/phoenix/2018/12/01/phoenixs-1st-latino-pride-festival-largest-latino-lgbt-gathering-arizona/2179247002; http://latinoprideallliance.org.

84. For example, at many Black-specific LGBTQ+ Pride festivals in various states, these organizers underscore their dance parties and musical acts with rapid HIV testing and advocacy, and emcees' speeches boldly address the negative effects of white supremacy and capitalism on Black LGBTQ+ youth. Latinx LGBTQ+ people, like Black LGBTQ+ people, have also created their own Latinx-specific Pride celebrations. Many Latinx LGBTQ+ organizers' missions are about empowering and educating LGBTQ+ Latinx communities. In 2018, the Latino Pride Alliance hosted a Pride festival in 2018 aimed to inform its attendees about Latinx-specific health and wellness initiatives, considering that Latinx folks accounted for 26 percent of all new HIV diagnoses. Addressing intersectional inequities at state and federal levels have been the cornerstones of Black and Latinx LGBTQ+ organizing, and some of the main missions of Black- and Latinx-specific Pride festivals, as well. For more on this, see the Centers for Disease Control and Prevention report *HIV and Hispanic/Latino People*, 2016, https://www.cdc.gov/hiv/group/racialethnic/hispaniclatinos/index.html; Center for Black Equity; La Marcha de la Diversidad; and the Latino Pride Alliance. For more on these organizations, please see https://centerforblackequity.org/black-lgbtq-prides; Emma Specter, "Thousands Rallied to Protect the Safety and Joy of Trans Youth at This Weekend's Brooklyn Liberation March," *Vogue*, June 14, 2021, https://www.vogue.com/slideshow/brooklyn-liberation-march-for-trans-youth-2021; https://www.brooklynliberation.com; Elli, "Pride Celebrations Are Happening Around the World and the Biggest Ones Are Taking Place in Latin America"; Hernandez, "'We're Making History Today'"; http://latinoprideallliance.org.

85. Aundaray Guess, "5 Reasons Why I Don't Celebrate Pride," *POZ Blog*, June 14, 2019, https://www.poz.com/blog/5-reasons-celebrate-pride.

86. Guess, "5 Reasons Why I Don't Celebrate Pride."

87. Guess, "5 Reasons Why I Don't Celebrate Pride."

88. Darnell Moore, "Angelica Ross Is Dreaming of a Free, Black Future," *Cassius Life*, June 15, 2021, https://cassiuslife.com/459794/angelica-ross-is-dreaming-of-a-free-black-future.

89. The Black LGBTQ+ academics that I am speaking of include, but are not limited to, Drs. E. Patrick Johnson, Roderick Ferguson, Alexis Pauline Gumbs, Eric Darnell Pritchard, Moya Bailey, Marlon Bailey, and Jeffrey McCune. The Black LGBTQ+ attorneys, artists, and creatives I am speaking of include, but are not limited to, Jaison A. Gardner, Preston Mitchem, George M. Johnson, Hari Zayd, Darnell Moore, Danielle Moodie, Aishah Shahidah Simmons, and Aisha Mills.

CHAPTER SIX: #WEALLWEGOT

1. Finbarr Toesland, "Police Departments Across U.S. Are Mandating LGBTQ Training," NBC News, September 25, 2021, https://www.nbcnews.com/nbc-out/out-news/police-departments-us-are-mandating-lgbtq-training-rcna2250.

2. Toesland, "Police Departments Across U.S. Are Mandating LGBTQ Training."

3. Toesland, "Police Departments Across U.S. Are Mandating LGBTQ Training."

4. Dawn Ennis, "The Full Scale of Anti-Trans, Anti-LGBTQ Bills in State Houses Will Shock You," *The Daily Beast*, May 26, 2021, https://www.thedailybeast.com/the-full-scale-of-anti-trans-anti-lgbtq-bills-in-state-houses-will-shock-you.

5. Kiara Alfonseca, "Record Number of Anti-LGBTQ Legislation Filed in 2023," ABC News, December 28, 2023, https://abcnews.go.com/US/record-number-anti-lgbtq-legislation-filed-2023/story?id=105556010.

6. Ennis, "The Full Scale of Anti-Trans, Anti-LGBTQ Bills in State Houses Will Shock You."

7. Belle Townsend, "Kentucky Legislators Have Introduced 14 Anti-LGBTQ+ Bills: Here's What to Know," *Queer Kentucky*, February 19, 2024, https://queerkentucky.com/kentucky-legislators-have-introduced-14-anti-lgbtq-bills-heres-what-to-know.

8. Townsend, "Kentucky Legislators Have Introduced 14 Anti-LGBTQ+ Bills."

9. Ryan Adamczeski, "Kentucky couldn't pass a single anti-LGBTQ+ bill this session-and it's not alone," The Advocate, April 16, 2024, https://www.advocate.com/politics/kentucky-anti-lgbtq-laws-fail.

10. Bruce Schreiner, "Kentucky Lawmakers Pass Ban on Youth Gender-Affirming Care," AP News, March 16, 2023, https://apnews.com/article/transgender-rights-health-care-kentucky-legislature-848343fe842e714dfc2bb734745f3cd5.

11. Spencer Jenkins, "Advocates to Fight Anti-LGBTQ+ Bills, Support State-Wide Fairness," *Queer Kentucky*, December 29, 2021, https://queerkentucky.com/advocates-to-fight-anti-lgbtq-bills-support-state-wide-fairness.

12. Jenkins, "Advocates to Fight Anti-LGBTQ+ Bills, Support State-Wide Fairness."

13. Dee Knight (@Dr.DeeKnight), "stop calling people resilient without calling out the systems that force them to be resilient or die," Twitter, March 31, 2021, https://twitter.com/DrDeeKnight/status/1377416499359412224.

14. Zandashé Brown (@zandashe), "I dream of never being called resilient again in my life. I'm exhausted by strength. I want support. I want softness. I want ease. I want to be amongst kin. Not patted on the back for how well I take a hit. Or for how many," Twitter, May 18, 2021, https://twitter.com/zandashe/status/1394805726825099279.

15. @DandyCommie, "Cis people stop calling trans people 'brave,' and 'resilient' . . . this shit is exhausting," Twitter, August 1, 2021, https://twitter.com/DandyCommie/status/1421895175052296196.

16. Danielle DeLoatch (@Freckle&Tea), "Stop calling Black people resilient as a compliment because 9/10 we shouldn't even have to be in the

circumstances to yield resilience," Twitter, April 12, 2021, https://twitter.com/FreckleAndTea/status/1381617352505167876.

17. The Oxford English Dictionary defines the word *resilience* as "1. The capacity to recover quickly from difficulties; toughness;" and "2. The ability of a substance or object to spring back into shape; elasticity." For more information, please see https://www.lexico.com/en/definition/resilience.

18. Merriam-Webster defines the terms *sib* and/or *sibling* as "a brother or sister considered irrespective of sex," https://www.merriam-webster.com/dictionary/sib. Accessed June 4, 2019.

19. Henry Jenkins, "Youth Voice, Media, and Political Engagement: Introducing the Core Concepts," in *By Any Means Necessary: The New Youth Activism*, ed. Henry Jenkins, Sangita Shresthova, Liana Gamber-Thompson, Neta Kligler-Vilenchik, and Arely M. Zimmerman (New York: New York University Press, 2016), pp. 1–60.

20. Jenkins, "Youth Voice, Media, and Political Engagement," 24.

21. The Black feminist theoretical contention of experiential knowledge is defined as the intelligence and authority that are gained through living one's life and critically analyzing those lived experiences. This reflexive praxis enables minoritized communities to become experts in their own experiences, empowering them to enact change in the larger world. For more on this, see Patricia Hill-Collins, *Black Feminist Thought: Knowledge, Consciousness, and the Politics of Empowerment* (New York: Routledge Press, 2000).

22. The Black and Latinx LGBTQ+ podcasts I am referring to include, but are not limited, to *Translash*, hosted by Imara Jones; *Democracy-ish*, hosted by Danielle Moodie; *The Laverne Cox Show*, hosted by Laverne Cox; *Never Before*, hosted by Janet Mock; and *Affirmative Reaction*, hosted by Xorje Olivares.

23. Phillip M. Ayoub and Jeremiah Garretson, "Getting the Message Out: Media Context and Global Changes in Attitudes Toward Homosexuality," *Comparative Political Studies* 50, no. 8 (2017): 1055–85, https://doi.org/10.1177/0010414016666836.

24. Ayoub and Garretson, "Getting the Message Out."

25. GLAAD, "Procter & Gamble and GLAAD Study: Exposure to LGBTQ Representation in Media and Advertising Leads to Greater Acceptance of the LGBTQ Community," May 27, 2020, https://www.glaad.org/releases/procter-gamble-and-glaad-study-exposure-lgbtq-representation-media-and-advertising-leads.

26. GLAAD, "Procter & Gamble and GLAAD Study."

27. The *#RepresentationMatters* study conducted in 2020 by the National Research Group found that 86 percent of Black Americans want more representation on television and feel as if this would increase anti-racist attitudes toward Black Americans. The 2021 study conducted by Horowitz Research, entitled *FOCUS Latinx: Consumer Engagement Report*, found that 64 percent of Latinx Americans want more representation on television and think that

this would decrease anti-Latinx attitudes and prejudices. For more on the *#RepresentationMatters* study, see Danielle Turchiano, "Two in Three Black Americans Don't Feel Properly Represented in Media (Study)," *Vanity Fair*, September 17, 2020, https://variety.com/2020/tv/news/representation-matters-study-nrg-black-americans-media-1234772025. For more on the 2021 *FOCUS Latinx: Consumer Engagement Report*, see Staff, "Research: Latinx Viewers Demand Better Representation," *Advanced Television*, January 26, 2022, https://advanced-television.com/2022/01/26/research-latinx-viewers-demand-better-representation.

28. GLAAD, "Procter & Gamble and GLAAD Study: Exposure to LGBTQ Representation in Media and Advertising Leads to Greater Acceptance of the LGBTQ Community," May 27, 2020, https://www.glaad.org/releases/procter-gamble-and-glaad-study-exposure-lgbtq-representation-media-and-advertising-leads.

29. Our podcast guests that I am referring to, who would often vocalize in their interviews the personal costs of creating the Black and Latinx LGBTQ+ content, include, but are not limited to, Janet Mock, Steven Canals, Patrik-Ian Polk, and Tarell Alvin McCraney.

30. The word *cishet*, as defined by The Queer Dictionary, is used as both an adjective and a noun and describes a person who is both cisgender and heterosexual. Further, it defines cishet "as a person who identifies with his or her assigned-at-birth gender," http://queerdictionary.blogspot.com/2014/09/definition-of-cishet.html.

31. For books about film and television's racist, sexist, homophobic, and transphobic histories, see Donald Bogle, *Toms, Coons, Mulattoes, Mammies, and Bucks: An Interpretive History of Blacks in American Films* (New York: Bloomsbury Academic Press, 2001); K. Sue Jewell, *From Mammy to Miss America to Beyond: Cultural Images and the Shaping of US Social Policy* (New York: Routledge Press, 1993); bell hooks, *Black Looks: Race and Representation* (New York: Routledge Press, 2014); J. Jack Halberstam, *Female Masculinity* (Durham, NC: Duke University Press, 1998); Jack Halberstam, *Gaga Feminism: Sex, Gender, and the End of Normal* (Boston: Beacon Press, 2012); E. Patrick Johnson, *Appropriating Blackness: Performance and the Politics of Authenticity* (Durham, NC: Duke University Press, 2003); E. Patrick Johnson, *No Tea, No Shade: New Writings in Black Queer Studies* (Durham, NC: Duke University Press, 2018).

32. George M. Johnson, "Black LGBTQ Visibility in Media Has Made Strides, But It's Time to Stop Ignoring Queer Violence," *The Grio*, February 21, 2018, https://thegrio.com/2018/02/21/black-lgbtq-movies-violence.

33. In 2020, the Bureau of Labor statistics reported that Black and Latinx families continued to live below the poverty line the United States, and well below white family incomes. For more on this, see Matt Saenz and Arloc Sherman, "Research Note: Number of People in Families with Below-Poverty

Earnings Has Soared, Especially Among Black and Latino Individuals," Center on Budget and Policy Priorities, July 15, 2020, https://www.cbpp.org/research/poverty-and-inequality/research-note-number-of-people-in-families-with-below-poverty.

34. According to *Fundable*, "The first recorded successful instance of crowdfunding occurred in 1997, when a British rock band funded their reunion tour through online donations from fans." See Fundable, "The History of Crowdfunding," n.d., https://www.fundable.com/crowdfunding101/history-of-crowdfunding. For more on the long history of mutual aid initiatives within colonized communities, see Jay Jones, "The Black Panthers and Young Lords: How Today's Mutual Aid Strategies Took Shape," *The Emory Wheel*, June 30, 2021, https://emorywheel.com/the-black-panthers-and-young-lords-how-todays-mutual-aid-strategies-took-shape.

35. Jones, "The Black Panthers and Young Lords."

36. Luis A. Miranda Jr., "Latino Communities Can Redefine American Generosity," op-ed, *Los Angeles Times*, November 26, 2021, https://www.latimes.com/opinion/story/2021–11–26/latino-philanthropy-u-s-remittances; Char Adams, "'Join, Support and Donate': Coalition of Minority Americans Come Together to Dismantle Hate," NBC News, March 12, 2021, https://www.nbcnews.com/news/nbcblk/how-black-people-can-be-strong-allies-asian-americans-right-n1260988.

37. According to Candid Learning, crowdsourced funding is defined as "a way to raise funds for a specific cause or project by asking a large number of people to donate money, usually in small amounts, and usually during a relatively short period of time, such as a few months." See "What Is Crowdfunding?" https://learning.candid.org/resources/knowledge-base/what-is-crowdfunding.

38. Matthew Whitley, "Why 'Mutual Aid'?—Social Solidarity, Not Charity," *Open Democracy*, July 14, 2020, https://www.opendemocracy.net/en/can-europe-make-it/why-mutual-aid-social-solidarity-not-charity.

39. In his YouTube video "What Is Mutual Aid?" Saint Andrewism asserts that the charity model has also been tainted with puritan notions of morality, and states that since "charity often has eligibility requirements, like the means testing of government welfare, these requirements for aid often demand sobriety, clean records, piety, curfews, job training, course participation, and cooperation with police to determine the worthiness or unworthiness of those in need." Saint Andrewism argues that this framework continues to pathologize and criminalize those communities in need, especially Black and poor communities, making the charity model inherently restrictive and dependent on the very systems that have made marginalized populations vulnerable in the first place. For more on this see Saint Andrewism, "What Is Mutual Aid?" YouTube video, March 24, 2021, https://www.youtube.com/watch?v=LlF-ZvRHa2o.

40. Saint Andrewism, "What Is Mutual Aid?"

41. Jia Tolentino, "What Mutual Aid Can Do During a Pandemic," *New Yorker*, May 11, 2020, https://www.newyorker.com/magazine/2020/05/18/what-mutual-aid-can-do-during-a-pandemic.

42. Tolentino, "What Mutual Aid Can Do During a Pandemic."

43. Molly Sprayregen, "Asanni Armon's Collective, for the Gworls, Gives Directly to Black Trans People in Need," *Forbes*, June 24, 2020, https://www.forbes.com/sites/mollysprayregen/2020/06/24/asanni-armons-collective-for-the-gworls-gives-directly-to-black-trans-people-in-need/?sh=210cb5fa6d50.

44. The gender identity *genderqueer* refers to any person who does not see themselves as fitting into our cultural binary gender identity norms. A genderqueer person may also identify as nonbinary, agender, pangender, genderfluid person, or another gender identity.

45. Sprayregen, "Asanni Armon's Collective, for the Gworls, Gives Directly to Black Trans People in Need."

46. Sprayregen, "Asanni Armon's Collective, for the Gworls, Gives Directly to Black Trans People in Need."

47. Nico Lang, "25 Fundraisers Giving Money and Hope to LGBTQ+ People During COVID-19," *Them*, April 28, 2020, https://www.them.us/story/25-fundraisers-for-lgbtq-people-during-covid-19.

48. Lang, "25 Fundraisers Giving Money and Hope to LGBTQ+ People During COVID-19."

49. Lang, "25 Fundraisers Giving Money and Hope to LGBTQ+ People During COVID-19."

50. For more information on Organización Latina Trans en Texas, see https://www.latinatranstexas.org.

51. For more information on the various mutual aid initiatives and crowdsourced funding campaigns that were established before and during the COVID-19 pandemic, see Lang, "25 Fundraisers Giving Money and Hope to LGBTQ+ People During COVID-19"; James Factora, "5 LGBTQ+ Mutual Aid Funds to Donate to This Giving Tuesday"; Jake Wittich, "Molasses, a Nightlife Collective, Is Creating Black Trans Liberation Through Art, Mutual Aid and Self-Defense Series," Block Club Chicago, October 29, 2020, https://blockclubchicago.org/2020/10/29/molasses-a-nightlife-collective-is-creating-black-trans-liberation-through-art-mutual-aid-and-self-defense-series; Adams, "'Join, Support and Donate'"; Quinn Meyers, "Chicago's Puerto Rican Community Emphasizes Solidarity in COVID-19 Fight," *Chicago News*, May 7, 2020, https://news.wttw.com/2020/05/07/chicago-s-puerto-rican-community-emphasizes-solidarity-covid-19-fight.

52. The term *global majority*, according to Rosemary Campbell-Stephens, refers to "people who are Black, Asian, Brown, dual-heritage, indigenous to the global south, and or have been racialized as 'ethnic minorities.'" For more, see Rosemary Campbell-Stephens, "Global Majority:

Decolonizing the Language and Reframing the Conversation About Race," Leeds Beckett University, 2020, https://www.leedsbeckett.ac.uk/-/media/files/schools/school-of-education/final-leeds-beckett-1102-global-majority.pdf.

53. Black Lives Matter, "Herstory," https://blacklivesmatter.com/herstory.

54. Queer theorist Julia Serano defines *transmisogyny* as "the way in which trans women and others on the trans female/feminine spectrum are routinely sexualized in the media, within psychological, social science and feminist discourses, and in society at large." Serano also asserts that transmisogyny "is [also] steeped in the assumption that femaleness and femininity are inferior to, and exist primarily for the benefit of, maleness and masculinity." For more on this, see Julia Serano, *Whipping Girl: A Transsexual Woman on Sexism and the Scapegoating of Femininity* (Emeryville, CA: Seal Press, 2007). The term *misogynoir* was coined by Black queer theorist Dr. Moya Bailey, and she has defined it as "the specific hatred, dislike, distrust, and prejudice directed toward Black women." For more on this, see Moya Bailey, *Misogynoir Transformed: Black Women's Digital Resistance* (New York: NYU Press, 2021).

55. Black Lives Matter, "Herstory."

56. Breonna Taylor was killed by Louisville Metro Police on March 13, 2020, and George Floyd was killed by Minneapolis Police on May 25, 2020. For more information on both Taylor and Floyd, see Alia E. Dastagir, "Breonna Taylor Has Been Gone a Year. Why We Need to Talk More About the Racial Trauma of Black Death," *USA Today*, March 13, 2021, https://www.usatoday.com/story/life/health-wellness/2021/03/11/breonna-taylor-george-floyd-and-racial-trauma-black-death/4630148001.

57. Wilborn P. Nobles III, "Black LGBTQ+ Activists March Against Transphobia, Racism in Baltimore on Saturday Afternoon," *Baltimore Sun*, June 27, 2020, https://www.baltimoresun.com/2020/06/27/black-lgbtq-activists-march-against-transphobia-racism-in-baltimore-on-saturday-afternoon/.

58. Nobles, "Black LGBTQ+ Activists March Against Transphobia, Racism in Baltimore on Saturday Afternoon."

59. Savannah Eadens, "Black Queer Pride: LGBTQ Kentuckians at the Forefront of the Black Lives Matter Movement," *Louisville Courier Journal*, June 25, 2020, https://www.courier-journal.com/story/life/2020/06/25/pride-month-2020-queer-kentuckians-lead-black-lives-matter-movement/3241602001.

60. Eadens, "Black Queer Pride."

61. Jennifer Medina, "Latinos Back Black Lives Matter Protests. They Want Change for Themselves, Too," *New York Times*, July 3, 2020, https://www.nytimes.com/2020/07/03/us/politics/latinos-police-racism-black-lives-matter.html.

62. Medina, "Latinos Back Black Lives Matter Protests."

63. Medina, "Latinos Back Black Lives Matter Protests."

64. The Black and Latinx LGBTQ+ academics I am referring to in this section include, but are not limited to, Drs. E. Patrick Johnson, Dwight McBride, Roderick Ferguson, Eric Darnell-Pritchard, Alexis Pauline Gumbs, Jose Munoz, Marshall Green, Jeffrey McCune, Marlon Bailey, C. Riley Snorton, Susana Morris, Cathy Cohen, Beth Richie, Francesca Royster, and Antron Mahoney.

65. Some of the educators, activists, cultural workers, and creatives that are erecting and executing counter-hegemonic narratives through their art, scholarship, and public activism in hopes that more folks begin to recognize not only the harms that come from anti-Blackness, misogyny, and anti-queer sentiments, but also how these harms are amplified and exacerbated by the neoliberal paradigm, which asserts that our politicized identities are irrelevant to collective freedom, include, but are not limited to, Drs. E. Patrick Johnson, Yaba Blay, Brittney Cooper, Joan Morgan and Treva B. Lindsey, Imani Perry, Kisese Laymon, Robert Jones Jr., Darnell Moore, Janet Mock, Dr. Tamura Lomax, Dr. Heidi Lewis, Dr. Eric Darnell-Pritchard, Dr. Alexis Pauline Gumbs, Lena Waithe, Issa Rae, Danielle Moodie, Dr. Farah Jasmine Griffin, Esther Armah, Shantrelle P. Lewis, Dr. Susana Morris, Dr. Anthony Monteiro, Aisha Mills, Charlene Carruthers, Dr. Koritha Mitchell, and Marshall Green.

66. Christine Emba, "Why Conservatives Really Fear Critical Race Theory," op-ed, *Washington Post*, May 26, 2021, https://www.washingtonpost.com/opinions/2021/05/26/why-conservatives-really-fear-critical-race-theory.

67. In Colleen Flaherty's "Being Watched," in *Inside Higher Ed*, Flaherty states: "The site, called Professor Watchlist, is not without precedent—predecessors include the now-defunct NoIndoctrination.org, which logged accounts of alleged bias in the classroom. There's also David Horowitz's 2006 book, *The Professors: The 101 Most Dangerous Academics in America*. But such efforts arguably have new meaning in an era of talk about registering certain social groups and concerns about free speech." For more, please see Colleen Flaherty, "Being Watched," *Inside Higher Ed*, November 22, 2016, https://www.insidehighered.com/news/2016/11/22/new-website-seeks-register-professors-accused-liberal-bias-and-anti-american-values.

68. Community Engaged Scholarship is defined by the University of Louisville as: "scholarly work done in full partnership with the community. It consists of research, teaching, and the application of scholarship for mutual benefits for the institution and community partner." For more on this, see https://louisville.edu/communityengagement/additional-resources/engaged-scholarship.

69. I define any academic discipline as a "non-traditional" discipline when activists, educators, and administrators had to argue, protest, or demonstrate for universities and colleges to make these disciplines integral to that institution. I use this term to discuss the disciplines of Black studies,

women's studies, gender studies, LGBTQ+ studies, and the like, as these disciplines had to be advocated for in order for them to become a part of an academic institution or community.

70. Cherrie Moraga & Gloria Anzaldua, *This Bridge Called My Back: Writings by Radical Women of Color* (New York: Kitchen Table/Women of Color Press, 1981); Akasha Gloria T. Hull, Patricia Bell-Scott, and Barbara Smith, *All the Women Are White, All the Blacks Are Men, But Some of Us Are Brave: Black Women's Studies* (New York: Feminist Press, 1982); Gabriella Gutierrez, Muhs Yolanda Flores Niemann, Carmen Gonzalez, and Angela P. Harris, *Presumed Incompetent: The Intersections of Race and Class for Women in Academia* (Boulder: University of Colorado Press, 2012).

EPILOGUE: ON TRANSCENDING THE RAINBOW AND LIVING BEYOND THE NOW

1. I define the Black and Latinx LGBTQ+ creative vanguard as any Black or Latinx LGBTQ+ person who is involved in producing, directing, and establishing media content that is diverse, robust, and three-dimensional as it relates to minoritized communities. This creative vanguard includes, but is not limited to, Black and Latinx LGBTQ+ creatives Patrik-Ian Polk, Tarell Alvin McCraney, Lena Waithe, Katori Hall, Steven Canales, and Billy Porter.

2. *Beverly Hills 90210*, created by Darren Star, Fox Network, 1990–2010; *Melrose Place*, created by Darren Star, Fox Network, 1992–1999.

3. *P-Valley*, *Pose*, *Twenties*, *David Makes Man*, *Boomerang*, *The Chi*, *Good Trouble*, *The L Word* reboot *Generation Q*, and *Claws* are all television shows on various networks that have either been produced, created, or written by Black and Latinx LGBTQ+ creatives in recent years or have characters that are either Black or Latinx and LGBTQ+.

4. Kimberly Wilson, "Da Brat Reveals Why She Waited 20 Years To Come Out: 'I Did It On My Own Terms,'" December 6, 2020, *Essence*, https://www.essence.com/celebrity/da-brat-coming-out; Asia Grace, "Queen Latifah Shares 'Love' for Partner Eboni Nichols at BET Awards," *New York Post*, June 28, 2021, https://nypost.com/2021/06/28/queen-latifah-shares-love-for-partner-at-2021-bet-awards; Trudy Ring, "R&B Star Tevin Campbell Comes Out as Gay," *The Advocate*, August 20, 2022, https://www.advocate.com/music/2022/8/19/rb-star-tevin-campbell-comes-out-gay.

5. *Ms. Pat Show*, *Loot*, *The Fresh Prince of Bel Air* reboot, as well as the reboot of the iconic *Roseanne*—now *The Conners*—are all streaming shows on various platforms that have either been produced, created, or written by Black and Latinx LGBTQ+ creatives in recent years or have characters that are either Black or Latinx and LGBTQ+.

6. Glenn Garner, "Beyoncé Dedicates 'Renaissance' Drop to Her Late Gay Uncle Johnny: 'To All of the Fallen Angels,'" *People*, July 29, 2022, https://people.com/music/beyonce-dedicates-renaissance-drop-late-gay-uncle-johnny; Lester Fabian Brathwaite, "On Beyoncé's Renaissance: To Be

Queer, Gifted, and Black . . . Oh What a Lovely, Precious Dream," *Entertainment Weekly*, August 4, 2022, https://ew.com/music/beyonce-renaissance-tribute-to-black-queer-culture-ball-scene; Lynnee Denise, "Beyoncé's Renaissance and the Case for Misery Resistance: The 16-Track Project Carries the Weight of Black Musical Genealogies and Geographies," *Oprah Daily*, August 2, 2022, https://www.oprahdaily.com/entertainment/a40786806/beyonce-renaissance-album-review.

7. Patricia Hill Collins, *Black Sexual Politics: African Americans, Gender, and the New Racism* (New York: Routledge, 2004); K. Sue Jewell, *From Mammy to Miss America and Beyond: Cultural Images and the Shaping of US Policy* (London: Routledge Publishers, 1992); Donald Bogle, *Toms, Coons, Mulattoes, Mammies, and Bucks: An Interpretive History of Blacks in American Films* (London: Bloomsbury Publishing, 1973).

8. Dan Mangan and Kevin Breuninger, "Supreme Court Overturns Roe v. Wade, Ending 50 Years of Federal Abortion Rights," CNBC, June 24, 2022, https://www.cnbc.com/2022/06/24/roe-v-wade-overturned-by-supreme-court-ending-federal-abortion-rights.html.

9. Deborah Yetter, "Abortion Ends in Kentucky as Supreme Court Strikes Down Roe v. Wade Due to Trigger Law," *Courier Journal*, June 24, 2022, https://www.courier-journal.com/story/news/local/2022/06/24/scotus-strikes-down-roe-v-wade-ending-kentucky-abortion-access/9928612002.

10. ACLU of Kentucky, "EMW Women's Surgical Center, P.S.C., et al. v. Daniel Cameron, et. al.," August 31, 2022, https://www.aclu.org/cases/emw-womens-surgical-center-psc-et-al-v-daniel-cameron-et-al.

11. Ivan Nechepurenko, "Brittney Griner Is Sentenced to 9 Years in a Russian Penal Colony," *New York Times*, August 4, 2022, https://www.nytimes.com/live/2022/08/04/world/brittney-griner-trial-verdict-russia.

12. T.J. Quinn, "Brittney Griner's book details harsh life in Russian prison," May 7, 2024, ESPN, https://www.espn.com/wnba/story/_/id/40071460/brittney-griner-wnba-phoenix-mercury-russia-detained-released-memoir.

13. Gershon Harrell, "Veterans Can Now Teach in Florida with No Degree. School Leaders Say It 'Lowers the Bar,'" *USA Today*, July 21, 2022, https://www.usatoday.com/story/news/education/2022/07/21/florida-education-program-military-veterans-teach/10117107002; Nicole Chavez, "Books About LGBTQ and Black People Were Among the Most Challenged Books in 2021," CNN, April 4, 2022, https://www.cnn.com/2022/04/04/us/american-library-association-most-challenged-books/index.html.

14. Matt Lavietes and Elliott Ramos, "Nearly 240 Anti-LGBTQ Bills Filed in 2022 So Far, Most of Them Targeting Trans People," NBC News, March 20, 2022, https://www.nbcnews.com/nbc-out/out-politics-and-policy/nearly-240-anti-lgbtq-bills-filed-2022-far-targeting-trans-people-rcna20418.

15. Anne Branigin, "Bette Midler and Macy Gray Upset Trans Advocates. Here's Why," *Washington Post*, https://www.washingtonpost.com/arts-entertainment/2022/07/06/bette-midler-macy-gray-transgender-advocates.

16. Wendy Medina, "P-Valley Co-Executive Producer Claps Back at Lil Duval for Homophobic Comments: 'The Gay Ain't Goin' Nowhere,'" *Black Enterprise*, July 2, 2022, https://www.blackenterprise.com/p-valley-co-executive-producer-claps-back-at-lil-duval-for-homophobic-comments-the-gay-aint-goin-nowhere.

17. Louis Pisano, "Dear White Gay Men, Please Stop Fetishizing Black Men," *Medium*, May 19, 2019, https://medium.com/@LPP1/dear-white-gay-men-please-stop-fetishizing-black-men-f71e9f9a7f29; Stefano Duc, "Sexual Racism: Dear White Queer People, Now You Have to Listen to Us," *Il Grande Colibrì*, January 8, 2021, https://www.ilgrandecolibri.com/en/sexual-racism-dear-white-queer-people-now-you-have-to-listen-to-us; Juwan J. Holmes, "A Block Party Protest Is Held Outside of Gay Bar Where Black Woman Was Dragged by Hair," LGBTQ *Nation*, June 26, 2022, https://www.lgbtqnation.com/2021/06/block-party-protest-held-outside-gay-bar-black-woman-dragged-hair.

18. Jamilah Lemieux, "Dave Chappelle and 'the Black Ass Lie' That Keeps Us Down," *Vanity Fair*, January 13, 2022, https://www.vanityfair.com/hollywood/2022/01/dave-chappelle-and-the-black-ass-lie-that-keeps-us-down.

19. Natasha Decker, "Now, T.D.: Backlash Erupts over Bishop Jakes' Sermon About Families Being in Trouble Because 'We're Raising Up Women to Be Men,'" *MadameNoire*, July 22, 2022, https://madamenoire.com/1319539/td-jakes-fathers-day-sermon.

20. Aja Romano, "The Racist Backlash to the Little Mermaid and Lord of the Rings Is Exhausting and Extremely Predictable," *Vox News*, September 17, 2022, https://www.vox.com/culture/23357114/the-little-mermaid-racist-backlash-lotr-rings-of-power-diversity-controversy.

21. Amber Phillips, "What Is Florida's 'Don't Say Bill'? Florida's Law Limiting LGBT Discussion in Schools," *Washington Post*, August 22, 2022, https://www.washingtonpost.com/politics/2022/04/01/what-is-florida-dont-say-gay-bill.

22. Associated Press, "Dictionary.com Anoints Allyship Word of the Year for 2021," NBC News, December 6, 2021, https://www.nbcnews.com/nbc-out/out-news/dictionarycom-anoints-allyship-word-year-2021-rcna7726.

23. Josh Gerstein, "Supreme Court Makes Gay Marriage a Nationwide Right," *Politico*, June 26, 2015, https://www.politico.com/story/2015/06/supreme-court-gay-marriage-119462.

24. Angie Franklin, "Ghosted by Allies: Why BIPOC Still Can't Trust White People with Social Justice," *Bold Italic*, February 4, 2021, https://thebolditalic.com/ghosted-by-allies-why-bipoc-still-cant-trust-white-people-with-social-justice-6a5d9edc6f52; Holiday Phillips, "Performative Allyship Is Deadly (Here's What to Do Instead)," *Forge*, May 9, 2020, https://forge.medium.com/performative-allyship-is-deadly-c900645d9f1f; Black Youth

Project, "The Bar for White 'Allies' Is Absurdly Low and I'm Tired of Watching Them Be Praised for Reaching It," December 7, 2018, http://blackyouth project.com/the-bar-for-white-allies-is-absurdly-low-and-im-tired-of -watching-the-be-praised-for-reaching-it; Shayla Lawson, "Your White Neighbor's Black Lives Matter Yard Sign Is Not Enough," *In These Times*, June 30, 2020, https://inthesetimes.com/article/black-lives-matter-yard -signs-white-neighbors-performative-allyship.

25. Phillips, "Performative Allyship Is Deadly."

26. For definitions of a social justice accomplice and its difference from allyship, please see Tai Harden-Moore and Kimberly Harden, "Moving from Ally to Accomplice: How Far Are You Willing to Go to Disrupt Racism in the Workplace?" *Diverse Issues in Higher Education*, March 4, 2019, https:// www.diverseeducation.com/opinion/article/15104148/moving-from-ally -to-accomplice-how-far-are-you-willing-to-go-to-disrupt-racism-in-the -workplace; White Accomplices, "Opportunities for White People in the Fight for Racial Justice, Moving from Actor to Ally to Accomplice," n.d., https://www.whiteaccomplices.org; Willie Jackson, "To Promote True Advocacy, Don't Be an Ally: Be an Accomplice," From Day One, December 10, 2019, https://www.fromdayone.co/2019/12/10/to-promote-true-advocacy -dont-be-an-ally-be-an-accomplice; Joyell Arvella, "Your Performative Empathy Does Not Equate to Justice for Black Life," *Medium*, June 11, 2020, https://medium.com/@joyell/your-performative-empathy-does-not-equate -to-justice-for-black-life-deb4f2e7b65.

27. Colleen Clemens, "Ally or Accomplice? The Language of Activism," *Learning for Justice*, June 5, 2017, https://www.learningforjustice.org /magazine/ally-or-accomplice-the-language-of-activism.

28. Annalee Schafranek, "What's the Difference Between an Ally and Accomplice?" YWCA Seattle, King, Snohomish, December 21, 2021, https:// www.ywcaworks.org/blogs/ywca/tue-12212021–1103/whats-difference -between-ally-and-accomplice.

29. Schafranek, "What's the Difference Between an Ally and Accomplice?"

INDEX